Palmetto Country

STETSON KENNEDY

Palmetto Country

Cover photography provided by John Moran, Florida Nature Photography. www.johnmoranphoto.com

ISBN 10: 1-886104-38-7
ISBN 13: 978-1-886104-38-9

The Florida Historical Society Press
435 Brevard Avenue
Cocoa, FL 32922
www.myfloridahistory.org/fhspress

P•R•E•S•S

To

Folk In General

And

Edith In Particular

This Edition

of this, my first book

is dedicated to

my last wife

Sandra

Appreciation is hereby tendered Dr. Alton C. Morris for making available a number of songs from his collection of *Florida Folksongs*; Dr. B. A. Botkin, Fellow in Folklore at the Library of Congress; *Directions, The Crisis*, and *Opportunity* magazines for permission to republish certain stories; and the Florida Writers' Project for access to its archives—particularly material collected by Robert Cornwall, Lindsay Bryan, Martin Richardson, Barbara Darsey, Zora Neale Hurston, and Veronica Huss.

CONTENTS

THE PALMETTO COUNTRY 1
   Grass-Water *15*
   Trembling Earth *20*
   Up from the Sea *26*
   Way-Way Down South *32*
   When the Sawgrass Blooms *36*

UNDER SEVEN FLAGS 49
   Fountains of Youth and Cities of Gold *49*
   Blood and Sand Dunes *53*
   San Augustin, the Ever Faithful *55*
   The Tories Take Over *59*
   Return of the Spaniard *62*

STARS AND STRIPES FOREVER 65
   Bad Characters *65*
   Statehood—with Liberty and Justice for All Whites *68*

SLAVE DAYS 73
   Mama Duck *73*
   Chips from the Smokehouse Floor *80*
   Slave-Breeding for Profit *81*
   New Names for Old Gods *82*
   The Man with the Branded Hand *85*
   "Whereas I Don't Give a Damn" *87*
   Rich Man's War, Poor Man's Fight *91*

THE OLD ORDER CHANGETH, SOMEWHAT 97
   The Net Proceeds *97*
   Lost: 40 Acres and a Mule *97*
   Carpetbaggers and Scalawags *102*
   Just Voters *106*
   Conservative Radicals *113*
   The Rising Tide of Demockkkracy.....................................*115*

MEET THE FOLKS 117

A MAN IN FULL 131
   Bullock County's Nine-Second Man *132*
   Captain Charlie Coker, Brute *134*

Quevedo 135
Big John the Conqueror 137
Uncle Monday 141
Daddy Mention 143
Kerosene Charlie 148
Old Pete 150
Roy Sold His Car to God 153

STUFF AND SUCH 155
The Sea Serpent of Cape Sable 157
West Hell 160
How Folks Got Their Colors 163
Why Folks Aint Got Tails 164
Why the World is so Wicked 165
Why Solomon Said, "Vanity of Vanities—" 166
Why Women Talk So Much 167
God and Moses 167
Samson versus Satan 168

BLACK MAGIC...169
Congo Talk 169
Conjure Shop 172
Who's Who in Hoodoo...174
Father Abraham 175
Aunt Memory 178
"Deliverer to Satan" 178
The Prophet of Maaii 179
The Gods of Yoruba..181
The Fire Dance 184

JOOK TOUR 189

RED LIGHTS GLOWING 201

WAITIN ON TIME 211

SOUTH ON THE RANGE 223
Cattle Kings 231
Hungry Land 236
Jackpot Herds 237
Tick Fever 240
To Burn or Not to Burn...241
Rolling Stock 243

The Spirit of Joe Stalin *244*
Sacred Highway Cows *247*
The Little Pigs Danced *249*
Hog Wild *251*

FISHERFOLK 255
Conch Talk *260*
"Wreck Ashore!" *264*
Sponger Money *266*
Conch Eats Conch and Grunts *270*
"When the Blues Is Runnin" *272*

TURPMTINE 275
The Story of Naval Stores *280*
The Man *284*

OUR CIGARS PUT FLORIDA ON THE MAP 287
"An Odious Spectacle" *293*
The Cradle of Cuban Independence *296*
"The Citizens Lost Their Patience" *297*
"We are Superfluous Here" *302*
Gravy on His Grits *306*
"Democracy is Damned Foolishness!" *308*
Gato Carried a Gun *311*
Custom Reigns *313*
Golden Jubilee *314*

ALL FOR ONE AND ONE FOR ALL 315
The Bread of Instruction *322*
"God is Very Discredited" *327*
"Cuba, Call Your Children!" *332*
Lolita Likes Bolita *335*
"Heck Yeah, I'm an American" *337*
An Unhealthy Place for Fascists *340*
Shotgun Shacks *343*
"I've Done My Duty by Uncle Sam" *344*
"I Destroyed the Cigarmakers' Union" *347*
"Man Should Not Be Enslaved" *350*

AFTERWORD 353
Retrospect and Prospect *355*

INDEX 363

ILLUSTRATIONS

01 PALMETTO COUNTRY. 3
02 "CROOK" PALM. 5
03 CUTTING DOWN TREES. 8
04 LUMBER MILL. 9
05 MAKING CYPRESS SHINGLES BY HAND. 10
06 RIVER OF GRASS. 16
07 SEMINOLE TRADERS. 19
08 SEMINOLE MOTHER AND CHILD. 22
09 ON THE CALOOSAHATCHEE. 27
10 LIVING OFF THE LAND CAN BE DIFFICULT. 29
11 HARD TRAVELLIN. 33
12 HARVESTING VEGETABLE CROPS, SOUTH OF MIAMI. 36
13 MAKING REPAIRS AFTER THE 1926 HURRICANE. 39
14 MIGRATORY FARM WORKERS' HOUSING, BELLE GLADE. 43
15 MIGRATORY FARM WORKERS. 44
16 NATIVE AMERICAN GIRLS. 52
17 FORT SAN MARCO 57
18 COQUINA STONE BUILDINGS. 58
19 FLORIDA CRACKERS WRESTLING AN ALLIGATOR. 72
20 MAUMA MOLLIE. 74
21 SLAVE MARKET. 77
22 BELL SCHOOL. 79
23 ROSEWOOD PLANTATION HOME. 84
24 SLAVE CABIN. 89
25 WALLS OF SLAVE CABINS. 90
26 WOMAN TRANSPORTING GOODS. 99
27 AFRICAN AMERICAN MAN AT HOME. 102
28 WALLACE RALLY 112
29 WALLACE RALLY 112
30 KLAN RALLY. 114
31 TIN CAN TOURISTS. 119
32 "WHITES ONLY" JOOK JOINT 121
33 RECREATION FOR TOURISTS. 122
34 BOYDS MODERN TOURIST COTTAGES. 124
35 TARPON SPRINGS SPONGE DIVER. 127
36 STORYTELLER ANNIE TOMLIN. 140
37 ZORA NEALE HURSTON. 162
38 AUNT MEMORY ADAMS. 177
39 WHITE JOOK JOINT. 191

40 JOOKING, MOORE HAVEN. 193
41 "SKIN" GAME, MOORE HAVEN JOOK JOINT. 196
42 CORA CRANE. 203
43 MAIN STAIRWAY, THE COURT. 207
44 BEDROOM, THE COURT 208
45 THE COURT. 210
46 REVENUERS DESTROY A STILL. 212
47 CHAIN GANG. 217
48 PENNED CATTLE. 224
49 REMINGTON DRAWING OF FLORIDA COWBOYS. 227
50 KING KONG SMITH. 228
51 LYKES BROTHERS. 230
52 FLORIDA REPRESENTATIVE IRLO BRONSON. 231
53 LEGENDARY CRACKER COWBOY BONE MIZELL. 233
54 KING OF THE BRAHMANS. 238
55 YOUNG KAY DAVIS WITH CHAMPION STEER "JACK". 239
56 CATTLE DIPPED FOR TICK FEVER. 240
57 DEER HUNTING PARTY. 242
58 SEMINOLE COWBOY CHARLEY MICCO. 244
59 GOVERNOR FULLER WARREN. 248
60 RAZORBACK HOGS. 252
61 BOYS FISHING. 256
62 MAN CASTING NET. 257
63 KEY WEST FISHING DOCK. 261
64 "TURNING TURTLES". 263
65 PRISONERS WORKING A TURPENTINE FARM. 276
66 1920'S WAUCHULA TURPENTINE STILL. 278
67 TURPENTINE STILL, CIRCA 1930. 279
68 STRIPPING BARK AND DIPPING SAP. 282
69 WAUCHULA TURPENTINE STILL. 285
70 KEY WEST CIGAR WORKERS PACKING CIGARS 289
71 WORKERS SELECTING CIGAR WRAPPERS. 292
72 MEETING OF CIGAR WORKERS ON STRIKE. 301
73 WPA MURAL. 312
74 CENTRO ESPAGNOL. 317
75 CENTRO ASTURIANO, YBOR CITY, TAMPA. 318
76 CUBANS IN EXILE. 320
77 SAN CARLOS INSTITUTE. 324
78 SIGNS OF THE TIMES. 329
79 HARLAN BLACKBURN, GAMBLING KINGPIN. 336
80 SHUCKING OYSTERS, APALACHICOLA. 355

PUBLISHER'S PREFACE

Any list of people who contributed significantly to the history and culture of Florida in the twentieth century would include environmentalist Marjorie Stoneman Douglas; novelist Marjorie Kinnan Rawlings; writer, folklorist, and anthropologist Zora Neale Hurston; and educator and civil rights activist Harry T. Moore. Also on that list would be Stetson Kennedy.

Like Marjorie Stoneman Douglas, author of the 1947 book *The Everglades: River of Grass*, Kennedy has demonstrated his concern for the environment through his writing and with the establishment of the Stetson Kennedy Foundation. Headquartered in Beluthahatchee Park, the Foundation is establishing walking trails, a nature observatory, and environmental demonstration programs to benefit "Fellow Man and Mother Earth." Marjorie Stoneman Douglas praised Kennedy's book *Palmetto Country* and its call for the protection of Florida's natural resources.

Marjorie Kinnan Rawlings, best known for the novel *Cross Creek*, taught a course in creative writing at the University of Florida in the mid-1930s. One of her students was Stetson Kennedy. Rawlings published her most famous work in 1942, the same year that Stetson Kennedy's *Palmetto Country* first appeared in print. Just as the novel *Cross Creek* provides a distinctive portrait of rural life in Florida in the early twentieth-century, *Palmetto Country* remains a unique and important social history by preserving the oral histories, folktales, songs, and lifestyles of a diverse group of Floridians from the same time period.

In 1937, Stetson Kennedy left the University of Florida to join the Works Progress Administration (WPA) Florida Writers' Project. At the tender age of 21, Kennedy was named head of the Florida Writers' Project unit on folklore, oral history, and socio-ethnic studies. As such, Kennedy was the supervisor and friend of another participant in that program: writer, folklorist, and anthropologist Zora Neale Hurston. As the author of acclaimed novels including *Their Eyes Were Watching God* (1937) as well as the collections of folklore *Mules and Men* (1935) and *Tell My Horse* (1938), Hurston is arguably the most significant cultural figure to emerge from Central Florida. Kennedy incorporated some of Hurston's anthropological work into *Palmetto Country*.

From 1937 to 1942, Stetson Kennedy dragged a coffee-table sized tape recorder through the cities, towns, and rural backwoods of Florida, capturing the thoughts and memories of cracker cowboys, migrant farm laborers, cigar factory workers, sponge divers, and many other diverse people. *Palmetto Country* documents Kennedy's important work during this period. This new edition of *Palmetto Country*, proudly published by the Florida Historical Society Press, features period photographs not found in previous editions of this work, and a new Afterword update with contemporary reflections by the author.

While *Palmetto Country* is Stetson Kennedy's first book about Florida history and culture, it is not his last. An activist as well as an author, Kennedy's books reflect his experiences as a participant in efforts to enact positive social change. After World War II, Kennedy infiltrated the Ku Klux Klan, sharing secrets he learned with the writers of the popular *Superman* radio program, which resulted in the Man of Steel battling the KKK during four episodes. Kennedy's 1946 book *Southern Exposure* is a critical indictment of the post-World War II south prior to the acceleration of the contemporary civil rights movement.

It was during the late 1940s that Stetson Kennedy met and befriended educator and civil rights activist Harry T. Moore. Before a bomb exploded under his home in Mims, Florida, on Christmas night, 1951, Harry T. Moore started the Progressive Voters League, traveling throughout the state registering African American voters. He founded the Brevard County branch of the NAACP, and later was an active state-wide leader in the organization. Harry T. Moore and his wife Harriette both died from injuries sustained in the unprosecuted bombing of their home. Prior to his death, Moore had offered his endorsement to Stetson Kennedy's 1950 independent write-in campaign for U.S. Senate from Florida, as a "colorblind candidate on a platform of total equality." Folk musician Woody Guthrie, best known for the iconic song *This Land is Your Land*, wrote the campaign's theme song *Stetson Kennedy*, which was rediscovered and recorded by Billy Bragg and Wilco in 2000.

It was Stetson Kennedy's infiltration of the Ku Klux Klan and other white supremacist groups that earned him national and international recognition. Using the name "John Perkins," Kennedy was able to secretly gather information that helped lead to the incarceration of a number of domestic terrorists. These experiences led to the 1954 book *I Rode With the Klan*, which was later republished under the title *The Klan Unmasked*. Much has been made of Kennedy's creative choice to integrate information obtained by another KKK infiltrator and additional interviews with Klan members with his own experiences, presenting them with one narrative voice. The accuracy of the information in Kennedy's book can not be effectively challenged, just the style in which the facts are presented.

As racial tensions were rising in the United States during the 1950s, Kennedy was having difficulty getting his books exposing bigotry published. The French existentialist philosopher Jean-Paul Sartre, best known for the play *No Exit*, published Kennedy's book *The Jim Crow Guide* in Paris in 1956. While living in Paris, Kennedy became close friends with Richard Wright, the self-exiled African American existentialist writer best known for the novel *Native Son* (1940) and the semi-autobiographical *Black Boy* (1945). Despite his international travels and connections to celebrated figures, Kennedy has never forgotten his roots as a native Floridian, born in Jacksonville on October 5, 1916.

Stetson Kennedy's contribution to the cultural heritage of Florida has been deservedly well recognized. He has received the Florida Heritage Award, the Florida Governor's Heartland Award, the NAACP Freedom Award, and he has been inducted into the Florida Artists Hall of Fame. His most recent books include *Southern Florida Folklife* (1994) with Peggy A. Butler and Tina Bucuvalas; *After Appomattox: How the South Won the War* (1995); and *Grits & Grunts: Folkloric Key West* (2008), winner of the Charlton Tebeau Award from the Florida Historical Society.

The relationship between Stetson Kennedy and the Florida Historical Society started in 1937, when Kennedy began his work with the WPA in Florida. That year a presentation on the WPA activities in Florida was given at the Florida Historical Society Annual Meeting in Palm Beach. The affiliation between Kennedy and the FHS has continued over the past seven decades. Most recently, the FHS sponsored the creation of a photography exhibition called *Stetson Kennedy's Palmetto Country*. The exhibition, featuring fourteen panels of images captured in Florida in the late 1930s, was prepared by Professor Michael Thomason at the University of South Alabama for the Florida Historical Society. The Stetson Kennedy Award, presented annually by the Florida Historical Society, recognizes books that "cast light on historic Florida events in a manner that is supportive of human rights, traditional cultures, or the natural environment." At the FHS Annual Meeting held in Pensacola, May 21-23, 2009, Stetson Kennedy and Rosalind Foster presented a well received special session called "Bringing Oral History to Life."

With this new edition of the classic Florida book *Palmetto Country*, the Florida Historical Society Press hopes to introduce a new generation of readers to the important work of Stetson Kennedy. We are presenting the book with eighty historic photographs never before published with this work to add a new dimension of enjoyment and understanding for both first time readers and people who have read previous editions of this text. An updated Afterword by the author provides the reader with additional historical context.

Perhaps most striking to the contemporary *Palmetto Country* reader is Stetson Kennedy's repeated suggestion, in 1942, that we should celebrate our cultural differences rather than try to assimilate all racial and ethnic groups into one homogenous society. The "melting pot" concept of a single, unified American culture was the prevailing view in this country for decades after Kennedy's call for the preservation of our many unique cultural attributes. Today, of course, we recognize the wisdom of the perspective that Kennedy expresses here.

A cautionary note is needed for the contemporary reader as well. Throughout this text, the "n" word appears frequently, and the term "Negro" is used often to describe African Americans. While these terms are now considered to be offensive and archaic, they provide an accurate portrayal of attitudes and social norms from the time periods being discussed. To excise these terms from this text to appease our modern sensibilities would be a misguided effort to change or forget an unfortunate part of Florida history.

A highly skilled group of very hard working people have made this edition of *Palmetto Country* possible. The Florida Historical Society Press Production and Design Team for this project was led by Paul Pruett, who was assisted by Chris Brotemarkle, June Geiger, Bob Gross, and Barbara West. Special thanks to the author, Stetson Kennedy, and his wonderful wife, activist and author Sandra Parks, for their participation in this labor of love.

Benjamin D. Brotemarkle
Executive Director
Florida Historical Society
August 20, 2009

PALMETTO COUNTRY

Anyone who has seen the Deepest South – Florida and the southern portions of Georgia and Alabama—knows that there lies the Palmetto Country.

Folks outside the region usually think of the palmetto as the tall palm which is locally called the swamp cabbage or cabbage palm. Rearing its tawny head like a shaggy-maned lion on the African veldt, this majestic palm gives the Palmetto Country much of its tropical singularity. An old-timer once described it in these glowing terms: " I tell you, there's no tree like the cabbage palm. It never dies of old age, and you can't see the end of it lessen you cut it down. The sun can't wither it, fire can't burn it, and moss can't cling to it. Have you seen one bend before the wind, lay all its fans out straight, and just give so's the wind can't find nothing to take hold of?"

Growing slowly to a maximum height of eighty feet, the cabbage palm readily adapts itself to salt marsh, fresh-water swamp, or high ground. Its range through Florida and up the coast to Cape Hatteras (North Carolina) has probably been established by the dropping of its seeds by migratory birds.

There are several reasons why the cabbage palm has come to be known as a palmetto to non-Southerners. One of the first writers to refer to it as such was John Bartram, a Pennsylvania Quaker whom Linnaeus called "the greatest botanist in the New World." Of his travels in the Palmetto Country in 1865, Bartram wrote:

"We now come to plenty of the tree palmetto which the inhabitants call cabbage tree and is much eaten raw and boiled. We felled three tall palms and cut out the top bud, the white tender part or rudiments of the great leaves. This tender part will be three or four inches in diameter, tapering near a foot and cuts as white and tender as a turnip. This they slice into a pot and stew with water, then when almost tender they pour some bear's oil into it and stew it a little longer, when it eats pleasant and more mild than cabbage. Our hunters eat it raw and live upon it several days. The long trunks when split it in two make excellent troughs or conduits to carry water above ground."

These things were taught to the pioneer settlers by the Indians, who not only ate the palm's bud, but also made molasses from its berries. When hard-pressed for bread-stuff, the Indians managed to beat a kind of flour from the palm's foliage, and from its trunk they obtained salt by a process similar to that used in making potash.

Modern natives, both black and white, are still fond of swamp cabbage. They also gather the buds for sale and three cents each, and the buds are then canned and shipped to appear on America's ultra-swank menus as "Heart-of-Palm Salad," usually at a dollar a plate. Nature-lovers and conservationists take alarm at the fact that the removal of the bud causes the death of the palm, which may have been a hundred years in the making.

The cut trunks of this and other palms are called palmetto logs, both within and without the region. They attracted national attention during the Creek and Seminole Wars, when they were used in the construction of fortifications – the spongy wood absorbed bullets and even cannonballs without splintering. Before that, Indians and settlers had used the logs for all kinds of construction. The fans are still used for thatching, and the logs for pilings, as they are virtually immune to destruction by marine worms.

The word palmetto is probably derived from the Spanish *palmito*, meaning diminutive palm, and is so used by Southerners. Shrub-like saw palmetto underlies the pine flatwoods from Florida northward into South Carolina and westward to Louisiana. Originating in the swamplands, it eventually planted its feet on higher ground, burying its reclining root-stem beneath the soil to escape destruction by fire. To folks who live

01 .... PALMETTO COUNTRY.
  Indian River, cabbage palms, and sunset were captured in this distinctive Palmetto Country scene. From the Stetson Kennedy collection.

among them, palmettos are a major problem in clearing land, while to non-residents they are merely an attractive or monotonous feature of the landscape.

Yet even the lowly palmetto has its uses. Since the first discovery of the region, palmetto berries have provided nourishment for folks with no other visible means of support. In *God's Protective Providence,* Jonathan Dickens relates how he and his shipwrecked English companions, while trekking along Daytona Beach in 1699, "being nigh the shore, went thither and found some ripe berries on the palm shrubs." The Minorcans of St. Augustine soak the berries in wine and serve them as delicacies, calling them "Minorcan plums."

Another low-lying palmetto—variously called the dwarf, needle, porcupine, blue, or creeping palmetto – has an ever wider range than the saw palmetto, extending from Florida to North Carolina and Texas. An inhabitant of low woods and swamps, its recumbent trunk is surrounded by needle-sharp spikes. This palmetto represents a very ancient form of plant life, and its nearest relative lives in southeastern Asia.

Only four kinds of native palms, including the low palmettos, are to be found throughout Palmetto Country, but Florida has fifteen native varieties, as well as 126 imported species, some of which have "gone native." The coconut palm, with pinnate fronds instead of palmate fans, grows as far north as Daytona, thriving best along the coast. Sometimes reaching a height of 100 feet, it is noted for its slender trunk and graceful curves. Together with the bathing beauty, it has become the symbol of Florida resorts.

The coconut palm may have been indigenous to the Florida Keys, but more likely its fruit floated to Florida from the West Indies. Copra—dried coconut kernel—yields an oil used in the manufacture of oleomargarine, cooking oil, soap, and candles; the only place it is produced commercially in the United States is on the Ten Thousand Islands along Florida's southwest coast. Burnt coconut shells make the finest grade of charcoal, which is indispensable in the manufacture of gas masks.

Falling coconuts are not always a laughing matter, as they have been known to fracture skulls and even cause death. The growing coconut is encased in a thick fibrous husk which adds greatly to its weight. Floridians prefer to pick their coconuts when the custard is just beginning to form. At this time the inner shell is soft, and the stem-end can be sheared off with a knife; after drinking the sweet "milk," the soft custard can be scooped out with a spoon. In Key West and Miami, delicious ice cream is made with this custard, after a West Indian recipe. Coconut milk is also used in the concoction of rum cocktails.

02.........."CROOK" PALM.
   Mother Nature's formula for making a "crook" palm tree is to whistle up a wind to blow one sideways. The palm does the rest, curving it's way back to an upright position. P.K. Yonge Library, University of Florida.

A native of surpassing beauty is the royal palm. Like the coconut palm, it has pinnated fronds and reaches a height of 100 feet. Its trunk, however, is regally erect, and shines like a polished grey concrete.

Besides being palmetto-fan provider for the nation, the Palmetto Country supplies the United States with most of its palms for Easter observances. This use of palm fronds dates back to the multitude's reception of Christ upon his triumphal entry into Jerusalem; but the general idea – based on the palm fan's resemblance to the human palm – was an integral part of much older religions.

Yet palms are only symbolic of the region, which is noted for the variety of its soil and vegetation. Of the 500 native trees in the United States, more than 330 are to be found in the Palmetto Country, and 100 of these occur exclusively in Florida. A great deal of the plant life in the frost-free southern part of the peninsula grows nowhere else in the United States. Throughout the region the vegetation is extremely sensitive to topography; in the pine flatwoods, poorly drained hollows give rise to "bayheads" and clumps of cypress, while sandy hills are usually topped with scrub oaks.

The predominant growth is long-leaf and slash pine, which blankets the flatwoods from Lake Okeechobee northward and constitutes the backbone of the lumber and naval stores industries. Next in extent are the hardwood hammocks which thrive on the richer upland and bottom soils. Oak, hickory, gum, maple, bay, ash, basswood, and magnolia are the outstanding hammock trees, and are often woven into a jungle of vines, creepers, and briars. Chinaberry trees grow near many old dwellings, where they were planted in the belief that they would dispel fever-spreading "miasma."

The mangrove, "the tree that walks on stilts," borders much of the peninsula's tide-washed sand and mud flats, especially along the southern coasts, Florida Keys, and Ten Thousand Islands. Its elongated floating seeds fall into the water and take root in the shallows, sending up rootstems that bear foliage above the waterline. As the tree grows it lets down adventitious roots from its branches, and these send up new stalks. The result is a gradual coalescence of adjacent thickets, and the spreading network of roots becomes a lodging place for all manner of flotsam and jetsam, gradually building up a foundation of debris and thus extending the shoreline.

The rolling sand hills which extend over much of the northern part of the region and down through the center of the peninsula as far as Lake Okeechobee support a stunted growth of scrub oaks and pines. It is in Big Scrub of Florida's central ridge section that Marjorie Kinnan Rawlings has staked out her literary domain. The life of the folk who live there is aptly epitomized in the prayer she recorded in *South Moon Under:*

> *Good God, with a bounty*
> *Look down on Marion County;*
> *For the soil is so poor, and so awful rooty, too,*
> *I don't know what to God the poor folks gonna do.*

Because the scrub has so few distinguishing landmarks, it is easy to become lost in it. In some sections there are not yet so many roads that a man cannot become lost for days and days, and this danger has made a place for itself in the folklore of the region. A "Song Ballad of the Lost Boy" still recalls how in 1880 Polk County (Florida), three-year-old Aaron Hart was lost in the scrub for four days and nights before being found by a party of sixty searchers.

Cleo Wynn O'Berry, an old-time cracker fiddler of Sebring (Florida), tells a similar story about the origin of a fiddle tune: "'Collier in the Scrub' was composed by Uncle Bunk Collier about eighty years ago. The story [is] that Uncle Bunk got losted in the scrub down around Lake Okeechobee. Come nightfall he got caught in a hard rain and lightnin-storm, and to keep hisself company he started to whistle. Pretty soon he was whistlin a particular tune which pleased him so much he kept right on whistlin it and plumb whistled hisself out of the scrub and back onto the road afore he knowed it. Soon as he got home he played the tune over and over on his fiddle until he had it be heart; and he called it 'Collier in the Scrub.'

"Another story told about the same piece is that Uncle Bunk was accused of cow-stealin and was a-hidin in the scrub from the sheriff. To keep hisself in spirit he began to whistle and made up that tune. – But that story never did seem just right to me. A man hidin from the law aint likely to do much whistlin."

One of the Palmetto Country's most valuable trees is the cypress, which grows in fresh-water swamps, often rising out of the shallow water itself. Its trunk is buttressed at the base for greater support, and the extensive

03.........CUTTING DOWN TREES.

Two-man handsaws were used to strip the Palmetto Country of its pine, oak, and cypress forests. Sawmills were a familiar sight throughout the Palmetto Country. From the Stetson Kennedy collection.

root system sends up gnarled "knees," presumably for aeration. Some poor folk eke a living by fashioning these knees into handcraft articles.

Dating back more than a million years to the ice age, the cypress is also the oldest living thing on earth, sometimes reaching an age of 6,000 years. They grow very slowly – about one inch in radius in thirty years. The oldest remaining cypress in the Palmetto Country is the Old Senator at Longwood (Florida), estimated to be 3,500 years old. Excavations of ancient rock strata have revealed pieces of cypress that were neither petrified nor decayed – pretty good evidence that it deserves its title, The Wood Eternal.

The boggy habitat of the cypress often requires that it be snaked out by means of oxen and two-wheeled carts. Worm-eaten "Pecky" cypress was once used only for fencing and stakes, but during the Boom it became popular and expensive as "antique" interior trimming. Though Pecky cypress is never less than one hundred years old (the borers do not attack younger

04........ LUMBER MILL.
Under the "cut-out and get-out" system which characterized the industry, as soon as the timber was exhausted in one area the mill would be dismantled and moved to another. Marion Post Wolcott photograph. State Library and Archives of Florida.

trees), its aged appearance can be artificially enhanced by sand blasts, acids, and charring by furniture makers.

Big Cypress Swamp, a vast morass covering 2,400 square miles west of the Everglades, is the largest wooded swampland in the United States. Its dense stands of cypress are studded with air plants and draped with festoons of Spanish moss. Undrained and largely inundated, the Big Cypress is inhabited only by a small band of Seminoles and, in season, by a few trappers and hunters.

Lumbering has been one of the main attractions of the Palmetto Country since its discovery. Menéndez built a ship at St. Augustine that sailed to

05 .... MAKING CYPRESS SHINGLES BY HAND.
Hand-cutting cypress shingles was once a major occupation, the same being widely used for siding as well as roofing. Homes shingled with "the wood eternal" are found in some areas of the Palmetto Country. Arthur Rothstein photograph. State Library and Archives of Florida.

Spain half a century before the Pilgrims made their appearance in the New World. Sizeable lots of timber were shipped by the early Spanish and British colonists, and a sawmill was operating at Cow Ford (Jacksonville) during the Revolutionary War. Many of the first towns were established near sawmill sites, and the early history of the whole region is in large measure a history of lumbering operations.

The live oak, with its thick trunk and long spreading branches, is one of the most handsome of the region's evergreens. Great live-oak forests, long held in reserve by the United States Government for naval construction during the days of wooden ships, were extensively cut during the 1830's. John James Audubon, in his *Delineations of American Scenery and Character* (1831-39), described "Live-Oakers" as being "mostly hale, strong, and active men from the eastern part of the Union." With the outbreak of the Civil War, the Confederates set fire to huge stores of live-oak logs which the Federal Government had buried along the river banks to season. When Florida lands were opened to homesteading in 1885, many other live oaks were felled to make way for agriculture.

A. G. Van Schaick, a prominent lumberman from the American Northwest, "was never more surprised in this life" than when he visited Pensacola in 1890 and saw no less than ninety-five square-rigged vessels loading lumber for foreign ports. During the previous year Pensacola had shipped 350 million feet of lumber by boat, and seventy-five million feet by rail. The orgy of cutting increased in tempo. Vast tracts of land were leased to be stripped under the "cut out and get out" system. For the most part these despoiled lands were then left idle and returned to the state via the delinquent-tax route.

One of the region's timber-land agents inserted this novel advertisement in a Pensacola paper in 1889:

CABLEGRAM

Yokohama, Japan

W. J. Van Kirk, Pensacola, Florida USA

His Royal Highness, the Mighty Mikado, Son of the Moon and Favorite of the Oriental Constellations, is fully persuaded that you are the YELLOW PINE KING of the United States, and cordially invites you, when you have sold Florida, Alabama, and Birmingham, to come to Japan and we will allow you a liberal commission to sell our Empire. *—The Mikado of Japan*

It is interesting to know that there has been a precedent for a Mikado seeking to dispose of his empire.

The comparative extent of the various types of surviving woodland in the Palmetto Country are indicated by the following figures on Florida: longleaf and slash pine, fifteen million acres; hardwood hammock, three million acres; and one and a half million acres each of scrub oak and scrub pine. These figures would be considerably higher—because of the region's exceptionally favorable conditions for rapid timber growth—were it not for the cattlemen's annual custom of "greenin up the woods" with fire. They are responsible for seventy-five per cent of the 20,000 forest fires which sweep the Palmetto Country each year, causing an annual loss of more than ten million dollars. Yet the region is still one of the most densely wooded areas in the United States, and lumbering continues to employ more folk than any other industry.

A new market for the Palmetto Country's second-growth pines was opened by Charles H. Herty, a Georgia chemist whose experiments at Savannah in 1933 proved that pulp made from these pines is admirably suited for the manufacture of kraft paper and rayon. Since then almost a dozen large pulp mills have been established in the region; representing an investment of $40,000,000, they give employment to 5,000 people.

For the past couple of centuries some very poor folk of the Palmetto Country have gleaned a meager income by gathering Spanish moss. Equipped with long bamboo poles tipped with wire, whole families range through the hammocks and gather the moss, which they sell to processors for a few cents per pound. The processors suspend the moss on racks in the sun and allow it to cure for six months. Some moss-gatherers do their own curing, and it is a common sight to see moss strung out on fences to dry. Ginning then removes the outer husk, and the finished product – highly resilient and unattractive to vermin – is used in upholstering furniture and automobile seats. In 1940 the income from the industry amounted to over a million dollars.

Spanish moss received its name when the region was Spanish territory. It is not a true moss, but a seed-bearing air plant related to the pineapple. Nor, contrary to popular belief, is it a parasite; once anchored, it grows very well on telegraph poles and wires. Its very bulk, however, often harms trees by covering their branches and cutting off sunlight.

Many of the Palmetto Country's streams and lakes are obscured by rafts of purple hyacinths. Though delicate enough to be mistaken for orchids, the lavish blooms wither quickly when plucked. The plant is not a true hyacinth, but is related to the pickerel weed. Equipped with bulbous floats, they mat their thick roots together to form rafts so dense that they will sometimes support a man. The plant also has the ability to drop its floats and take root in boggy ground.

They were cultivated by the Dutch in the sixteenth century, but did not exist in the United States until 1884, when they were brought from Venezuela and exhibited at the New Orleans Cotton Exposition. Samples were distributed, and within four years the hyacinth had spread through many of the streams of Alabama, Mississippi, and Texas. In 1890, a woman living on the St. Johns River near Palatka (Florida) introduced them to her fish pond. They increased rapidly, and she opened a veritable Pandora's box by tossing the surplus into the St. Johns – in ten years they had covered fifty million acres of the river and its tributaries. Seeing that cattle fed on the hyacinths, cattlemen distributed them to lakes and streams all over the region. It was later discovered that the plants contain so few solids that they have little value as stock feed.

By 1897 they had become such a hindrance to navigation that Congress authorized an investigation into ways and means of controlling them. Poison was tried, but was discontinued in 1905 because it endangered cattle and fish. A temperature of twenty-eight degrees will kill the hyacinth tops, while a few degrees less will kill the entire plant; consequently they are less numerous after severe winters. Apparently they have no parasitic enemies, and the secret of their success is that one square yard of them can increase a thousand-fold in six months.

In the past forty years the Government has expended one million dollars on hyacinth control. The Jacksonville office of the United States Engineers is spending about $200,000 annually for control work throughout the peninsula, and estimates that without such work many of the region's rivers would be utterly impassable in ten years. The Engineers employ what they call "destroyers" – fifteen-foot boats equipped fore and aft with circular saws which slash through the hyacinths (and moccasins) at the rate of ten acres per day.

Another symbol of the Southland is the mockingbird, whose liquid trills and skillful mimicry have inspired volumes of poetry and prose. The old argument as to the relative singing ability of the mockingbird and nightingale was settled in 1931, when European nightingales were imported to the Bok Tower sanctuary near Lake Wales (Florida). The mockingbirds in the neighborhood immediately added the songs of the nightingales to their own repertoire. After being selected by school children as Florida's State Bird, the mockingbird was so designated by the 1927 State Legislature.

Folklore has it that no mockingbirds are to be seen on Fridays, and the story goes like this: "Once there was a man who was very bad. He robbed and stole and was always gettin in fights and killin people. But he was awful good to birds, and mockinbirds was his favorites. At last when somebody killed him he went straight to hell. The birds hated to see him in hell, and they tried to get him out. But the fire was too hot and pretty soon they gave up—all except the mockinbirds. They got together and decided to tote sand until they squenched the fire. So they set a day and all agreed on it. And that's why nobody don't never see a mockingbird on Friday. They aint on earth that day—they all gone to hell with a grain of sand in their mouth."

Even this old lullaby, as sung in the Palmetto Country, has had a mockingbird verse added to it:

Hush, little baby, don't say a word
Papa's gonna buy you a mockinbird;
If that mockinbird don't sing,
Papa's gonna buy you a diamond ring;
If that diamond ring turns to brass,
Papa's gonna buy you a lookin glass;
If that lookin glass gets broke,
Papa's gonna buy you a billygoat;
If that billygoat runs away,
Papa's gonna buy you a horse and dray.

There is a superabundance of insects in the Palmetto Country, and many of them exert a terrific influence on the life of the region. The malarial mosquito, for example, gives Florida a 20.3 incidence of malaria—six times higher than the national average.

The Mediterranean fruit fly, discovered in Orlando in 1929, enjoyed a brief year of notoriety at the expense of the Federal Government, which appropriated $4,725,000 for its eradication. Squads of eradication workers invaded groves and backyards, spraying all trees and cutting those which were infected. Many Florida folk resented these activities, and even tried to turn back the squads at the point of a gun. On the highways, National Guardsmen stopped all cars and gave them a perfunctory spraying, and searched luggage for hidden fruit. Since the campaign ended, the fruit fly has been the subject of many jokes. Some folks say the flies have always been present, while others assert that the sole specimen to reach Florida is in a bottle at the Plant Inspection Bureau. The general belief is that the campaign was a gigantic boondoggling project. As late as 1942, Florida congressmen were making political capital by trying to get Congress to consider an appropriation of ten million dollars for the compensation of grove owners.

In fact, natives refuse to take any insects seriously, except the boll weevil. As the cracker said to the bugologist, "What's the use in namin all them bitin and stingin critters? I've lived here all my life and aint run up agin nary one of em, ceptin of course redbugs and 'skeeters and scorponiums and sich trash that don't count, only to make a feller scratch and cuss."

The old saying that once folks get Florida sand in their shoes they always come back should include a footnote about something else often acquired in the Palmetto Country. The Conchs have a riddle for it: "A man was goin along a road not lookin for nothin but he found somethin, picked it up, carried it along, but didn't see it. Then he put it down again and went on without it. What was it?" Answer: a sandspur.

Grass-Water

Florida's Everglades occupy a nearly level plain which slopes from fifteen feet above sea level at the southern shore of Lake Okeechobee to sea level at the tip of the peninsula. Covering 4,472 square miles, it is by far the most extensive swampland in the United States. *Pay-hai-o-kee* the Seminoles call it, meaning Grass-Water, and for the most part that is what it is.

06 .... RIVER OF GRASS.
Florida's Everglades is by far the most extensive swamp land in the United States. From the Stetson Kennedy collection.

The whole drowned plain is blanketed with tall growths of sawgrass, and differs from most swamps in that trees are generally confined to small clumps or islands.

It was in this remote region that the final chapters of the Seminole wars were written. The chieftains established strong-holds on hidden islands in its interior, and one of them, Sam-Jones-Be-Damned, sent word to the American commander that "he has never signed a treaty and never would; that he and his people would fight it out forever." When the American forces sought to invade the 'Glades, the Seminoles led them on a disastrous chase, tauntingly marking their trail with palmetto fans traced with two muskets point to point. After much suffering from the sun, water, sawgrass, snakes, and mosquitoes, the soldiers found the Seminoles had taken a stand in a cypress hammock fronted by a deep sawgrass slough. The soldiers attacked, but were completely routed.

Other expeditions met with only minor military success, but served the purpose of partially exploring the 'Glades. One force of 100 American soldiers captured a chief and five warriors, and proceeded to hang and scalp them. Bloodhounds were imported from Cuba at $150 each, but they had been trained to trail Negro slaves, and made no headway at all in following Seminoles. Though all intercourse with the tribes was forbidden, they continued to receive supplies by a secret water route into the 'Glades which was not discovered until many years later.

Although the Seminole Wars officially ended in 1843, after thirteen years of peace a group of Americans under Lieutenant Hartsuff destroyed a banana grove upon which big chief Billy Bowlegs had lavished years of care. When Bowlegs accused the men of the outrage, they said they had done it "just to see how old Billy would cut up." This touched off further hostilities and in 1858 the Secretary of the Interior had to admit that "these Seminoles have completely baffled the energetic efforts of our army to effect their subjugation and removal."

But in that year a delegation of forty-six Indians from Arkansas was brought in and persuaded Bowlegs and 164 of his followers to go West. About one hundred Seminoles refused to leave, and remained hidden in the 'Glades under the leadership of Sam Jones. This band, which now numbers more than 600, has never formally concluded hostilities with the United States.

In 1850, when Congress deeded to the states all unsold swamp and over-flowed lands within their boundaries, the grant to Florida was the largest ever made by the United States to any state.

Thirty years later, a Philadelphia capitalist named Hamilton Disston saved Florida from bankruptcy by purchasing four million acres of land in the 'Glades area at twenty-five cents per acre. He had agreed to drain 15,000 acres, and some canals were dug, but the work was discontinued after Disston's death. Drainage plans were carried on, however, by the Everglades Drainage District in 1905, and the Okeechobee Flood Control District in 1929. After a total expenditure of twenty-two million dollars, thousands of acres of muckland were reclaimed and are now producing truck crops for Northern winter markets. More than 30,000 acres are planted in sugar cane.

But the drainage of the 'Glades has also resulted in periodic muck fires which have destroyed more than 500,000 acres of valuable farm land. Most of the fires have been set by alligator hunters in order to locate the 'gator caves. In dry weather the peat-like muck burns deep beneath the surface, and it is sometimes weeks and months before the fires are extinguished by heavy rains. Thick palls of smoke rise in the air, turning the sunsets red over Miami and other coastal cities. The smoldering fires are hard to locate, except at night when dim glows show from crevices. It is dangerous to approach the vicinity, because what appears to be safe ground may suddenly collapse into a pit of fiery ash.

Stretching in almost a straight line across the 'Glades, the Tamiami Trail is one of the great memorials to the workers and engineers whose labor and skill have provided America with highways across regions where not even foot-travelers could pass before. The Trail's name was derived by compounding the names of Tampa and Miami, the major cities it connects, and was completed in 1928 after the expenditure of thirteen years of labor, thirteen million dollars, and three million pounds of dynamite.

Seminoles guided the first surveyors of the routs, and a contractor observed that it would take three "m's" to build the road —"men, money and machinery." A newspaper paraphrased this to "muck, misery, and moccasins," and someone said the project presented a perfect example of what was meant by "hell and high water."

A canal was blasted ninety miles across the limerock of the 'Glades and this material was used to build the road beside it. Advance guards preceded the work crews, destroying all moccasins in sight. To keep from losing their way, laborers moving from one camp to another had to build smoke signals. The construction company could only maintain communications with Miami by radio. At night the tired works slept in the open around campfires, and many of them were killed by dynamite, drowning, fever, and snakebite. Slowly they hacked their way with ax and machete. When things went well the highway progressed at a rate of two miles per month.

A frequent cause of delay was the sinking of heavy machinery into the mud, requiring days to extricate it. It was here that the "swamp buggy" was evolved, a contraption that moves with equal facility on water, high-

07 .... SEMINOLE TRADERS.
For centuries after the European occupation, the Seminoles periodically emerged from the fastnesses of the Everglades to trade alligator hides for white folks' commodities. From the Stetson Kennedy collection.

way, or bog. An armored version of the swamp buggy is seeing service with the United States Marines.

The Tamiami Trail affords motorists an awe-inspiring panorama of Grass-Water, beside which the road and canal seem insignificant. Over all is the vast dome of the sky and the loud silence of remote places. Occasionally a Seminole is seen poling his dugout along the canal, but the only other signs of life are the circling and wading water birds, and such animals as the raccoon, opossum, and swamp rabbit.

In 1934 Congress authorized the formation of the Everglades National Park, which will embrace 1,300,000 acres of the only tropical wildlife habitat in the United States. Already the Royal Palm State Park is affording protection to a large part of the Grass-Water.

Trembling Earth

The Okefenokee Swamp—locale of Vereen Bell's *Swamp Water*—is about forty miles long from north to south, and twenty miles wide. Covering 660 square miles, seven-eighths of it are in Georgia, while the remainder lies in Florida. Okefenokee is a corruption of the Indian name *Owaquaphenoga*, meaning Trembling Earth. Like most Indian names, it is appropriate. Swamp folk drop the last syllable, calling it the Okefenoke, and this was also done on a map of 1810 which labeled it the Eckonfinook.

A major portion of the Okefenokee consists of water-covered "prairies" choked with marsh grasses, lilies, and bonnets. The stretches of prairie are interspersed with "bays" of cypress, and islands or "houses" of trembling earth which support a variety of trees and other plant life. There are about twenty-five larger islands of white sand—such as Cow House, Billy's, Bugaboo, Black Jack, Floyd's, and Honeybee—which support heavy growths of gum, oak, bay, and pine. Smaller islands have such names as John's Negro Island, Roastin Ear Island, and Soldier Camp Island. The latter got its name by serving as a haven for some of the Palmetto Country's menfolk who felt no urge to fight for the Confederacy.

The swamp lies on what is geologically known as the Okefenokee Terrace, which was formed some seventy million years ago and now lies from 100 to 130 feet above sea level. It is dotted with innumerable lakes which vary in depth from two to forty feet and in length to more than three miles.

Two rivers rise out of the swamp—the famous Suwanee flows southward to the Gulf, and the St. Mary's, forming part of the Georgia-Florida border, winds 175 miles to reach the ocean which is but sixty-five crow-fly miles from its source.

Both rivers are noted for the purity of their water. The Suwanee is the color of light coffee because of suspended organic matter, but contains little sediment. In the old days, sailing vessels ventured up the St. Mary's to take on water, and for a time the river's water was also hauled to Fernandina (Florida) and sold to ships at one cent per gallon. Much of the Okefenokee Swamp water is also drinkable, and "swampers" have a trick of deftly plunging a tin can an arm's length beneath the surface, and bringing it up full of cool water. And anyone can obtain drinking water by digging a shallow hole almost anywhere in the swamp.

The Okefenokee has always attracted men as a hunting ground and place of refuge. Burial mounds reveal that the swamp was inhabited by prehistoric tribes whose men were well over six feet tall. Their pottery, tools, and weapons show their culture was definitely superior to that of the tribes which came later.

A Spanish map of 1765 made this note of the region: "Lagoon and Island of Ocone, in which there is a village of Indians of the Nation of Timuquanos, whose forebears were all Catholics. In the first years of the present century, when the British attacked St. Augustine, these Indians moved to the Lagoon area where they have since lived without Catholic communion. All that is known of them is they retain the Catholic faith, wearing large Rosaries around their necks."

William Bartram, writing in 1791, reported: "There is a story concerning the inhabitants of this sequestered country, that they are the posterity of a fugitive remnant of the ancient Yemassees, who escaped massacre after a bloody conflict between them and the Creek nation, and here found an asylum, remote and secure from the fury of their conquerors."

Bartram also related a legend about the swamp which is still current in wide variety. His version was as follows: "This vast accumulation of water contains some large islands of rich land, one of which the present generation of Creek represents to be the most blissful spot on earth. They say it is inhabited by a peculiar race of Indians, whose women are incomparably beautiful. This terrestrial paradise has been seen by some of their enter-

21

08.........SEMINOLE MOTHER AND CHILD.
   The Seminoles were the last Native Americans to inhabit the Okefenokee.   From the Stetson Kennedy collection.

prising hunters, who, lost in the inextricable swamps and bogs, and on the point of perishing, were unexpectedly relieved by a company of beautiful women, whom they called 'Daughters of the Sun.' These women kindly gave them oranges, dates, and some corn-cakes, and then enjoined them to fly for safety to their own country, for their husbands were fierce men and cruel to strangers.

"The Creeks further say that these hunters had a view of the women's settlement, situated on an elevated promontory in a beautiful lake, but in their endeavors to approach it they were involved in perpetual labyrinths. Like enchanted land, it seemed to fly before them, alternately appearing and disappearing. At length they resolved to leave the delusive pursuit. When they reported their adventures to their tribesmen, their young warriors were inflamed with an irresistible desire to invade and make conquest of so charming a country, but all their attempts have hitherto proved abortive, never having been able to again find that enchanting spot. Yet they say they meet with frequent signs, such as the building of canoes and the footprints of men."

The Seminoles were the last Indians to inhabit the Okefenokee. When they made raids on surrounding settlers in 1830 a detachment of Georgia militia pursued them into the swamp; but the militiamen were no match for the Indians in traveling over the trembling earth, and had to abandon the chase. Other raids occurred in 1838, and this time a "corduroy" road was built into the swamp by laying cypress logs side by side. The Seminoles attacked, but were defeated, and since then the swamp has seen no more of red men. The Corduroy road is still in use.

Until 1889, the Okefenokee was the property of Georgia, but in that year it was sold to the Suwannee Canal Company for fourteen and a half cents per acre. The company set out to fell the valuable timber, and to reclaim part of the swampland for agriculture by digging drainage canals. Swamp folk insisted that the latter project could never succeed because in many places there was more water below the trembling earth than there was above it. Prime mover in the drainage project was Captain Harry Jackson, an Atlanta financier. At a cost of many thousands of dollars, a main drainage canal fourteen miles long, and a branch canal eight miles long, were scooped out. Then in 1893 Jackson died and the project expired with him.

While compiling a history of the Okefenokee, A. S. McQueen searched at length for an explanation as to why the drainage plan was not carried out. Finally he got the answer from an old Negro who had been on the spot as cook for a steam-shovel crew. It seems that after the canals were dug it was discovered that the water was not moving toward the near-by St. Mary's, but was running slowly back through the swamp toward the far-off Suwannee. Completion of the canals might have raised the water level instead of lowering it. The last of the company's buildings was destroyed by a fire in 1923, and now only the plant-choked canals remain.

Some of the swamp's islands have interesting histories. Cow House Island, the largest, received its name during the Civil War when settlers hid their cattle there from foraging Federal forces. A colony was established, and the island became the headquarters of some of the Okefenokee's most famous hunters and trappers. Bill's Island, in the heart of the swamp, was named after Billy Bowlegs, who encamped there with his band before leaving for the 'Glades. After that the island was uninhabited until Dan Lee settled there with his wife in 1833. He raised corn, sugar cane, and potatoes, and fished, hunted, and trapped. Occasionally he made trips to the mainland to sell his furs and lay in a few provisions. He and his wife raised fifteen children without the benefit of a doctor.

In 1908 all of Okefenokee in Georgia was sold to the Hebard Lumber Company, which proceeded to strip the swamp of its timber. Some forty miles of railway were built on pilings, and a community of worker's shacks, a school, church, and even a motion-picture theater spring up on Billy's Island. All this was too much for the Lee family, and they moved away; but within a year they were driven back by homesickness. At the peak of the lumbering activities 1,500 men were working in the swamp. After seventeen years the job, so far as it could be profitably pursued, was done. The buildings on Billy's Island were torn down, and the wilderness moved in. Today only a fisherman's lean-to and the wooden markers of Dan Lee's family burial ground remain. Through the swamp, rotting cross-ties and rusting rails are silent remainders of the days when the ring of the ax and whistle of the locomotive mingled with the cry of the water-bird, the scream of the panther, and the bellow of the 'gator.

The swamp continued to attract swampers—kinfolk of the neighboring people—who made a living by fishing, hunting, and trapping. Bears, deer, wildcats, raccoons, opossums, mink, otters, and foxes were plentiful, and the swampers sold their hides for cash money in Waycross. More than fifty kinds of fishes, including the large-mouth black bass, war-mouth bream, pickerel, and speckled perch abound in the swamp waters.

Transportation through the Okefenokee is accomplished in flat-bottomed "weed-boats" or *bateaux*. From ten to sixteen feet long and drawing only a few inches of water, these craft are propelled from the stern by a pole tipped with two prongs to prevent it from sinking in the spongy bottom. A great deal of skill is required to snake them through the winding passages between the cypress trees and over the clinging grass beds.

Hamp Mizell, a typical swamper, says: "My father was one of the first to try a boat to get through the swamp instead of the old way of wading and jumping from one clump of bushes to another, all the time bogging from knee to armpits. He built a boat with just enough room for two men, dogs, guns, blankets, sweet potatoes, and a side of bacon. He always carried a small pole about eight feet long with an old bayonet on the end which was used to fight off 'gators that would attack the boat in an attempt to drag out the dogs. Bacon and sweet potatoes were carried because they keep in good shape, wet or dry. When it was time to cook, a board was placed across the end of the boat and covered with wet mud or muck, and upon this a fire was built."

Swamp folk usually got their fish by "striking" them at night from a boat poled slowly through the shallows. The fish were sighted by pine-knot torches, and impaled on a spear. The swampers also had their own method of deer hunting, which was to hide their boat in tall reeds and wait for the deer to wade far out into the prairie to feed. Then the hunters would pole their boat swiftly between the deer and the trembling earth "houses," and the frightened deer, with its escape cut off, would flounder in the prairie and be overtaken by the men in the boat. Communal bear hunts were frequently held at night along the swamp's edge, and attracted men and hounds from the farms for miles around.

Hunters tell amusing stories of encountering bears far from their swamp fastnesses, "staggerin around like a man, gruntin like they was talkin to themselves, and not payin nobody no nevermind." After killing the staggering animals, the hunters would find them reeking with the odor of fermented mash which the bears had devoured at some moonshine still in the swamp.

The folkways of the Okefenokee swampers are similar to those of swamp folk everywhere, though one belief which seems to be peculiar to the region is that stuttering can be cured by eating mockingbird eggs. It is also believed that a screech owl can be made to stop screeching by turning pockets inside out, turning shoes upside down, or tying a knot in a corner of the bedsheet.

In 1937 President Roosevelt set aside most of the Okefenokee as a wildlife refuge, and since then hunting and trapping have been forbidden. About the only occupation remaining for the swampers is to sell their services as guides to fisherman, cameramen, and nature students. The United States Biological Survey is making numerous improvements so that the Trembling Earth will be more easily accessible to visitors.

Up from the Sea

At the bottom of any region's culture and way of life are its natural resources. Climate, soil, minerals, water—these are the things that primarily determine how folk live, and usually these elements were themselves determined by the manner in which the land came into being.

"The world is as ignorant of the geology and topography of Florida as of Central Africa," it was written in 1885, and the observation continues to be quite true in spite of the fact that much has been said on these subjects and even though millions of tourists have explored the coastal regions. To add to the general confusion, some folk have made a practice of ridiculing the Palmetto Country's physical aspects. For example, Carl Dann, a prominent citizen of Orlando, opens his chamber of commerce speeches with this story, "just to show how important the Danns are."

"My grandfather drove down the Florida in a covered wagon in the 1860's, but bein born and raised up in Kentucky, he didn't like such a flat country. So he got down on his hands and knees and scraped up the sand and built all the hills you see scattered around. Sometimes he scared me with his diggin, and I said, 'Grandpa, you better not dig up all that sand—you know there are a lot of places down here where you have to use a ladder to climb up to the ocean.' But he wouldn't pay no attention to me, and went right on with his hill-makin.

"Bein born and raised up in Wisconsin, another thing Grandpa didn't like about Florida was the scarcity of rivers and lakes. So he hitched up his ox team and went over to the coast, dipped up some water with gourds, carted it back and filled up all those holes he had dug. That's how he made all these rivers and lakes with the unmentionable names—the Caloosahatchee, Withlacoochee, Oklawaha, Tsala Apopka, Weohyakapka, Thonotosassa, Okonlockhatchee, Hickpochee, Lockapepka, Hatcheneeha, Econlockhatchee, Tildepucksassa, Peaatlecahah, and Istokpogayoxie."

The Palmetto Country rests upon what is geologically knows as the Floridian Plateau, which, compared to the rest of the continent, is a mere infant of some forty-five million years. Contrary to popular belief (founded upon superficial examinations of early geologists), the Floridian Plateau was not built up out of the sea as a coral reef. For ages the entire Plateau rested beneath the sea—much as it still does—and the foundation rock was covered with successive layers of limestone skeletons and microscopic marine life.

On The Caloosahatchee, Entrance to Lake Okeechobee.

09.........ON THE CALOOSAHATCHEE.
Old postcard with the title "On the Caloosahatchee. Entrance to Lake Okeechobee." Florida Historical Society.

After reaching a thickness of 4,000 feet, these layers rose above the surface to form a large island. Winds and waves built up protective coastal dunes, and the island's interior became a vast fresh-water lake, teeming with aquatic plant life. Lake Okeechobee is the remnant of this lake, and the 'Glades muck-lands owe their existence to the lush flora of those prehistoric ages. At length the island became joined with the mainland (whose coastline had roughly corresponded with the northern boundary of the Palmetto Country). The peninsula this formed extended only as far as the bottom rim of Lake Okeechobee, while the land and islands below this were later built up as coral reefs on top of the limestone layers—a process which still continues.

Layers of sand, and red, black, and white clay were washed down over the region from the mountains of Georgia and Alabama. The low hills of the Palmetto Country were not upheaved, but generally stand out because the surrounding terrain has settled or eroded away. The coastal lowlands comprising a great part of the region are for the most part less than one hundred feet above sea level, and the highest hill in Florida has an elevation of only 330 feet. The region's largest commercial, industrial, tourist, and port cities are along the coast, but otherwise the coastal lowlands are thinly populated. Most inland towns are marketing centers for agricultural areas, though a few inland Florida towns attract tourists.

It was during the Pleistocene era—the Age of Man—that the glacial ice sheet advanced from the North Pole to cover the northern part of what is now the United States, driving great hordes of animals southward into the Palmetto Country. Among those present were camels, horses, oxen, swine, hippopotami, rhinoceroses, elephants, mastodons, sloths, mammoths, and such carnivorous animals as saber-toothed tigers, lions, and wolves. Fossil remains of these animals are frequently found in the region, and in the underlying marine deposits there are shark teeth, whale bones, and fossil oysters two feet long.

The spotty nature of the region's soil has resulted in extremes of exaggerated folksay. "Things grow big around here," it is said in one area. "My old man planted sweet potatoes one year, and when it come 'tater-diggin time, one of em was so big we had to make a sawmill job out of it. He built the sawmill and put a lot of men to work cuttin up that potato. That year everybody had houses made out of sweet potato slaps. And what you reckon they ate? They all lived off potato pone made from the sawdust."

On the other hand there are stories like this: "The land is so poor around Ocala my old man had to give away a piece of land he bought there. It was so poor he couldn't get nothin but a church to take it. Well, they built a church and called a preacher, but that land was so poor they had to telegraph Jacksonville for ten sacks of commercial fertilizer and spread it on the ground before could raise a tune."

The limestone strata which crop to the surface in many places vary somewhat in their composition and appearance. Some are almost pure lime phosphate, and the surface wash-mining of this phosphate employs about 2,000 men. About two and a half million tons—sixty percent of the world's supply—are produced in the region each year. Other types of limestone are widely used for road beds and surfacing, while others are mixed

10 .... LIVING OFF THE LAND CAN BE DIFFICULT.
There wasn't much in the way of left-overs, but it was important for a shoat to eat, too. From the Stetson Kennedy collection.

with cement and molded into construction blocks. Additional non-metallic minerals mined in the Palmetto Country include Fuller's earth, kaolin, titanium oxide, diatomite, and silica.

The solubility of the limestone accounts for much of the region's pitted topography, sinks, potholes, and 30,000 lakes. It also provides underground reservoirs that hold an abundant supply of potable water. Underground waterways often cause the land surface to cave in, exposing streams like the Santa Fe and Alapaha Rivers, which disappear into the earth to reappear miles beyond. Enormous underground caverns have been washed out of the limerock, and a few of them have been partially explored. Names and dates carved into the walls of same of these caverns testify that they served as a hideout for Confederate draft dodgers.

The region has more coastline and surface water than any other in the United States. Florida's coastline alone—including islands, bays, estuaries, and other tidal reaches—extends 3,751 statute miles. Lake Okeechobee, with an area of 717 square miles, is the second largest body of fresh water lying entirely within the United States. Altogether, three million acres of Florida's surface are under water.

The Palmetto Country is dotted with springs, the largest of which is Silver Springs near Ocala (an Indian name meaning water's edge), with a daily flow of 800 million gallons. Next in size are Rainbow Springs near Dunnellon and Itchetucknee Springs near Lake City. Such springs either form or swell the region's rivers, about fifty of which are navigable. The Apalachicola, Escambia, and Choctawhatchee Rivers have their sources in the hills of Georgia and Alabama, and were important arteries of travel to the Gulf during ante-bellum days. The entire Atlantic coast of the region is bordered by a series of lagoons, through which winds the Intracoastal Waterway; a popular scenic route for pleasure craft, the Inland Waterway was used during World War II as a safe means of transporting petroleum by barge.

The disappearance of lakes is a periodic phenomenon, the best explanation of which is that debris clogs the openings in limestone lake bottoms, and from time to time rots away, allowing the water to drain off underground. When the holes again become clogged the lakes refill. Lake Neff in Hernando County (Florida) has gone through this process three times since 1917, and Payne's Prairie near Gainesville (Florida) has often been a lake. Its water drained off suddenly in 1823, 1870, and 1892, and on the latter date a small lake steamer was left high and dry. The Great Alachua Sink derived its middle name from the Indians; it means Big Bottomless Jug. Folks who live in the vicinity of disappearing lakes look forward to the opportunity to scoop up stranded fishes by the basketful, and salt down the surplus for future use.

Another characteristic feature of many lakes in the Palmetto Country are floating islands (see those in Orange Lake, Florida). These islands are formed when decaying masses of vegetation lying under water generate enough gas to force them to the surface. The buoyant roots of bonnets, which grow as large as a man's leg, are also said to play a large part in setting and keeping the islands afloat. When the masses break loose from the bottom they come "boiling" to the surface. Resembling muck, they protrude several inches above the water, and range in size up to several hundred square feet.

Soon their fertility gives rise to a heavy growth of trees and shrubs which sometimes reaches a height of twenty-five feet, and whose weight either anchors the mass or causes it to sink. The islands have every visible semblance of solidity, but tremble or sink underfoot. Often the vegetation acts as a sail, causing the islands to drift about—but the birds which nest on them somehow manage to keep track of their particular island. The Indians often buried their dead on floating islands, believing that when the islands sank they took the departed souls on a short cut to the Happy Hunting Ground.

The Palmetto Country has not been without its geological mysteries. One occurrence which caused much speculation was the appearance of a column of smoke and a red glare over Florida's Wakulla Swamp in August of 1886, and its disappearance immediately after the Charleston earthquake. The presumption is that lightning had ignited a flow of natural gas, and that the vent was closed by the quake. Less spectacular are a series of "chimneys" near Brooksville (Florida). About thirty-six inches in diameter, and filled almost to the top with sand and humus, their rims are blackened at the top, yet show no indications of ever having undergone volcanic heat.

Way-Way Down South

I'm goin where that chill wind never blows,
Lord, I'm goin where the climate suits my clothes,
And I aint gonna be treated thisaway.

That song of the migratory farm workers who move down into the Palmetto Country each winter reveals something of the relation between climate and life. Geographically, the Palmetto Country is the Deepest South. The northernmost part of Florida is farther south than the southernmost part of California, Jacksonville lies in the same latitude as Shanghai and Cairo, and the entire peninsula is hundreds of miles nearer than Rome to the Equator.

With the exception of a few spots in Florida, the region is also psychologically the Deepest South. Even Florida is not so sophisticated as she pretends to be. Recently when a prominent speaker opened his address at the University of Florida by saying "Down here in the sticks—" he was interrupted by an indignant howling, hissing, whistling, booing, and stomping that could not be quelled for fifteen minutes. As a university professor observed the next day, "If there was any doubt about Florida being in the sticks, there was none whatever after that idiotic demonstration."

For a long time the Gulf Stream was given much of the credit for the region's mild climate, but its reputation in this respect has now fallen into disrepute. Ponce de León was the first to record encountering the current around the tip of Florida. In 1771 it was labeled the Florida Stream by an English map-maker, but it was later named the Gulf Stream by Benjamin Franklin. It is actually an enormous river whose volume exceeds that of all other rivers in the world combined. At times the waters of the Gulf of Mexico are three feet higher than in the ocean; forming a mighty stream 350 fathoms deep and fifty miles wide, they push through the Florida Straits and up along the Atlantic coast. Vessels traveling southward keep close inshore to avoid the current, while northbound ships take advantage of it.

The quantity and quality of the region's sunshine have been overexploited, and there is no reason for flaunting the chamber of commerce school of writing on this particular subject. With a daily average of more than six hours of sunshine, Florida calls herself "The Land of Sunshine,"

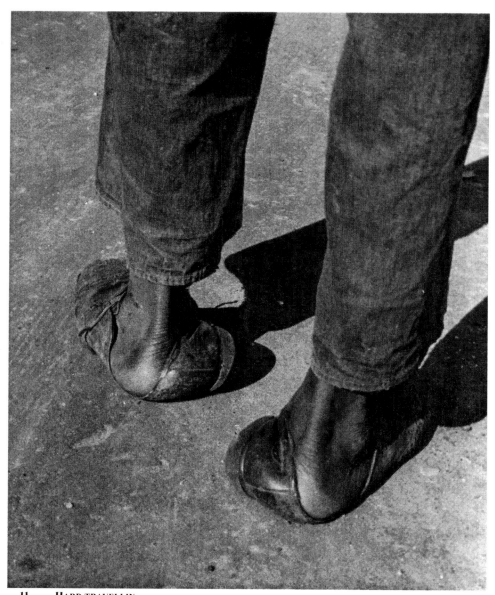

11 ....Hard Travellin.
America's legendary folk balladeer Woody Guthrie sang "Now I been doin some hard travellin, Lord! I'm goin where the climate suits my clothes, and I ain't a-gonna be treated this-away!" From the Stetson Kennedy collection.

while Miami is "Where the Summer Spends the Winter," the Florida Keys are "Where the Tropics Really Begin," and the 'Glades area is "The Empire of the Sun."

St. Petersburg has spent no less than a million dollars advertising itself as The Sunshine City, with such effectiveness that letters so addressed promptly reach their destination. Since 1910 the St. Petersburg *Independent* has given away its entire edition each day the sun failed to shine before its 3 p.m. presstime. In twenty-six years this has only happened an average of five times per year. The city's green benches, which have won such wide fame in fiction and in the proceedings of swindle and divorce cases, have become an institution whose contours are standardized by ordinance.

According to the American Meteorological Society, "Florida has the sunniest winter climate in the eastern U. S. The Florida peninsula not only has the highest percentage of possible sunshine—over 60 percent in winter and over 70 percent in spring—but also the most intense sunlight of any lowland east of Texas. In December, the intensity of sunshine exceeds that in the North by over 50 percent."

There may be some connection between this and the fact that the process of making artificial ice was worked out in the Palmetto Country. The inventor, Dr. John Gorrie of Apalachicola, built his ice-making machine in 1845 to cool the rooms of fever patients. He is one of the two Floridians who have been given a niche in Statuary Hall at Washington, D. C.

During tourist season the sea breezes become laden with the heavy sweet scent of sun-tan lotion. Hotels, apartments, and even cabin camps feature roof sun-decks, and solariums for nude sun-bathing attract numerous patrons and 'planes. These modern sun-worshipers are following in the footsteps of the Indians of the Palmetto Country, who gave pre-eminence to the sun god, as contrasted to the Plains Indians who worshiped a sky god.

July and August, with an average temperature of about 81 degrees, are the warmest months in Florida; thereafter the temperature declines to an average of 59 degrees in December and January. Even in South Georgia the temperature only falls below freezing an average of 22 days each year. All this does not mean Palmetto Country is never cold; severe freezes have changed the way of life in whole areas, and many poor folks suffer terribly each winter.

In 1766 a freeze killed the orange groves in North Florida, where inhabitants referred to the light snow as "an extraordinary white rain." By 1835 new groves had been planted, but in that year the temperature dropped to seven degrees below zero, permanently driving the citrus industry out of the northern part of the state. Another "Big Freeze" in 1895 killed the groves deep into the peninsula. A bright landowner in the Miami area sent a bouquet of unharmed orange blossoms to Henry M. Flagler, head of the Florida East Coast Railway. Impressed, Flagler visited Miami—then a few sand trails through the palmettoes—and was enticed by large land grants to extend his railroad there in 1896.

Colonel V. E. Stolbrandt, one of the first graduates of West Point and an old Indian fighter who was "transferred two days before Custer's Last Stand," told his high school classes in Jacksonville, "After spending three years in Alaska where the temperature went to 30 below zero, I came to Florida and almost froze to death." It is the Palmetto Country's excessive humidity, arising from its countless lakes and encircling waters, that causes a damp coldness which penetrates clothing and flesh in a manner not known in cold dry climates.

Yet the summer heat is greatly mitigated by a general atmospheric drift from ocean to gulf—the region is really "The Land of Ocean Breezes" and "Down Where the Trade Winds Play."

Ever since the Fountain of Youth myth was associated with Florida, miraculous curative properties have been ascribed to the region's sunshine, salt air, pine groves, and springs. In 1885 the Florida Investment Company proclaimed, "Here is a land of open pine forests studded with crystal-clear lakes, and marked by an absence of fever, mosquitoes, and negroes." In 1941, W. T. Couch of the University of North Carolina said, "I hardly know what to say when a Southerner tries to tell me the South is not the Nation's Economic Problem No. 1. It makes me feel as though I were wading through a ditch with a man who insists we are standing on a mountain top." Geography and people are mixed up in more ways than one.

When the Sawgrass Blooms

One of the most widely believed bits of folksay about the natural phenomena of the Palmetto Country is that when the sawgrass blooms in the
Everglades, the Seminoles interpret it as a sign that a hurricane is coming,
and so migrate to higher ground until the danger has passed. This story,
dramatically retold each year by the Associated Press, never fails to create
a flurry of excitement. As a matter of fact, the sawgrass blooms every year,
and the Seminoles simply have sense enough to leave the lowlands during
the hurricane season.

Superstitious folk also think there will be a hurricane when: animals
become restless; sand crabs migrate from mangrove thickets; ants are

12........HARVESTING VEGETABLE CROPS, SOUTH OF MIAMI.
    In the Everglades mucklands below the frost line, three crops per year are possible. Up until mid-
century, this sort of "stoop labor" was provided by black and white Americans. Since then, Mexican
immigrants have predominated. State Library and Archives of Florida.

unusually busy storing food in their nests; ants invade a house; horseflies infest beaches in spring; cats perch on high furniture or fences; the summer is wet; the summer is dry; there is a good mango crop. On the other hand, a good citrus crop is said to indicate there will be no hurricane.

Florida editors, with their weather eye focused intently on the tourist trade, once bent their talents to subduing the howling hurricanes into gentle zephyrs, but they now render the public (and themselves, through added circulation) a service by giving headline prominence to "tropical disturbances," as they still prefer to call them. The University of Miami has even gone so far as to proudly name its football team the Miami Hurricanes. Most hurricanes are bred in that incubator of ill winds, the Caribbean, and Florida editors register legitimate kicks when a hurricane that has never been near the Florida coast sweeps northward and in on New England, to be branded by newspapers all over the country as a "Florida hurricane."

A popular bit of doggerel defines the hurricane season thus: June—too soon. July— stand by. August—look out you must. September—remember. October—all over.

The hurricane season actually includes August, September and October. It is then that Florida's south Atlantic coast and Keys are most hurricane-conscious, and storm-insurance sales reach their peak. The windows of tourist hotels and other establishments which remain closed during summer are tightly boarded. Radios and barometers are frequently consulted, but hurricane warnings give rise to little action until it seems certain that the storm is headed for the mainland. Then shop-owners take down their signs and board their widows. The windows of homes are likewise boarded, or metal storm shutters—like outside Venetian blinds— are tightly closed. Chimneys are capped, trees and shrubbery are braced.

Bath tubs are filled with water as a precaution against failure of the piped supply, and oil stoves, lanterns, and candles are made ready for emergency service. People in outlying districts often come into town to camp in churches, schools, libraries, auditoriums, and other substantial public buildings. Liquor package houses do a rushing business as folk stock up for "hurricane parties." Before the hurricane strikes, electric power is shut off to eliminate the danger of fallen live wires.

A heavy sky blacks out the sun, and torrential rain is driven by lashing wind. The hurricane proper is in the shape of a doughnut, with a body of wind rushing at high speed about a center of calm air. Fortunately, the forward speed of the whole averages about twenty miles per hour or less, giving ample time for protective preparations. Places in the direct path of a hurricane experience three phases of it: the racing wind in one direction, the dead calm, then the same circling wind, but coming from the opposite direction. These characteristics are responsible for much loss of life among those who leave their shelters during the intervening calm.

The damage wrought by hurricanes is not done by the wind alone, however; the accompanying tidal waves and torrential rains are even more destructive of life and property. In the 1926 hurricane, for example, an eleven-foot tidal wave covered Miami Beach, and Miami was inundated by eight feet of water. More than 150 persons drowned when the same winds forced the waters of Lake Okeechobee through its dikes to wash out the town of Moore Haven. Tidal waves were likewise responsible for most of the death and destruction in the blows of 1928 and 1935.

When the hurricane is over it is sometimes days before communications, except by short-wave radio, are re-established with the rest of the world. The National Guard is usually called out to maintain order, the Red Cross leads in rehabilitation work, and public and private agencies co-operate on the job of reconstruction. Material evidence of the damage is speedily removed, with the exception of long stretches of leaning trees and gaunt trunks which point the path of the hurricane.

But there is no erasing the vivid impressions left on the minds of the folk who go through the storms. The oral tradition of the region is filled with tales of the hurricanes' fabulous feats of destruction. As the Negro bean-pickers in the 'Glades say about the big blow of '28: "It blowed so hard it blowed a well up out of the ground, blowed a crooked road straight, and scattered the days of the week so bad that Sunday didn't get around till late Tuesday mornin." Another delightfully Negroid anecdote has it: "The hurricane met the storm in West Palm beach, and they ate breakfast together. Then the hurricane said to the storm, 'Let's breeze on down to Miami and shake that thing!'"

There is scarcely a place in the whole region that does not have its true local legends about boats blown so far inland and automobiles blown out to sea; boards driven through trees; railway tracks stood on edge like a picket fence; two-ton bridges lifted from their moorings; cows, horses, and pigs carried away on the wings of the wind, never to be heard of again; and houses lifted from their foundations to be turned in mid-air and set down intact again on the same foundations, but facing the opposite way.

One story tells of an incident in the hurricane of 1906, when Miami was a frontier settlement. Judge Robert R. Taylor was reputedly playing pool in Hill's Place, when the sky suddenly took on a pinkish glow. The terrified Negro population thought Judgment Day was at hand. When the hurricane struck Judge Taylor ran for his office in the Fussell Building. Across the hall he found Judge George A. Worley on his knees praying. After listening apprehensively for a few minutes to Judge Worley's praying and the hurricane's howling, Judge Taylor cried, "Get up from there, George—you aint doin a damn bit of a good! Let me try it!"

13.........Making repairs after the 1926 Hurricane.
The 1926 Hurricane brought extensive damage to Fort Lauderdale. Here linemen work to restore electricity to the area. Historical Association of Southern Florida.

Hurricanes have left their marks not only upon the folkways of the region, but also upon its literature. Examples of this are Theodore Pratt's *Big Blow,* Zora Neale Hurston's *Their Eyes Were Watching God*, and Laurie Havron's *Hurricane Hush.*

For the past half-century Florida has been damaged by an average of one hurricane per year. The three most disastrous in recent years were: the 1926 hurricane which affected Miami, Okeechobee, and Pensacola areas, causing the death of 327, injuries to 6,327 and property damage estimated at $150,000,000; the 1928 hurricane over the West Palm Beach and Okeechobee areas, which killed 1,810, injured another 1,849, and did $10,000,000 worth of damage; and the 1935 Florida Keys hurricane which caused about 800 deaths and the partial destruction of the Oversea Railroad. Most of the above estimates are by the arch-conservative Red Cross, whose death figures are largely limited to bodies found, and do not include all missing persons. The whereabouts of these missing persons is clarified from time to time as skeletons are discovered in remote places.

The sea-level barometer reading during the Keys hurricane was 26.35, the lowest ever recorded in the Western Hemisphere. The direct path of this hurricane was forty miles wide, and its wind velocity probably reached 200 miles per hour. The 1926 hurricane had a velocity of 115 m.p.h., and the 1928 hurricane brought winds of 150 m.p.h.

For a combination of reasons, the 1926 Miami blow is known as Florida's Great Hurricane, even though the loss of life and velocity of wind were considerably less than in '28 and '35. First among causes of the '26 hurricane's pre-eminence was the enormous property damage affecting many people in all parts of the country. Then there was the twenty-four-hour blackout of all communication with the area, and the dramatic break of the news. The scarcity of real news gave rise to sensational but false reports that the entire city had been flattened, that looters were being shot, and that the whites were lynching the blacks.

The national campaign for relief funds also played an enormous part in publicizing the hurricane, as indicated by the public contributions of $3,818,281 to the Red Cross—the second largest fund ever raised in the United States. (Largest: 1905 San Francisco earthquake and fire: $9,279,953.) After the hurricane the Governor of Florida visited the area and declared, "The damage is not as bad as has been reported"; whereupon the national director of the Red Cross complained that his statement had hindered the collection of relief funds, and intimated that the Governor and real estate agents were trying to cover up the situation.

Though not as bad as some reports, the situation was ghastly enough. Most notable wreck was the Meyer-Kiser Building, eighteen stories high, which was laid open and virtually stripped of the wall facing Biscayne Bay. Countless other large buildings were seriously damaged, and whole blocks were condemned. Scarcely a plate-glass window was left intact. The flimsy constructed Boom buildings, usually made of stucco or light concrete blocks, were, for the most part, damaged, de-roofed, and demolished. Many pioneer wooden dwellings came through almost unscathed, and this was attributed to the soundness of their timbers as well as their low, solid construction. One such building had long been condemned as unsafe; it withstood the blow while the Boom buildings around it were flattened.

All vessels in Biscayne Bay and the Miami River were either sunk, carried out to sea, or tossed far inland. Among those sunk was the *Nohab*, a luxurious yacht given by Bertha Krupp to the Kaiserin; for a nominal admission charge it had been opened to the public, which seemed most intrigued by the silver bathtubs in which the German nobility had bathed.

Among the freaks of the storm were two beach umbrellas left standing in the open amid the ruins of demolished buildings; a steel flagpole bent into a triangle; and a man who complained for several days about a "crick" in his neck until it was found to be broken—and he didn't even know how it had happened. A sudden jerk would have killed him.

For the first few days following the hurricane the National Guard and American Legion were on guard to prevent looting, and a curfew required everyone to stay off the streets after 6 p.m. Profiteering in foodstuffs was rigidly prohibited by a city proclamation which pulled no punches. It read:

"Anyone found guilty of profiteering in food supplies will be subject to immediate arrest, their places of business closed, license revoked, and all food supplies on the premises confiscated. Citizens are urged to report any violations of this proclamation."

Cuba sent a relief mission aboard one her battleships, with 250 tons of supplies, 50,000 typhoid inoculations, a $6,000 contribution, and a corps of doctors and nurses. The Chicago *Herald-Examiner,* in a special train donated by the Illinois Central Railroad, sent a mercy expedition of about one hundred doctors, nurses, and X-ray technicians, together with chlorine for disinfecting water, clothing, and other supplies. Trainloads of used clothing poured into Miami—far more than was needed. Several thousand persons who wanted to leave the area were given free transportation by the railroads.

Fifteen thousand persons were homeless, and five tent colonies were established to care for them. Tents, cots, blankets, and other supplies were provided by the Army and National Guard. The Red Cross rendered assistance to 60,000 people, and administered 50,000 typhus inoculations which not only prevented an epidemic but lowered the normal incidence of the disease for many months to come. No less than 60,000 letters and telegrams were received and handled from people requesting information about friends and relatives.

The Great Hurricane is commemorated by the following folksong which is still widely sung in the area.

MIAMI HURRICANE

The rich white folks and well-to-do
Were playin five-up and pool;
God-Almighty got angry, and glory—
They forgot each other's move.

Some was floatin on the ocean,
And some was floatin on the sea;
And some was cryin on bended knee,
"Lord, have mercy on me!"

Ships swam down that ocean,
It was most too sad to tell;
Ten thousand peoples got drownded,
And all but twelve went to hell.

And the lady left Miami,
She left in lightnin speed;
Ev'ry time the lightnin flashed,
She thinks bout her dirty deeds.

Yon stands the lady,
Standin in the back door
Singin, "If I get back to Georgia,
I won't go to Florida no more."

Chorus:
God-Almighty moved on the water,
And the peoples in Miami run.

The 1928 hurricane is less renowned than its predecessor because the property damage was less and also because the great majority of those killed were Negro migratory agricultural workers, many of whom were natives of the Bahama Islands. After passing over West Palm Beach the hurricane swept a tidal wave from Lake Okeechobee over the 'Glades mucklands where the workers were caught in their flimsy shacks with no

14.........MIGRATORY FARM WORKERS' HOUSING, BELLE GLADE.
    Car models have changed for the better since the 1930s, but farm workers housing has not. Marion Post Wolcott photograph. State Library and Archives of Florida.

43

means of escape. Said to be a public-health menace, the bodies of the victims were hastily piled, drenched with kerosene, and burned.

There is also a folksong which tells of this storm.

> *The 1928, or West Palm Beach, Storm*
> *On the sixteenth day of September,*
> *In 1928,*
> *God started ridin early;*
> *He rode till very late.*
>
> *He rode out the ocean,*
> *Chained the lightnin to his wheel;*
> *Stepped on land at West Palm Beach,*
> *And the wicked hearts did yield.*
>
> *I tell you wicked people,*
> *What you had better do:*
> *Go down and get the Holy Ghost,*

15 .... MIGRATORY FARM WORKERS.
The 1928 Hurricane killed many African American migratory farm workers. From the Stetson Kennedy collection.

And then you live the life, too.

Over in Pahokee
Families rushed out at the door,
And somebody's poor mother
Haven't been seen anymore.

Some mothers looked at their children,
And they began to cry;
Cried, "Lord, have mercy,
For we all must die!"

Out around Okeechobee
All scattered on the ground,
The last account of the dead they had
Were twenty-two hundred found.

South Bay, Belle Glade, and Pahokee,
Tell me they all went down,
And over at Chose,
Ev'rybody got drowned.

Some people are yet missin,
And haven't been found, they say;
But this we know: they will come forth
In the Resurrection Day.

When Gabriel sounds his trumpet,
And the dead begin to rise,
We'll meet the saints from Chose,
Up in the heavenly skies.

Chorus:
In the storm, oh, in the storm,
Lord, somebody got drowned.

Another variation of this song centers about a localized disaster of 1936:

THE GAINESVILLE STORM

On April 6, 1936,
God swept through Gainesville, Georgia,
And left the people in a fix.

God got tired the way some people do,
So he went sweepin through there
And left only a few.

People were runnin and hollerin—
Oh, what a mighty sound!
Ev'ry time God gave a whirl,
The buildins hit the ground!

When God began his work,
The telegrams fell down;
People there in Gainesville,
Couldn't get no news from town.

So all you people who want work to do
Can go to Gainesville, Georgia
Where God prepared plenty good work for you.

In some respects the 1935 Keys hurricane was the saddest of all. Of the 800 victims, more than half were World War veterans—Depression "hunger marchers" on Washington. The Government had put them to work on the Overseas Highway on the mosquito-ridden Florida Keys. The veterans had no shelter but the small board shanties in which they were housed, and these were smashed flat by the first gusts. Some of the men lashed themselves to the low mangrove trees, while others tied themselves to the railroad tracks. But the eighteen-foot tidal wave which swept over the Keys covered everything. Most of those who saved themselves did so by clinging to floating debris.

Although some food was dropped by plane, it was several days before the survivors could be reached by boat. Funeral pyres were again ignited, in spite of the protests of Miami morticians who said that cremation was motivated only by the desire of the Government to save an embalming fee of about fifty dollars per victim.

An official Congressional investigation was held in an effort to fix responsibility for the tragedy. Survivors testified that camp officials had refused to let them leave in several trucks that were available. After much delay, the camp had sent a request for a special evacuation train; the request marked hours of precious time in Miami and St. Augustine (headquarters of the railroad) before it was granted. Because it was Labor Day, more hours were lost in Miami rounding up a train crew. The train eventually departed, but was overturned before arriving. Official verdict: "The disaster was an act of God."

Most of the deaths and much of the destruction caused by hurricanes has been due to flimsy housing, the inability and failure of people to get out of danger zones, inadequate publicizing of storm warnings, and lack of public instruction as to precautionary measures. Improved methods of charting storms, greater prevalence of radios, and the construction of more hurricane-proof buildings have helped decrease the danger, but there is really nothing to prevent the recurrence of such "acts of God."

The Negroes have a story which comes about as close to the truth as the "act of God" verdict. "It was the day before Christmas, and God was on his way to Palatka. It happened the Devil was travelin the same road, and when he seen God comin he jumped behind a stump—He wanted to catch God 'Christmas gift' so God would have to give him a present. God was sorta busy in his mind, countin over how many new angels he had to buy presents for, so he wasn't payin no attention to stumps. When God passed by, the Devil jumped out an hollered 'Christmas gift!'

"'You done caught me for once,' God said, lookin back over his shoulder. 'Take the East Coast.'—And that's why the Florida East Coast has so many hurricanes—it belongs to the Devil."

UNDER SEVEN FLAGS

Fountains of Youth and Cities of Gold

The tall tale about Ponce de León discovering the North American continent while searching for a miraculous Fountain of Youth is a legend often accepted as historical fact. The legend of a fountain whose waters bestowed eternal youth was current among the Indians of Puerto Rico, and it was they who reputedly passed it on to Ponce de León. The fountain was said to be in Bimini, as the Indians called the land to the north, and from time to time Puerto Rican Indians set out in their canoes to find it. Fontenada reported in 1580 that there were whole villages of West Indians in South Florida who had come there in search of the magic spring; their descendants were observed by explorers as late as 1722. One West Indian, Andreas the Bearded, told the New World's first historian, Pedro Martyr, that his father had actually found the fountain at some time before 1524, and had returned home with renewed youth and vigor.

The idea of such a fountain existed among the folk legends of many parts of the world, including Europe. Prester John, the mythical king of central Asia, was alleged to have written the Christian Pope that in his realm "at the foot of Mount Olympus bubbles a spring, just three days' journey from Paradise, out of which Adam was driven. If any has tasted twice of the fountain, from that day he will feel no fatigue but will as long as he lives be as a man of thirty years." When the first maps of the New World were drawn they showed the Americas as part of Asia, so it was natural for the explorers to think they might find the fountain. Whether or not Ponce de León was seriously searching for it is a question. At any rate, tourists are now able to take their choice of several Fountains of Youth, where they may imbibe freely of sulphurous waters.

Ponce de León embarked upon his voyage of exploration in 1513, and sighted the mainland on March 28. He named the land *La Florida* because of its cool level woodlands and also because the discovery was made during *Pascua Florida*—Flowery Easter. Leonardo da Vinci's map of 1513 used the name Terra Florida, and so the entire continent was known for more than two hundred years. A typical map of 1560 showed Florida as extending from the Rio Grande indefinitely up the Atlantic Coast to the Polar Sea.

Ponce de León returned in 1521 with a group of colonists, but their preoccupation with searching for cities of gold, and their disdain for agricultural pursuits, soon led to trouble with the Indians. Ponce de León was wounded in a battle with the natives, and when he prepared to leave for Cuba his entire colony insisted on going along.

The cities of gold idea was based upon a legend which was very widely believed at the time, to the effect that during the eighth century seven Christian bishops and their followers had fled Moorish persecution in Spain, and had sailed across the unknown western seas to a new land where they founded seven cities of fabulous wealth.

In another attempt to find wealth in Florida, Spain dispatched an expedition under Pánfilo de Narváez in 1528, which landed with 300 soldiers in the vicinity of Tampa Bay. At first the Indians thought the Spaniards were gods. Like the Mexican Indians, their religion included a belief that some day white men would come to rule them wisely and well. The Spaniards seemed to have abundant signs of divinity: they came in great cloudlike ships from over the water; they carried miraculous death-dealing sticks and spoke with thunder, fire and smoke; they were clad in shining armor, and some of them (on horse-back) seemed to have four legs and two heads. Narváez himself was a one-eyed giant of a man with flaming red hair—the symbol of the sun god.

The Indians soon discovered, however, that the Spaniards were more inhuman than superhuman. Learning of their greed for gold, the Indians told them that to the north they would find the Ocalis—men so powerful that birds on the wing were felled by their shout. Such strength, they said, had brought the Ocalis great riches in gold, silver, and pearls. Narváez and his men speedily set out for Ocali-land. Their tortuous trek carried them through many difficult swamps and jungles, but eventually they reached the land of the Ocalis.

Dunchanchellin, their chief, met Narváez with great pomp and ceremony. The latter was disappointed to learn that the Ocalis had lots of corn, but no gold, silver or pearls. Dunchanchellin quickly caught on, and told Narváez that the city of gold he had in mind was farther to the west, in the land of the Apalachees. Their country, he said, was so rich that its southern boundary, the *Guasaca-Esqui* (River of Reeds—now the Suwannee), flowed over beds of gold. Again the fairy tale worked like a charm, and the Ocalis were soon rid of the troublesome Spaniards. Dunchanchellin personally conducted them to the territory of his rivals, the Apalachees, and then, like the Pied Piper, he vanished.

One-third of Narváez' men fell victim to Indian arrows, fever, hunger, and privation. When the survivors finally came out on the Gulf they built boats and attempted to sail down the coast to their ships, but most of them perished in the storm. Among the survivors was Alvar Núñez Cabeza de Vaca, two other Spaniards, and Estebanico—a Moorish Negro slave from the west coast of Morocco, who was probably the first Negro to reach the North American continent. This group wandered eight years before reaching Mexico. Later, in 1539, Estebanico acted as advance agent for Fray Marcos de Niza who preceded the Coronado expedition into the American Southwest.

It was also in 1539 that Spain sent Hernando de Soto to look for the cities of gold which lured Narváez to his doom. De Soto, having spent seventeen years in Peru, was thoroughly enamored of the metal. Like Narváez, he landed in the vicinity of Tampa Bay and marched northward. Traversing the length of the peninsula, he marched through Georgia, cut the corners of the Carolinas and Tennessee, and entered Alabama to fight a disastrous battle with the Indians in the vicinity of Mobile. Going on to discover the Mississippi River, he was stricken by fever and buried in its waters. Four

16 .... NATIVE AMERICAN GIRLS.
When the Spanish came to La Florida looking for gold, Native American tribes already populated the Peninsula. From the Stetson Kennedy collection.

years after the beginning of the expedition, its remnants reached Mexico—without having found any cities of gold.

Blood and Sand Dunes

The French put in a claim to the region in 1562, when an expedition led by Jean Ribaut landed at the mouth of the St. Johns River and erected a stone pillar engraved with the French King's coat-of-arms. Ribaut made a good impression on the local Indian chieftain by presenting him with a robe of royal blue embroidered with the fleur-de-lis in gold, plus assorted trinkets for the tribesmen. When the Frenchmen sailed away the Indians treated the stone pillar with reverence, adorning it with boughs and placing fruit and corn at its base. A Spanish Captain Hernando Manrique de Rojas came searching for the pillar in 1563, but the Indians hid it from him.

In reporting on his expedition, Ribaut wrote, "We inquired of them [the Indians] for a certain town called Cibola—whereof some have written not to be far from here—and they showed us by signs that they might go there with their boats by rivers in twenty days. It is said there is a great abundance of gold, silver and precious stones, and that the people tip their arrows with turquoise."

In 1564, René de Laudonnière, who had accompanied Ribaut, set out from France with 300 colonists, most of them Huguenot Protestants, but there was no minister along because the settlement was to be nonsectarian. They also landed at the mouth of the St. Johns, and were welcomed by the Indians. With the colonists were four women—probably the first female Protestants to reach North America.

A fortification was built, which they called Fort Caroline, but too many of the colonists were adventurous young sons of wealthy French Huguenots. Like the Spaniards, they were more interested in looking for gold than in procuring food. When the Indians grew tired of feeding the colony, Laudonnière made the mistake of imprisoning their chief.

In 1565, Sir John Hawkins, homeward bound after a slave-trading trip to the West Indies, stopped at Fort Caroline to take on water. The custom of smoking tobacco, now an international folkway, was noted in Hawkins' ship's log as follows: "The Floridians when they travaile have a kind of herbe dried, who with a cane and an earthen cup on the end, with fyre and dried herbes put together, doe suck through the cane the smoke thereof, which smoke satisfieth hunger, and therewith do live four or five days without food or drinke."

Hawkins offered to transport the discontented French colonists back to Europe, but they declined, rightly suspecting him of coveting the land in which they had gained a foothold. Yet he was scarcely out of sight before the Frenchmen began making their own preparations to depart. But then Jean Ribaut made an appearance with seven vessels and about 700 colonists. A week later, however, a Spanish fleet under Pedro Menéndez de Avilés attacked the colony. The French vessels slipped their cables and outdistanced their pursuers, and when Menéndez returned to attack on Fort Caroline he found the French artillery ready for him. Consequently he retired to the nearest harbor, in the vicinity of St. Augustine.

Ribaut manned his returning ships and sailed down the coast to look for the Spaniards, but a violent storm drive his ships ashore. When Menéndez learned that the French fleet had been driven southward, he moved overland through the storm and took the remaining defenders of Fort Caroline by surprise. One hundred and thirty-two of the French, including women and children were killed in the battle. Thirty French survivors were hung by Menéndez to oak trees, "not as Frenchmen, but as Huguenots." A few Frenchmen escaped by ship and eventually made their way to France.

Upon returning to St. Augustine, Menéndez was told that the French fleet had been wrecked and that the survivors were gathered on the beach a few miles to the south. Taking forty soldiers, Menéndez surrounded the 150 Frenchmen, and "promised them solemnly under the pledge of his word that if they surrendered themselves to his mercy, he should do with them as his Lord commanded him." This sounded like a Christian offer, so the shipwrecked Frenchmen accepted. Menéndez then tied them in bunches of ten, ferried them across the inlet—since called *Matanzas* (Massacre)—and slaughtered them all behind the sand dunes.

Twelve days later, he learned that 200 more survivors of the French shipwreck had gathered at Matanzas. This time he took 150 soldiers with him. Finding Ribaut in charge, he offered them the same proposition of dealing with them as God commanded him. Knowing nothing of the previous massacres, the Frenchmen again placed themselves at Menéndez' mercy. On the march to St. Augustine they were suddenly halted, and

Menéndez suggested that they make their confessions. Ribaut replied, "From earth we come, and unto earth we must return; twenty years more or less of little account. Do with us as you wish." The massacre began and the sand dunes were again drenched with blood. Ribaut and about seventy other Frenchmen were slain, while the remainder escaped into the woods, never to be heard of again. Menéndez spared four men who professed to be Catholics, and several musicians.

When news of all these events reached King Philip of Spain, he wrote, "As to those Menéndez has killed he has done well and as to those he has saved they shall be sent to the gallows."

In 1568, a Frenchman named Dominique de Gourgues outfitted three ships at his own expense and set out to avenge the massacres. He captured the Spanish Fort San Mateo which had been erected on the site of Fort Caroline, deliberately killing all of the Spaniards except thirty, whom he hanged on the same oaks on which Menéndez had hanged the thirty Frenchmen. Over their bodies Gourgues hung a tablet reading: "Not as Spaniards, but as traitors, thieves, and murderers."

San Augustin, the Ever Faithful

St. Augustine, the oldest permanent white settlement in the United States, was founded by Menéndez in 1565. He remained in Florida until 1572, ruthlessly suppressing all further efforts of the French to settle the region. The Spaniards established four settlements of import: St. Augustine and Fernandina on the north Florida coast, and St. Marks and Pensacola on the Gulf; and also an extensive system of missions and trading posts. They were indefatigable in their efforts to catholicize the Indians, and also taught them farming and stock-raising.

At first Indians were used as slaves, but they proved so intractable that they were gradually replaced with Negro slaves, who were required to "accept Catholicism" before being admitted to the colony. Probably there were a few Negro slaves in St. Augustine from the very first. It is known that in 1581 the Spanish King sent Negro slaves to erect platforms for the artillery of St. Augustine's Fort San Marco, and that a Negro slave was attached to the friary in 1589. In 1594 the Spanish Governor of Florida asked the Governor of Cuba for a detachment of soldiers "and a few slaves"; and in the first hospital built in North America, completed at St.

55

Augustine in 1597, a Negress slave in the royal service "tended the sick—soldiers, Indians and Negroes." By 1603, there were thirty-two Negro slaves in the city, five of whom were women.

The old city of gold tale cropped up again in 1586 when Sir Francis Drake sacked and burnt St. Augustine. Nicholas Burgoigne, one of the French musicians spared by Menéndez, rowed out to Drake's ship playing the Protestant "March of the Prince of Orange," to show he was a friend. He told Drake that twenty days' journey northwest of St. Augustine, among the mountains of gold and crystal, there was a great rich city. But the British freebooters were never taken in by the folklore of Florida's riches, and mockingly referred to it as "Stolida, the Land of Fools," and "Sordida, the Land of Muckworms." English tars carousing in taverns often made this toast:

Have you not herd of floryda,
A Coontre for bewest,
Where savage pepell planted are
By nature and by hest,
Who in the mold
Fynd glysterynge gold
And yet for tryfels sell?

Yet all along the watere syde,
Where yt dothe eb and flowe,
Are turkeyse founde and where also
Do perles in oysteres growe,
And on the land
Do cedars stand
Whose bewty dothe excell.

The defeat of Spain's "Invincible Armada" in 1588 paved the way for England's efforts to colonize the Atlantic coast of North America. Despite violent Spanish protests, Jamestown (Virginia) was settled in 1607. In 1665 the British Crown boldly defined its Carolina colony as including northern Florida, Georgia, and all land westward to the Pacific Ocean. By that time Spain's grip on Florida had slipped to such an extent that British sources described St. Augustine as "a place where 200 Spaniards and Indians are in hiding." In a treaty of 1670, Spain officially conceded for the first time England's right to colonize a portion of North America, and an immediate result was the founding of Charleston.

In the following years an interesting association of Indians and Negroes took place in Florida. Negro slaves, as well as Creek and Yemassee Indian slaves, escaped from their British owners in the Carolinas and Virginia and made their way to Florida. The Spaniards of St. Augustine helped them build a fortification—Fort Moosa—a few miles north of their own Fort San Marco. Completed sometime between 1687 and 1695, Fort Moosa became the center of a prosperous agricultural and stork-raising colony of Indians and Negroes. Those Negroes who associated with the Indians, intermarried with them, and spoke their language, came to be known as Maroons (probably an Anglicized rendition of the Spanish word *morenos*—browns).

The outbreak of war in Europe in 1702 put an end to a brief period of amicability between Spanish St. Augustine and British Charleston. Co-operating French ships from Mobile and Spanish ships from St. Augustine attacked Charleston, but failed to capture it. Governor James Moore of South Carolina then laid siege to St. Augustine by land and sea, aided by 600 Yemassee Indians. After thee months the approach of two Spanish ships frightened Moore away. Arrotomakaw, chief of the Yemassees, scornfully told Moore's abandoned soldiers: "Though your governor leaves

17.........FORT SAN MARCO.
   Construction on the Spanish Fort San Marco (Castillo de San Marcos), photographed here in the late 1880's, began in 1672 in St. Augustine. Ellen Press Murdock Collection, Florida Historical Society.

you, I will not stir until I have seen all my men before me." The land forces carried back many Florida Indians and Negroes for sale in the Charleston slave market, and this inspired Moore and other Carolinians to make periodic raids into Florida which carried them as far west as Tallahassee and southward to Lake Okeechobee.

In 1719 the French of Mobile, no longer friendly with the Spanish, destroyed Fort San Carlos which the Spanish had built at Pensacola in 1698, and it was four years before Spain regained control of the place. Then in 1725 the British Colonel George Palmer led an attack from Georgia against St. Augustine, and though he captured many slaves, he did not succeed in taking Fort San Marco. The British again encroached on Spanish territory in 1733 by establishing Savannah below the boundary agreed upon in the treaty of 1670.

18.........Coquina Stone Buildings.
    St. Augustine's coquina stone buildings, photographed in 1888, were built by the Spanish and the English. 1888 Scrapbook Collection, Florida Historical Society.

The continuing escape of slaves from the British colonies led to the establishment of Georgia in 1738 as a colony where slavery was forbidden; the idea was to get the runaways to stop there, and not make a clean get-away into Spanish Florida. But the prosperous colony of Indians and Maroons around Fort Moosa continued to attract new refugees, and in 1740 Governor James Oglethorpe of Georgia launched an attack on it and St. Augustine. Colonel Palmer, leading a band of eighty Scotch Highland-ers, captured Fort Moosa, but it was soon retaken; Palmer was killed and the twenty survivors of his garrison were stripped and incarcerated in the dungeons of Fort San Marco. The siege of the fort lasted thirty-eight days before the British withdrew.

Three years later, Oglethorpe tried again, but with no more success. San Marco seemed impregnable, and the Spanish King gratefully bestowed the title of The Ever Faithful on the city of St. Augustine. To the British, how-ever, St. Augustine was "a den of thieves and ruffians, a receptacle of debt-ors, servants, and slaves, the bane of industry and society."

A scant eight years after Georgia had been set up on a non-slave basis, the rapid spread of cotton plantations caused its conversion into a slave-holding colony.

Havana fell before a British attack in 1762, and by the Treaty of Paris (1763) Spain traded Florida for the return of the Cuban capital. And so the Spaniards who had defended the peninsula for 200 years prepared to depart. The entire Spanish population of Pensacola was transported to Vera Cruz, Mexico, and the Spaniards of St. Augustine left in a body for Cuba, taking with them many of their Indian friends. When the British Tories occupied St. Augustine, they found that scarcely five Spaniards remained, and these were said to have missed their boat because they were so long in rounding up their horses.

The Tories Take Over

The Tories brought steep gabled roofs to St. Augustine, but coquina rock (pulverized sea shells naturally cemented with limestone) continued to be the most popular building material for both fortifications and dwellings. The newcomers also moved the living rooms in the Spanish-built houses down to the first floor, and installed fireplaces.

The British Crown, anxious to promote the settlement of its new colony, offered generous land grants as an enticement, and Florida began to experience her first boom. Promoters and land agents bestirred themselves in England, and published the first of the extravagant line of literature that made Florida "the best lied-about state." In 1765, the famous King's Road (now State Highway 4) was completed from New Smyrna below St. Augustine to Colerain, Georgia, thus establishing overland communication with the other British colonies.

In the same year Denys Rolle, a member of Parliament, having personally surveyed much of the peninsula, finally selected his 20,000-acre royal grant near the mouth of the St. Johns. There he brought a group of derelicts, prostitutes, and other unfortunates from the slums of London, with the aim of rehabilitating them. They established Rolletown, called Charlotia by its founder, but disease and dissatisfaction among his colonists soon put an end to his hopes of founding a Utopia. Rolle, however, continued to purchase land, and eventually controlled 80,000 acres. After adopting slave labor he managed to ship considerable quantities of rice, corn, beef, lumber, naval stores, and orange wine.

The first of a series of schemes to colonize Florida with Mediterranean peoples was launched in 1765 under the leadership of Dr. Andrew Turnbull, who brought in 1,500 colonists of Spanish, Greek, and Italian descent. About 1,200 of them came from the Spanish island of Minorca, where they had just undergone a severe famine. Lord Grenville, First Lord of the Treasury, was an ex-officio backer of the colony, and the British Government provided land grants exceeding 100,000 acres, 4,500 in cash, and a sloop of war for transportation.

Turnbull's colonists were landed at New Smyrna, and their status was that of "indentured servants" (debt slaves) who were under obligation to work until the "cost" of their transportation had been paid. For ten years they toiled, clearing the dense underbrush, raising indigo, digging drainage canals, and building roads (some of which are still in use). They endured many hardships, chief among which was cruel treatment at the hands of overseers who had been accustomed to handling Negro slaves, and who did not even speak the language of the Minorcans. When some of the colonists protested, they were beaten and executed. Privation and disease finally reduced their number to 600; they revolted, burnt the plantation, and moved to St. Augustine, where many of the men joined the British militia. The story of the Minorcan colony formed the basis of Stephen Vincent Benét's novel *Spanish Bayonet* (1926).

When the news of the American Declaration of Independence reached St. Augustine, John Hancock and Samuel Adams were burned in effigy in the public square. Four years later, three signers of the document—Arthur Middleton, Edward Rutledge, and Thomas Heyward—were sent to St. Augustine as prisoners and placed in the dungeon of the old fort.

There were about a thousand white Floridians at the time, and some 3,000 Negro slaves. Mostly newcomers from the British Isles and the recipients of land grants, the whites were generally loyal to the Throne. The Revolution caused more than 7,000 Tories to flee to Florida from the American colonies. Some came overland by wagon, while others made the journey in small coastal vessels.

Among them were Thomas Browne—a large planter from the Savannah River who had been given a tar-and-feathering by the "Liberty Boys" of Augusta—and Daniel McGirth of South Carolina. McGirth had been a scout in the American Army, but had been court-martialed after a row with an officer who had appropriated his favorite mare, Gray Goose. McGirth escaped and came to Florida with his brother and Gray Goose. He was instrumental in organizing the loyal East Florida Rangers, and became as noted for his pillaging as for his bravery.

St. Augustine was crowded with refugees, and feeling against the "rebels" ran high. When an army of 3,000 Americans invaded Florida in 1778 they were repulsed by a force of 1,210 British regulars, Indians, and backwoodsmen. Most of the original "Spanish" Indians of north Florida had by now been replaced by Creeks from south Georgia, who were allies of the British.

A noteworthy result of the Revolution was the establishment of the Scotch firm of Panton, Leslie and Company in Pensacola. William Panton, the senior partner and North America's first millionaire, planned to monopolize the Indian trade of West Florida. This he succeeded in doing by aligning himself with Alexander McGillivray, the son of Lachlan McGillivray (of a good Scotch family) and a French-Indian mother. Educated in Charleston, he became the chief of 6,000 Creek warriors, not to mention the fact that from time to time he was a colonel in the British Army, a colonel in the Spanish Army, and a brigadier-general in the American Army. Through him the firm of Panton, Leslie and Company extended its trade as far as Tennessee, and became more powerful than any government in the territory.

After the American colonies had won their independence, Florida remained the only loyal British colony on the mainland south of Canada. Britishers and Loyalists who had fought in the war were offered land grants in Florida according to their rank, and many of them accepted. The colony prospered until Spain seized Pensacola in 1781. With increasing American pressure from the north, Spanish pressure from the south, and Spanish-French encroachments on the west, England decided she could not afford to try to hold Florida.

So in 1783, after two decades of British rule, Florida was ceded back to Spain. At the time there were about 15,000 Britishers in the colony, and the majority of them packed up their livestock, Negroes, and other movable property and went to the Bahamas, Jamaica, or some American state. Only the Minorcans, looking forward with pleasure to Spanish Catholic rule, remained in St. Augustine.

Return of the Spaniard

Spain encountered little but trouble during her comeback in Florida. Since few Spaniards were willing to return, generous land grants were offered to American settlers who would swear allegiance to the Spanish King. Thomas Jefferson, then an American cabinet member, wrote President Washington: "I wish a hundred thousand of our inhabitants would accept the invitation. It may be the means of delivering to us peaceably what may otherwise cost a war. In the meantime we may complain of this seduction of our inhabitants just enough to make them [the Spaniards] believe we think it very wise policy for them and confirm them in it."

Quite a few southern folk—mostly woodsmen and cattlemen—took advantage of the offer, but there were few planters of means among them. Even those Americans who swore allegiance to Spain did so with their fingers crossed—most of them were descend from Spaniard-hating frontiersmen who had taken part in Oglethorpe's raids into Florida. The Seminoles, who hoped for a return of British rule, also remained aloof from the Spaniards.

The first treaty made under the Constitution was concluded with the Georgia Creeks on August 1, 1790, and bore the signature of President George Washington. It set aside certain lands for the Creeks, and required them to return all runaway slaves. Since they had few if any such slaves among them, the Creeks began making raids into Florida to capture Maroons to be turned over to American slavers.

The importation of additional slaves into the United States was prohibited after 1808, but as they could still be brought into Florida under Spanish law many Americans began smuggling them across the border into Georgia and Alabama. The slavers who landed their human cargoes in Fernandina had to first run a gauntlet of American gunboats, and then such pirates and hijackers as Pierre and Jean la Fitte.

As the War of 1812 became imminent, President Madison took steps to forestall British seizure of Florida. He sent an agent, General George Mathews, to Fernandina to forment a "Patriots' Rebellion." Two hundred "patriots" were rounded up, and under the leadership of John McIntosh they obtained the surrender of the Spanish garrison without bloodshed, and the Republic of Florida was proclaimed under a white flag bearing the figure of a soldier with fixed bayonet and inscribed with the motto: *Salus Populi—Suprema Lex*. Mathews had promised McIntosh payment and protection, but at the vigorous objections of Spain and England the "patriots" stepped down and Fernandina was again Spanish.

In the latter part of 1817 a chain of exciting events took place in Fernandina. Gregor MacGregor, a thirty-one-year-old Scotch promoter of South American independence, put into port with five vessels. The Spanish garrison surrendered, and MacGregor set up a government composed of men from Savannah and Charleston. Then he proceeded to offer his cargoes for sale. When the Spaniards finally mustered a striking force, MacGregor sailed away. Therupon Jared Irwin, who had been a congressman from Pennsylvania, gathered together the privateers of Fernandina, and defeated the Spaniards.

After a few weeks, Luis Aury, a pirate of French ancestry, arrived with thirteen ships and loot worth $60,000. He took possession of the town, appointing Irwin his "Adjutant-General." Having been the first Governor of Texas under Mexican rule, and still being a Mexican official of sorts, Aury raised the Mexican flag. In December the American ship under secret orders from President Monroe made its appearance, and Aury hauled down his Mexican flag and sailed away to resume his career as a pirate. The Americans stuck around, and Spain granted "local autonomy" to the northeast corner of Florida. This is said to have been the first time representative government was granted a Spanish colony.

Things were also happening fast in West Florida, which declared itself independent in 1810. John H. Johnston, member of a West Florida convention, said that "after annexation" the territory would submit in all things to the Federal Constitution, but suggested that a general amnesty be granted to all Tories, deserters, and fugitives from justice.

Meanwhile there had been a noteworthy strengthening of the bonds between the Seminoles and Maroons. Many of the latter were now several generations removed from the original runaway slaves, and had built up prosperous villages along the Suwannee and Apalachicola Rivers. Living a communal, unsupervised existence, they raised crops and livestock, paying annual tribute to Seminole chieftains.

In 1814 the British were permitted by the Spanish to land at Pensacola, where they began drilling Seminole recruits in the public square. A spectator wrote: "Such scenes of preposterous costuming, tripping over swords, and mad marching can hardly be imagined. The British might as well attempt to drill the alligators of the Florida lagoons." The British also built the Maroons and Seminoles a fort, mounted it with guns, and stocked it with powder. This inspired General Andrew Jackson to take it upon himself to lead a force of volunteers into Florida, which drove the British from Pensacola.

Two years later Jackson returned, this time he gave orders to General Duncan Clinch to attack the Negro fort, blow it up, and "return the niggers to their rightful owners." After a four-day siege by land and water, a heated cannonball pierced a powder magazine inside the stockade, and all but sixty of the 334 persons were blown to bits. Only three escaped injury. Two of the survivors, one Maroon and one Indian, were executed as "leaders."

In 1819 Spain ceded Florida to the United States, and the latter merely assumed responsibility for $5,000,000 in damage claims which Americans had filed against Spain during the troublous "Republic of Florida" period.

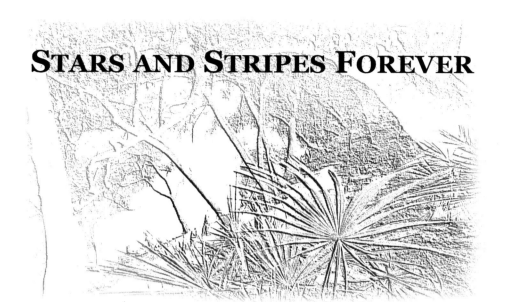

STARS AND STRIPES FOREVER

Bad Characters

When the American flag was raised over Florida in 1821 the territory had a population of about 8,000 whites, most of whom were Spanish. The number of Anglo-Saxons in the peninsula was considerable, however. For the most part they were backwoodsmen, who from time to time had been subjects of Great Britain, the United States, and Spain; but since none of these governments had bestowed any particular benefits on them, they naturally "didn't give a damn" what flag they lived under. These citizens led Surveyor-General George Clark to report in 1821: "The St. Mary's River has long been a jumping-off place of a large portion of bad characters who gradually sift southwardly; warm climates are congenial to bad habits." A similar opinion was expressed by Governor W. C. Claiborne of New Orleans, who wrote in 1810, "My impression is that a more heterogeneous mass of good and evil was never before gathered in the same extent of territory."

These "bad characters" were the forerunners of American civilization, and it was they who acquired the name "cracker" which even then was applied to poor white folk of Florida, Georgia, and Alabama. Probably the true story about how the crackers got their name is that when their "bad character" forebears first began to filter into Florida they were quite naturally called *cuácaros* (Quakers) by the Spaniards, and it was a simple matter, phonetically, for the Anglo-Saxons to conclude that they were being called "crackers."

There are two other stores about the origin of the term. The most popular has it that crackers got their name from their skill at cracking whips used to drive their cattle and the oxen which were the long source of haul-power in the region. The other story says that they got their name from the cracking and grinding of corn to make grits and meal, their chief staples.

Crackers are mainly descended from the Irish, Scotch, and English stock which, from 1740 on, was slowly populating the huge Southern wilderness behind the thin strip of coastal civilization. These folk settled the Cumberland Valley, the Shenandoah, and spread through every Southern state east of the Mississippi. That branch of the family which settled in the Deep South was predominantly of Irish ancestry, and their modern cracker descendants still sing songs in which their immigrant ancestors expressed hope for a better life in America:

> *Come to my arms, Norah darling,*
> *Bid your friends in old Ireland goodbye,*
> *And it's happy you will be,*
> *In the dear land of the free,*
> *Living happy with your Barney McCoy.*

As is the custom of folk everywhere, the newcomers were subjected to good-natured ridicule by songs like these:

> *Larry went out to plow in his corn,*
> *Wishing to his soul he'd never been born;*
> *Weeds was so think he couldn't get through,*
> *Saying, "Haw, haw Paddy, this will never do."*

> *Now it's I must finish my song:*
> *All the blamed Irishmen ought to have been hung;*
> *They come to this country and done as they please;*
> *They stocked it all up with their damn lice and fleas!*
> *Whoa, whoa, whoa Larry, whoa!*

> *My mother and father was Irish*
> *And I am Irish too.*

They kept a pig in the parlor,
And that was Irish too.
They had a bottle of whiskey,
And that was Irish too.

The early crackers were the Okies of their day (as they have been ever since). Cheated of land, not by wind and erosion, but by the plantation and slavery system of the Old South, they were non-essentials in an economic, political, and social order dominated by the squirearchy of wealthy planters, and in most respects were worse off than the Negro slaves.

To these crackers the opening up of Florida brought a promise of dirt-cheap land, most of it free to homesteaders, and so they poured into the peninsula from all parts of the Southland. The first settlements grew up at the natural deep-water harbors, and then along the inland waterways which served as the main arteries of intersectional transportation. Cow Ford became Jacksonville in 1822, Quincy was settled in 1825, Monticello in 1828, Marianna and Apalachicola in 1829, and St. Joseph in 1836. The latter was later changed by yellow fever from a thriving port with 4,000 inhabitants into a ghost town.

But the crackers were not the only ones who came to Florida to seek their fortunes. With them came many wealthy planters whose slaves raised cotton, corn, sugar cane, rice, and tobacco, creating new wealth for their masters. In a very short time the region was marked by the same wide class disparities which characterized the rest of the South, and the poor folks continued to eke a living from their garden plats, firearms, and fishing lines.

All of the settlers, rich and poor alike, proceeded at once to the pleasant and profitable business of robbing the "pesky Injuns" of their lands and herds. The Seminoles fought back with admirable fortitude in 1835 to 1842, when the majority of them agreed to emigrate to Western reservations. The campaigns, which were marked by repeated treachery on the part of the Americans, cost the lives of some 1,500 American soldiers and the loss of $40,000,000 in expenditures and property damages. It was the longest war ever waged by the United States.

Many Florida cities still bear the names of the forts which were erected along the navigable waterways. The first Florida railroad—Tallahassee to

St. Marks—was chartered in 1831, and in spite of the Seminole Wars the territory's population increased more than fifty-six per cent in the following decade.

Statehood—with Liberty and Justice for All Whites

In 1845 Florida was admitted to statehood along with Iowa, in accordance with the national policy of admitting an equal number of slave and free states. According to a writer of the times, "There was no hope of anything like a comfortable maintenance then, but what a change came over the country before 1860." The census of that year revealed that there were 78,000 whites in Florida, 25,000 of whom were slave-owners. Of these, 250 owned more than fifty slaves, and forty-seven owned more than 100 slaves. There were seventy-seven plantations of more than 1,000 acres each. Approximately half of the population was native born, twenty-two per cent was from Georgia, eleven per cent from South Carolina, and five per cent from North Carolina.

The preponderance of settlers from Georgia was reflected in the lyrics of such fiddle dance tunes as:

I Want To Go Back To Georgy

The coon he takes a ringy tail,
The possum takes a slick un,
Oh, the coon he eats my new-ground corn,
And the possum catches chicken.

I wouldn't have you to save your life,
Because you are my cousin,
And I can get a-plenty more,
For eighteen cents a dozen.

The higher you climb the cherry tree,
The riper is the berry,
The more you court that pretty li'l gal,
The sooner she will marry.

Chorus:

I want to go back to Georgy,
And I want to go back to Georgy.

There has always been keen rivalry between Florida and Georgia, in everything from country-cured "ham-what-am" to football. Florida crackers often seek to put Georgia crackers in their place by telling them, "You may have been born and bred in Georgia, but you're nothin but a crumb here."

In the ante-bellum period the north-central Florida counties attracted the most settlers, who were said to have been a "moderately cultured and eminently forceful lot of people." According to *Verdad*, an anonymous correspondent writing from Gainesville in 1860, "The first settlers of middle Florida were generally enterprising, educated gentlemen who emigrated there some 40 years ago from Virginia, North and South Carolina. The population which has flowed into East Florida in the last 15 years has emigrated chiefly from Georgia, Alabama, and the Carolinas, and the proportion of first-class planters which it embraces forms a large and controlling element in the society of that section."

Tallahassee had changed somewhat since 1827, when Ralph Waldo Emerson described it as "a grotesque place, selected three years since as a suitable spot for the capital, and since that day rapidly settled by public officers, land speculators, and desperadoes." Along with Madison, Monticello, and Quincy, Tallahassee became the center of "a new Southern aristocracy (and the headquarters for the Methodist and Episcopal conversion of the section).

The "Tournament of Love and Beauty" was an annual Tallahassee affair in the '60s and '70s and was usually held at Christmas time. Three posts were erected about fifty years apart, an arm extended from each pole, and from these a hinged slat held lightly a small iron ring wrapped with red flannel. The rings hung at shoulder height of a mounted man, and gaily costumed "knights," riding at top speed, sought to pick them off on the tip of a slender lance. Each knight "rode at the rings" three times, and occasionally someone scored nine ringers. He who scored highest won the privilege of crowning the "Queen of Love and Beauty," while runners-up named her maids of honor. The events were climaxed by a gala ball during the evening.

From Jefferson County came such gallants as the Knight of Ravenwood, Knight of the Border, Roland of Avenel, and the Knight of the Golden Fleece; while James Fitz James, the Unknown Knight, and the Knights of the Red Cross, Malta, and Greenwood came from Leon County. In a word, the uppercrust society of the section was medieval.

The crackers who made up the mass of the white population were of a different sort, and their folksongs and ways reflected their predominant Irish and Scotch background. Some were recent immigrants who had been driven overseas by the Irish potato famine of 1848. The grim memory of that event is perpetuated in this folksong:

THREE GRAINS OF CORN

Give me three grains of corn, Mother
Only three grains of corn,
To keep the little life I have
Till coming of the morn.

I'm dying of hunger and cold, Mother
Dying of hunger and cold,
And half the pain of such a death
My lips have never told.

I dreamed of bread in my sleep, Mother
The sight was Heaven to me,
I woke with eager, hungry lips;
But you had no bread for me.

What has poor Ireland done, Mother,
The rich man and the great?
O give me just three grains of corn,
Before it is too late!

Come closer to my side, Mother
Come closer to my side,
And hold me fondly, as you held
My sister when she died.

I cannot see you now, Mother

My breath is almost gone;
This breath I have will never last
Till coming of the morn.

Once in America, the Irish immigrants were able to look back on their sufferings with admirable humor, as in this song:

OVER THERE

Oh, they raise potatoes small, over there,
Oh, they raise potatoes small
And they dig them in the fall
And they eat tops and all, over there.

Oh, they chew tobacco thin, over there,
Oh, they chew tobacco thin
And it runs down on their chins
And they lick it in again, over there.

Got a gal named Dinah, over there,
Got a gal named Dinah
And her cheeks are painted China,
You can have her if you can find her, over there.

Before the Civil War, crackers were often called "sand-lappers," because their children "contracted the habit of eating dirt." This "habit," now known to be a symptom of hookworm infection, has by no means disappeared; in many counties the entire rural population is infected at some time during life.

A hard-drinking, hard-fighting, hard-loving lot, the crackers are nevertheless ferociously addicted to piety. Mostly Baptist and Methodist fundamentalists, their favorite hymnal has been the folksy *Original Sacred Harp,* as contrasted with the sedate hymn-books of the big planters. They hold frequent singing festivals where they try to "sing each other down" with the largest repertoire, and at periodic square dances they "dance the pigeons off the roof." They are also fond of such festivities as family reunions, fence raisings, cane grindings, taffy pulls, corn huskings, bear hunts, chicken pileus, barbecues, and the like.

19.........FLORIDA CRACKERS WRESTLING AN ALLIGATOR.
Florida crackers are "fond of such festivities as family reunions, fence raisings, cane grindings, taffy pulls, corn huskings, bear hunts, chicken pileus, barbecues," and as this 1880s photograph demonstrates, alligator wrestling. State Library and Archives of Florida.

SLAVE DAYS

Mama Duck

I wanta tell you all I can about slave days," said Mama Duck, "and I wanta tell it right. I done prayed and got all the malice out of my heart, and I aint gonna tell no lies for em or on em."

In 1935, at her shack in "The Scrub" on the outskirts of Tampa, Mama Duck claimed she was 110 years old. She complained that when she first took over the abandoned shack she had trouble driving off young couples who had been using it as a "courtin-house." She complained further that the relief office had blacklisted her because she refused to go to the poor house with her trunk of "valuables." But let her continue her story about slave days:

"My whippin-boss was Mister Joe Sylvester. He had his pets among the women, and let em off light. The worst he ever give em was a bop over the head with a battlin-stick—You know what a battlin-stick is: to stir clothes in boiler pots. He had his pets among the menfolks, too, and sometimes he would only strap em over a barrel and give em a few licks with a bull whip. But those who tried to run away got frammed-out plenty. He would tie a rope around their wrists and hoist them up until only their toes touched the ground. Then he beat em all over the back and rump with a heavy wooden paddle drilled full of holes. Every hole made a blister. Then he made em lie down on the ground and he taken a rawhide whip and busted them blisters one at a time. After that he throwed salt brine all over em."

20 .... MAUMA MOLLIE.
Brought to South Carolina on a slave ship from Africa, Mauma was purchased by John and Elza Partridge, who brought her to Jefferson County, Florida in the 1830s. State Library and Archives of Florida.

Besides flogging, there was the "buck-and-gag" method of punishing slaves, whereby they were doubled about a hoe, shovel, or board, and left to lie in the hot sun. Stocks with apertures for the neck, wrists, and ankles were used in the same way. An ingenious device was a cabinet so contrived that the slave enclosed in it was prevented by its small dimensions from either standing erect or sitting. Slaves with a propensity for running away were often fitted with connecting iron bands around their waist and neck, with a bell attached to the neck band.

Gangs of "patrollers," composed of thrill-seeking hoodlums, plied a lucrative trade of capturing, punishing, and returning runaway slaves. These predecessors to the Klansmen were especially active during the Civil War, when most of the white man-power was away from home. A former slave named "Parson" Andrews recalled an incident in which a party of patrollers entered a slave cabin and accused a group of visiting slaves of having run away. One of the "runaways" reached into a bed of hot coals and threw them into the faces of the patrollers, and in the resulting confusion the slaves escaped and returned to their own cabins.

Some patrollers were slave-raiders in disguise. Florida Clayton, the daughter of a white father and Negro mother, recalled that a large covered wagon made periodic visits to the section around Tallahassee. In it came a band of men who told white folks they were patrollers, and told Negroes they were abolitionists, and thus succeeded in kidnapping many slaves whom they sold in Alabama. The leaders of the outfit were widely known and feared by the Negroes as "Mister Nimrod and Mister Sheehee."

Slaves reacted to cruelty in different ways—by running away, openly rebelling, or by passive resistance and sabotage. One woman, tired of being beaten by her overseer, turned on him and hacked him to death with a hoe.

The pursuit of slaves provided a popular theme for folk-songs like the following one from Micanopy, Florida:

RUN, NIGGER, RUN!

That nigger run, that nigger flew;
That nigger tore his shirt in two.

Nigger and white man running through the fiel';

Couldn't see nothin but the nigger's heel.

White man run like a railroad car;
Nigger run like a shootin star.

I run that nigger, I run my best;
I run my head in a hornets' nest.

Nigger and white man playin seven-up;
Nigger beat, but the white man wouldn't give up.

Some folks say that niggers don't steal;
But I caught one in my corn fiel'.

Some folks say that gals don't climb;
But I caught seven up a short-leaf pine.

I went down to my pea patch,
To see if my old hen had hatched.

When I get there she'd fell in the stream,
And Mellie was beatin on the tambourine.

Chorus:
Run, nigger, run!
The patterole'll ketch you!
Run, nigger, run, it's almost day!

White labor was more widely employed during slave days than is generally realized. Planters were especially anxious to employ whites to do dangerous work that might cause the illness or death of their slaves. But the
competition with slave labor led the whites to monopolize certain occupations, and their skilled craft unions barred Negroes from membership, just
as they do today. The growing political strength of the laboring whites was
reflected in laws enacted between 1845-60 restricting the activities of free
Negroes. Nevertheless, a considerable number of Negroes became profi-
cient at skilled trades and found employment in the larger towns. In most
cases, however, it was impossible for a free Negro to earn more than ten

dollars per month, while free Negro children were paid five dollars per month for farm labor.

Such conditions led many free Negroes to enter servitude voluntarily. One free Negro in St. Augustine became indebted to the amount of $850, and entered a three-year period of slavery to liquidate it. Cato Smith, a free Connecticut Negro traveling in Florida, became a slave for seven years in order to obtain the freedom of the woman he wanted to marry.

George Proctor, a free Negro who came to Tallahassee from the Bahamas, entered business as a contractor and built many of the city's finest homes, including those widely known as "The Three Sisters." In 1849 he resolved to go to California to look for gold. He did not have enough money to make the trip, so he mortgaged his wife and six children. When he failed to find gold the members of his family were sold as slaves to George Rutgers, a banker. Proctor died before the outbreak of the Civil War, without having seen his family again.

One of his sons, also named George, was still living in Tallahassee in 1942. George was born free, sold into slavery, emancipated, served six years as a member of the Florida Legislature, and at the age of ninety-four was subsisting on an old-age pension of ten dollars per month. "When Pa left to go to California he never meant for us to be sold. We was born free!" he declared. Asked about his memories of slavery, he replied, "It didn't

21 ....SLAVE MARKET.
1893 view of the slave market in the cathedral plaza of St. Augustine Florida. State Library and Archives of Florida.

seem much different from any other time—I've always had to work hard to live." He had never attended a motion picture, but had read rather extensively; at the time he was rereading *Pilgrim's Progress*. As for his thoughts about the War for the Four Freedoms, John said, "I don't think of it—I don't have much truck with wars."

Curfew ordinances for Negroes were common. In Key West in 1840—when there were ninety-six slaves and seventy-six free Negroes in the town—an ordinance forbade any slave to be on the streets after sundown without written permission from his owner, and free Negroes were required to have permission from the mayor or an alderman. Negroes were also forbidden to play fiddles, beat drums, or make any other noise after the five-minute ringing of the curfew bell. Every white citizen was empowered to apprehend any Negro who failed to reach home before the bell stopped ringing, and take him before the mayor or an alderman and obtain an order committing him to jail. The penalty was optional with the victim: a whipping, or three days' work on the city streets.

By 1850 this ordinance was being enforced by James Filor, the provost marshal. He locked his victims in the "market house," a sweat-box frame building twelve feet square with a single barred window overlooking the ocean. Townspeople who saw Negroes running for home would taunt them by singing:

> *Oh, Filor's as sly as a mouse—*
> *Locked the niggers in the market house;*
> *Kept them there till have past nine—*
> *Five dollars was their fine.*
>
> *Run, nigger run! Filor will get you!*
> *Run, nigger, run! Filor will get you!*
> *Wish I was in Filor's place,*
> *To give them niggers a longer race!*

The Florida Legislature of 1853 passed a law prohibiting a Negro or mulatto from purchasing more than one quart of liquor at time, and then only with a written order from a white person. Later in the same year the Legislature amended the law, prohibiting the sale of liquor to a Negro under any circumstances. Though an oversight, mulattoes were not mentioned in the amendment, and so were still allowed to purchase one quart under the original provision. This situation was protested by Mayor W. C. Maloney of Key West, who addressed a letter to James Filor, then representative of Monroe County, in which he said:

"Such a state of things, if desirable everywhere, must be intolerable here. The inequality between the owner of a negro and owner of a mulatto, on the same errand, is certainly surprising. This will suggest to you the necessity for legislation on the subject."

Education for slaves was strictly vocational, and was designed to increase their value to their owners. On a plantation in Pensacola, slaves caught attempting to write had their fingers chopped off. A former slave named Annie Trip said, "The white folks sure didn't like no nigger what could read and write. Miss Jane used to teach us Sunday school, but she never would let us look at the book or touch it with our hands."

"I remember old Uncle George Bull could read and write," recalled another one-time slave. "They used to take him and beat him just because of it. They would beat him and take him down to the lake and put him on a log and shove it out. Uncle George couldn't swim, but he always managed to get back somehow. Sometimes they beat him till the blood ran out, then throwed him in a ditch and covered him up, head and all. After they had

22 .... BELL SCHOOL.
This school near the Florida-Georgia border was built during Reconstruction to provide an education to newly freed slaves. State Library and Archives of Florida.

gone away I would go dig him out and he would say thank you, brush off the dirt, then get his hoe and go on back to work."

In spite of such treatment, a mulatto named Robert Meacham went about the plantation of his white owner-father near Quincy, and—secretly by candlelight—taught many of the slaves to read and write. Such efforts were generally regarded by slave-holders as connection with the abolition movement.

Chips from the Smokehouse Floor

White man kill miscogee duck;
Give the nigger the bones to suck.
A cold cup o coffee and the meat's mighty fat;
The white folks growl if we eats much of that.
White man in the dinin room, eatin cake and cream;
Nigger in the kitchen, eatin good old greasy greens.

The food afforded slaves was extremely meager; their subsistence diet consisted very largely of the cheapest commodities and least desirable and left-over portions of meat. When the work signal sounded early in the morning, many slaves had to "grab it and run," that is, snatch a sandwich or hunk of corn bread and eat it on the way to the fields. The lunch period was likewise brief, and the slaves had to eat rapidly in order to get a few minutes' rest.

Supper was eaten in the slave's cabin with whatever family he might have. Salt pork, fresh vegetables, potatoes, and corn bread were the usual fare. The corn bread was sometimes cooked in an "iron spider," a large pan with a compartment for hot coals. Potatoes were wrapped in tannion leaves or green corn husks, and baked in an open fire. "Coffee" was made from parched corn or corn meal, or even from okra seed or burnt potatoes.

A former slave named Hattie Thomas, residing in 1942 in Miami's slums, recalled that, "They used to pour milk into a wooden trough and thrown corn bread in it; then us children would line up at the trough and those who could eat the fastest got the fattest."

The slaves' Sunday menu showed but slight improvement over their week-day fare. A frequent addition was potato bread, made of boiled sweet potatoes, which were mashed, mixed with grease and corn meal, and baked until brown. Few slaves of the Palmetto Country were given sugar; their usual "long sweetening" was molasses.

Salt was another rare commodity among slaves. On many plantations the slaves scraped the smokehouse floor and every opportunity to get salt, and when they scrubbed the smokehouse floor they saved the scrub-water and used it for seasoning. The floor boards were also chipped, and the chips when used for seasoning imparted a flavor of both salt and meat.

The slaves' wardrobe was invariably limited and plain. The indigo plant provided blue coloring for cloth, and the poke berry made an attractive red. Oak bark provided various shades of brown, and walnut made a fadeless dark brown. Colored clothing was a rarity among slaves, however, and they carefully preserved such "Sunday-go-to-meetin'" garments for special occasions.

A description of slaves at work was given by a traveler in the South in 1856: "They were dressed in coarse grey gowns, generally very much burned and dirty. On their legs were pieces of blanket or bagging lashed with thongs, and they wore heavy shoes. The overseer rode about among them on a horse, carrying in his hand a rawhide whip. I had never before witnessed anything more revolting than the whole scene. " Yet the slaves somehow managed to keep alive their sense of humor, as evidenced in work songs like the following from Fernandina:

> *I knocked a man from the eastern shore,*
>   *Ho, ho, come along;*
> *I heard him fall in Baltimore,*
>   *Ho, ho, come along.*
>
> *Mosquito eat a bellyful of buckwheat dough,*
>   *Ho, ho, come along;*
> *Then turn right 'round and beg for more,*
>   *Ho, ho, come along.*

Slave-Breeding for Profit

Many slaves were married by the simple process of "jumping over the broom," a ritual probably imported from Africa. A broom would be placed on the floor, the bride would leap over it, then the groom, and so they were married.

It was customary for slave-owners to encourage or force the marriage or breeding of their slaves, for the same reasons they bred their livestock. To increase the number of one's slaves was to increase one's wealth and prestige. Besides those who bred slaves for themselves, there were others whose business was the breeding of slaves to supply the market; this industry boomed after the importation of slaves was forbidden.

The strongest and most intelligent Negroes were selected as "breeders," and some slave-holders saw to it that their strongest Negro man fathered the children of all their woman slaves. The women selected as breeders were maintained primarily for that purpose, and often were required to do only light housework. The white slave-owners and overseers also mated with the breeders, and their mulatto offspring were valued as house servants.

Another plantation job was that of the "suckler," a woman with an abundant supply of milk whose duty it was to nurse the babies of slave mothers who worked in the fields. Many prospective slave mothers were not allowed to leave the fields until their labor pains started. Their babies were taken from them and given to a suckler when only a few weeks old, so that they could return to the field work.

New Names for Old Gods

For a long time there was suspicion among slave-owners that proponents of religion for Negroes were abolitionists in disguise. The intensive Catholic teaching among the Negroes of St. Augustine during the Spanish reigns had such lasting effect that Protestant missionaries who later appeared among them were severely beaten. In many places slaves were forbidden to attend or conduct religious services. At the hamlet of Sixteen (Florida), a slave mother saw her son killed for attending church, and was threatened with death herself if she did not cease her weeping.

But the slave-owners were not long in recognizing that religion had a practical value in increasing the productivity of their slaves, and by 1856 religious services for slaves were compulsory on most plantations. "The preachers, white and colored, was all the time tellin us to mind our masters and not steal, and we'd be saved; but they never told us nothin about

Jesus," said a former slave. The slaves were assured of heavenly bliss if they followed the prescribed code; if they did not, they were given to understand that they faced an eternal damnation of fire and brimstone, not to mention the more immediate and familiar forms of punishment at hand.

Judging from the response of the slaves, they were sadly in need of some form of religious outlet and consolation, no matter how remote and ephemeral the benefits. Something of the compensation psychology created by these religious teachings is revealed in the following slave work song from Fernandina:

> *We have a just God to plead our cause,*
> *Plead our cause,*
> *We have a just God to plead our cause,*
> *For we are the chillun of God.*

> *Come along, I tell ya, doncha be afeard,*
> *Doncha be afeard,*
> *Come along my people, doncha be ashamed,*
> *For we are the chillun of God.*

There were many slaves, however, whom the spirit failed to move. One such individual, who was still living in 1942, complains that "After we had done worked in the fields from 4:30 in the mornin to 6:30 at night for six days a week, we had to get up at seven o'clock Sunday mornin to listen to the preacher." Another ex-slave reported that a full-time preacher on his plantation was exceedingly unpopular with the other slaves "cause he wore a big high hat and was all the time snoopin around and tellin the master everything we done."

A few white churches permitted slaves to enter by a separate door and sit in a separate section, while other churches conducted a "special" service for slaves after the regular service for whites was over. But for the most part the slaves conducted their own meetings, usually in the open air around a campfire. In some instances, pliable young saplings were trimmed to serve as "jerkin poles" to which the "prayin brethren and agonizin sistern" could cling during their spiritual convolutions.

Baptismal ceremonies were frequently held at near-by lakes and streams. The candidates, robed in dress-like garments, were led in a singing procession down to the water's edge. The preacher and his assistants remained in the water about waist-deep, and the candidates were led out one at a time for submersion. Some candidates resisted, and had to be forcibly ducked, and sometimes the reluctant ones succeeded in ducking the preacher.

Meanwhile the congregation on the bank sang and the awaiting candidates worked themselves into real or simulated seizures of spiritual frenzy, many of the "falling out" unconscious. When all the candidates had been immersed, a triumphant procession marched back to the quarters. This entire baptismal procedure has survived without change in many rural communities of the Palmetto Country.

But the Negro merely accepted the external form of the religion of his masters, and unconsciously used it as a cloak for his inherited paganism. In reality, he stood before new altars and called upon his old gods by new names. The Christian concept of the heavenly triumph of the meek and

23 .... ROSEWOOD PLANTATION HOME.
This plantation home was built by slaves in the late 1840s on 1,000 acres of land in Jefferson County. State Library and Archives of Florida.

submissive combined easily with the paganistic acceptance of the might as right; and the two together admirably served the purposes of the institution of slavery.

The Southern Negro did not long retain his organized African religious cults, but he did preserve an elaborate body of superstitious beliefs that affected every aspect of his life. An interesting sample of such beliefs is provided by a former slave. "My Uncle July mixed some graveyard dust and lightwood splinters and smeared it on his feet before he ran away, and that kept Mister Bob Amos' bloodhounds from ketchin him. And while he was hidin in the woods he sprinkled cotton-seed on the ground to keep the cold away."

Other beliefs widely held by the slaves were that hogs could see the wind, and that it appeared blood-red to them; that every Christmas morning all animals could speak fluently; that a pearl button or watermelon rind worn around a child's neck would eliminate pain during teething; that a concoction made of boiled wasps' nests and vinegar would help a child learn to walk, that occasional breast nursing of older children would help build sound bones and teeth, and that so long as a woman was nursing she would not become pregnant.

The Man with the Branded Hand

> Then lift that manly hand,
> Bold bloughman of the wave;
> Its branded palm shall prophesy,
> Salvation to the slave.
>
> Hold up its fire-wrought language
> That whoso reads may feel
> His heart swell strong within him,
> His sinews changed to steel.

Those lines penned by Whittier in 1846 have immortalized Jonathan Walker, the Man with the Branded Hand, but the events which led to his being branded are not so widely known.

Born a free Negro on Cape Cod in 1799—the year George Washington died—Jonathan Walker spent much of his early life at sea. In 1835 he went to Mexico to assist in colonizing Negroes who had escaped from slavery in the United States. The "underground railroad" had been established about 1832, and Walker served as one of its "conductors." During the six years prior to 1844 he lived with his family in Florida.

In that year he took on board his small open boat seven runaway slaves from Pensacola, and set sail on an 800-mile journey to the British Bahamas where the slaves could find freedom. They succeeded in rounding the Florida Keys, but then Walker suffered a sunstroke. The slaves, believing him to be dead, covered his body with canvas. Not knowing anything about navigation, they drifted helplessly for days. Meanwhile a reward of $1,700 had been offered for their capture and return; the announcement was accompanied by the comment that Walker had been absent from his family for two years "without apparent necessity," and that "he seems to have had no reasonable or proper business here."

As Walker later wrote his wife, "We were overhauled by a wrecker, the sloop *Catharine* from Key West, and by force taken to that port. I was carried before a justice of the peace, and thence to jail where I was kept for four days. Then I was put into the hold of a steamboat, among rubbish and filth, the heat being extreme, placed in heavy irons both hands and feet, and kept six days in which time the vessel steamed to Pensacola. There I was taken to court, and again to jail, where I now am, secured to a large ring-bolt by a chain made of half-inch iron and with a five-pound shackle around my ankle."

The *Pensacola Gazette* reported Walker's arrival as follows: "The U.S.S. *General Taylor* arrived Thursday evening bringing as a prisoner Jonathan Walker, charged with recently having abducted the seven negro slaves. When the prisoner landed on the wharf the crowd was immense. As he was escorted to the court-house the crowd thronged the streets and sidewalks, and the court-room was filled to overflowing by a highly excited mass of people. No doubt Walker's punishment will be severe."

Actually, Walker was saved from lynching by the Sheriff and deputy who held the mob at bay with drawn revolvers. His boat was confiscated, and the slaves were returned to their owners. Unable to post bond, he spent four months in jail awaiting trial. About his imprisonment he later said, "My sickness and the treatment I had received had reduced me to a skeleton. Many times I grasped around my leg above the knee, over the trousers with one hand so that my thumb and fingers met. The hungry mosquitoes tried hard to draw a little support from my emaciated form."

The United States District Court sentenced Walker to be taken from the prison, placed for an hour in the pillory on the public highway and pelted with rotten eggs; from thence to be returned to his cell, to the bars of which his right arm should be lashed, and in the palm of it be branded with a red-hot iron the letters "SS," signifying "Slave Stealer." In addition he was sentenced to one year in prison for each of the seven slaves and also fined $600 for each slave, plus the costs of trial.

During the egg-pelting someone removed a covering that had been placed over Walker's eyes, and a boy who cried shame at the act was arrested and fined. The first blacksmith who was asked to make the branding iron is reported to have replied, "I make irons to brand horses, mules, and cattle, but to burn the flesh of a fellowman—by the living God, I will not!" Another blacksmith made the iron, but refused to heat it at his forge. "There is only one fire in the universe fit to heat such and iron," said he.

From 1845 to 1849 Walker went about the North lecturing against slavery, and his branded hand came to mean "Slave Savior." When he died in 1878, Photius Fisk, chaplain of the United States Navy, erected a monument at his grave which is engraved with the branded hand and Whitter's lines. Frederick Douglass, the leading Negro emancipator, paid tribute to Walker, saying, "I knew him well. He was a brave but noiseless lover of liberty."

"Whereas I Don't Give a Damn"

"Whereas I am of sound mind and disposing memory and know what I am doing, and whereas I know perfectly well that it is against the laws and conventions of life to marry a colored person, and whereas this is my property and it is not anybody's damn business what I do with it, and whereas I have an African wife, and believe that the amalgamation of the white and colored races is to the best interests of America, and whereas I know that what I am about to do is going to bring down tremendous criticism, but I don't give a damn; now therefore I give to my wife, Anna Madgigiane Jai Kingsley, one-twelfth of my estate, one-sixth to our son John Maxwell Kingsley, and one-third to our son George Kingsley; also one-sixth to Flora

H. Kingsley and her children who I acknowledge are mine, and one-twelfth to Micanopy, my son by Sarah Murphy Kingsley. I further leave ten thousand dollars to each and every child which my wife might have by a white husband after my death.

"I do hereby order and direct that my body be buried in the nearest and most convenient place without any Religious ceremony whatsoever, and that it may be excused from the usual indiscreet formalities and parade of washing, dressing, &c., or exposure in any way.

"I do hereby authorize my Executors to allow any of my slaves the privilege of purchasing their freedom at one-half the price of their valuation, on consideration of their migrating to Hayti, if they cannot be allowed to stay as free in this Territory.

"I do solemnly enjoin my children, that seeing the illiberal and inequitable laws of the Territory will not afford to them and to their children that protection and justice which is due in civilized society to every human being: Always keep by them a Will, ready-made and legally executed, directing the disposal of their property after their death until they can remove themselves and property to some land of liberty where the conditions of society are governed by some law less absurd than that of color.

"This I strongly recommend, nor do I know in what light the law may consider my acknowledged wife, as our connubial relations took place in a foreign land, where our marriage was celebrated and solemnized by her native African custom altho never celebrated according to the forms of Christian usage; yet she has always been respected as my wife and as such I acknowledge her, not do I think that the truth, honor, integrity, moral conduct, or good sense will lose in comparison with anyone."

The foregoing may not be a true and exact copy of the last Will and Testament of Zephaniah Kingsley, but it was published as such in the *Florida Times-Union*. Certain it is that most of its provisions are correct.

Born in 1765 in Scotland, Kingsley spent his early manhood in Brazil and the West Indies amassing a fortune as a coffee merchant and slave-trader. He acquired Fort George Island in the mouth of the St. Johns River in 1817, and for over twenty years it was the headquarters of his slave-trading. In time he came to own 5,000 acres in East Florida.

On the north end of Fort George Island he built a comfortable home, now known as the "Homestead," and a crescent of coquina slave huts. He operated his own fleet of slave ships, building many of them at Fort George and near-by Mayport. He had contracted with an African tribal king to deliver slaves to his partner, a man named Reuter, at the mouth of the Congo. After bringing them to Fort George, he put the slaves through a rigorous course of vocational training and conversational English. Kingsley spoke a number of African dialects, and his graduates, known throughout the South as "Kingsley's niggers," brought premium prices at slave marts. His slaves cost him from fifty cents to fifty dollars per head in Africa, and he sold them for $1,000 to $1,500 each.

It was on one of his African slaving expeditions that he married Anna Madgigiane Jai, daughter of a Senegalese Negro tribal chief. He brought her to Fort George, where she was mistress of his home and plantation and was served by many slaves. They had four children: George, John, Martha,

24.........SLAVE CABIN.
A reconstructed slave cabin at the Kingsley Plantation, Ft. George Island, Florida. Florida Historical Society.

and Mary, the last of whom married John S. Sammis, a Scotch ship-builder and owner of a plantation at Arlington (Florida). Rumor has it that Kingsley gave Sammis a handsome dowry, and that the wedding was performed on the high seas to remove it from the jurisdiction of the Territorial laws.

Sammis and his wife also had four children: Egbert, Edwin, George, and Martha. Sammis provided a private school for his children, and permitted the children of free Negroes to attend with them. Later he sent his children to New York for higher education.

Kingsley's other daughter Martha married a well-to-do white man named Oran Baxter from Cold Springs, New York. They, too, settled on the St. Johns River, and were frequently visited by "Ma'am Anna," as Kingsley's wife was called.

25 .... WALLS OF SLAVE CABINS.
The original tabby walls of slave cabins at the Kingsley Plantation still stand in ruins today. Florida Historical Society.

At the height of his career Kingsley wrote a book, *The Patriarchal System of Society,* in which he extolled the merits of slave-holding as a means of disseminating certain benefits among uncivilized peoples. The book ran through four editions.

When the "Patriots' Rebellion" took place, Kingsley was asked to contribute $250 to the cause, or have some of his property sold to raise that amount. After Florida became part of the United States he was paid $73,222 for the damages he claimed to have suffered during the rebellion.

Kingsley's son George married a wealthy French woman named Anatoile V. Travers, and their four children were named Georgiana, Etoile, George, and Zephaniah, all of whom were born in the United States except Zephaniah, who was born at Yorsica, near Puerta Plata, Dominican Republic.

In 1839 Ma'am Anna and her sons John and George went to Haiti to live, taking with them George's family and Micanopy, Kingsley's child by the Negress Sarah Murphy. Kingsley died in New York City at the age of seventy-eight in 1843, and eight of his collateral kin petitioned that his will be broken on the grounds that the beneficiaries were slaves and were residing outside the United States. But the Duval County (Florida) court ordered confirmation of the Will, charging the petitioners $14.06 court costs. The courts later sustained the attack on the document on the grounds that it was "against the public policy and institutions of America." The case went to the Florida Supreme Court, and a settlement was finally reached.

George Kingsley spoke for the members of his family in opposing the collateral kin. He wrote his brother-in-law Sammis, "I wish you to hold out that if ever there is a likelihood of my losing my property *I am going straight to Boston where I can be near the family of Kingsley.*" These Boston Kingsleys were most prominent, and George's presence there would have been quite embarrassing.

But in one way or another Kingsley's collateral kin gained possession of much of his property, and thus were established the fortunes of some of the region's most prominent families.

Rich Man's War, Poor Man's Fight

> *Jeff Davis rides a big white horse,*
> *Abe Lincoln rides a mule,*

> *Jeff Davis is our president,*
> *Abe Lincoln is a fool!*

With an agricultural economy dependent upon slave labor, and with its legislature dominated by wealthy planters, it was to be expected that Florida would go along with the secession movement. A Democratic convention held in Tallahassee in 1860 resolved that "negro slavery is a necessary institution, and it is the duty of Congress to protect slavery and to enforce the fugitive slave law." A celebration at Madison voiced the same sentiments. The "toast" of the day was, "A seceder in '32, the same in '51; may peace be our motto until war is inevitable. In consequence of Northern fanaticism, if the irrepressible conflict must come we are prepared to meet it; we would sacrifice our lives before we would submit to a black Republican Party."

Florida was the third state to secede from the Union, the ordinance being passed by a vote of sixty-two to seven on January 10, 1861. The population at the time was about 77,000 whites and 66,000 Negroes. Though some 15,000 Floridians served in the Confederate armies, the sentiment that the conflict was "a rich man's war and a poor man's fight" was more widespread than had been admitted, and many of those who served had to be conscripted. To poor white folks, Negro slavery meant cut-throat competition. Large slave-holders were exempt from conscription on the ground that they were vitally needed to supervise the production of crops.

Though no decisive battles were fought on the peninsula, the Federals captured many port towns and made a number of inland penetrations in an effort to cut off the cotton, salt, beef, turpentine, lumber, and other products which Florida supplied the Confederacy after the imposition of the Federal blockade. This blockade not only affected the Confederate armies, but also prevented the home folks from living in the style to which they had been accustomed. The ladies glorified their predicament by adapting this old folksong:

THE HOMESPUN DRESS

> *Yes, I know I'm a Southern girl, I glory in the name,*
> *And that I prize far greater than glittering wealth and fame.*
> *I envy not the Northern girl her robes of beauty rare,*
> *Though pearls bedeck her snowy neck, and diamonds fill her hair.*

My homespun dress is plain, I know; my hat is palmetto, too;
But now you see what Southern girls for Southern rights can do.
We sent the bravest of our land to battle with the foe,
And we lend a helping hand; we love the South, you know.

Our Sunny South's such a glorious land, and ours a glorious
*   cause,*
So here's three cheers for Southerners and for your Southern
*   boys!*
We sent our sweethearts to the war, but dear girls never mind,
The soldier boy will not forget the girl he left behind.

Now Northern goods are out of date since Old Abe's blockade;
We Southern girls can get along with those by Southerners made.
We scorn to wear a bit of silk or a bit of Northern lace,
But we make our homespun dresses up and wear them with much
*   grace.*

Chorus:
Hurrah! Hurrah! For the Sunny South so dear;
Three cheers for the homespun dresses the Southern ladies wear!

Salt was so scarce it often sold for a dollar a pound, and rich and poor alike resorted to the Negroes' method of scrubbing the smokehouse floor to obtain brine. Those whose smoke-houses had dirt floors actually boiled the dirt and evaporated the brine. Along the coasts, sea water was evaporated in boilers and iron kettles such as those used in boiling sugar cane juice. Men engaged in this business were exempt from conscription, with the result that the coastal population boomed. Each fall, inland folks from all parts of the Palmetto Country drove their ox carts to the coast to boil down a supply of salt and brine.

The Confederate Government at length had in operation $3,000,000 with of salt distilleries along the Florida Gulf coast. Federal forces sent into the St. Andrews Bay region to destroy the mills reported, "The sky was lit up for miles, the glare being reflected from the fires of countless salt works along the shores."

On another occasion when the Federals marched from Jacksonville to Baldwin, a popular Confederate song was localized to fit the event:

I Can Whip The Scoundrel

The Yankees came to Baldwin,
They came up in the rear;
They thought they'd find old Abner,
But old Abner wasn't there.

So lay ten dollars down,
Or twenty if you choose;
For I can whip the scoundrel
That stole old Abner's shoes.

The Yankees took me prisoner,
They used me rough, 'tis true;
They took from me my knapsack,
And stole my blankets, too.

The Yankees took me prisoner,
But if I could get parole,
I'd go right back and fight them,
I would, upon my soul!

Negro volunteers, many of whom had been slaves in the Palmetto Country, comprised a major portion of the invading Federal forces, and were particularly valuable because of their knowledge of the territory. Eventually there were three Negro battalions stationed in Florida. An interesting picture of these Negro soldiers was given in 1865 by Colonel T. W. Higgenson, a white Northerner who commanded the first force of Negroes to be employed against the Confederacy.

Even the North had been taken in by the Southern propaganda that the use of Negro troops would result in unspeakable atrocities, and was apprehensive. In their first encounter with their former masters, along the St. Mary's River, the Negroes showed their eagerness to fight for freedom. "It was difficult to make them cease firing," wrote Colonel Higgenson. "One of them was heard to mutter indignantly, 'Why the Cunnel order cease firin when the Secesh keep on blazin away at the rate of ten dollars a day?'"

A colored Corporal Adam Ashton later recalled, "When I heard the bombshells a-screamin through the woods like Judgement Day, I said to myself, 'If my head gets took off tonight, they can't put my soul in torments unless God is my enemy.' And when the rifle bullets came whizzin, I cried, 'God help my congregation! Boys, load and fire!'"

Higgenson gave a vivid description of another of his colored corporals, Robert Sutton. "He was a Florida man, and he had been employed in lumbering and piloting on the St. Mary's. Down this stream he had escaped in a dugout, and then returned to bring away his wife and child. 'I couldn't leave my family, Cunnel,' he said. He yearned and pined for intellectual companionship beyond all ignorant men whom I have ever met. I believe he would have talked all day and all night, for days together, to any officer who could instruct him. His mind was at work all the time, even when he was singing hymns, of which he had an endless store."

The meeting of Sutton and the wife of his former owner at Woodstock was described as follows by Higgenson: "Calling up my companion, I said I believe she had previously been acquainted with Corporal Robert Sutton? I never saw a finer bit of unutterable indignation than came over the face of my hostess, as she slowly recognized him. She drew herself up, and dropped out the monosyllables of her answer as if they were so many drops of nitric acid, 'Ah,' quoth my lady, '*we* called him Bob.' Corporal Sutton simply turned from her, touched his hat to me, and asked if I would wish to see her slave-jail.

"At Fernandina I found building after building crowded with costly furniture, just as it was sent from St. Mary's when that town was captured. And here were my men, who knew that their own labor had earned for their masters these luxuries, and that their own wives were still sleeping on the floor, yet they submitted, almost without a murmur, to the enforced abstinence."

Later, when Federal troops occupied Jacksonville and some of them got out of control and indulged in rioting, a Confederate observer reported, "It gives me pleasure to state that the Negro troops took no part in this vandalism, and were merely silent spectators at a sad spectacle."

A story about one of these Negro troopers at Jacksonville has been given wide currency. While shooting his way through some "Debatable Land," as the Negroes called it, he captured a fine domestic goose. Unwilling to forego his prize, he clamped its head between his crotch and continued to advance and fire, with the goose hissing and squawking at every step.

More pathetic was Higgenson's account of his men's reception of the Emancipation Proclamation. "When we received a printed supply of the Proclamation the colored men seemed overjoyed. Though very few of them could read it, they all seemed to feel more secure when they held it in their hands."

The whole history of the war was succinctly summed up in this Confederate soldiers' song:

JOHNNIE, FILL UP THE BOWL

In 1861
The cruel war had just begun.
In 1862
We all had enough to do.
In 1863
Old Lincoln swore the niggers was free
In 1864
We drove em back to Baltimore.
In 1865
Scarcely a Rebel was left alive.
In 1866
Old Marse Jeff was in a damn bad fix.

Chorus:
So come up boys and we'll all take a drink.
Hussah! Hussah!
We'll give Marse Jeff the one-eyed wink,
And we'll all drink stone-blind.
Johnnie, fill up the bowl!

THE OLD ORDER CHANGETH, SOMEWHAT

The Net Proceeds

"The big gun fired on Saturday, and meant that the Yankees had come and the slaves was free," said Margret Nickerson in 1940, who was among those present. "Niggers came out of the woods from all directions. The next day Mr. Carr got us all together and read a paper to us that didn't none of us understand except that it meant we was free. Then he said that them what would stay and harvest the cotton and corn would be given the net proceeds. Them what did found out that the net proceeds wasn't nothin but the stalks."

Such were the bitter fruits of freedom given to trusting Negroes all over the Palmetto Country. Some planters who were not under the immediate surveillance of Federal officers actually held their Negroes in slavery until the crops had been harvested, while many other planters contrived to get free Negro labor "by hook or crook."

Lost: 40 Acres and a Mule

The assassination of Lincoln placed the task of reconstructing the South in the hands of Johnson, whose Presidential Plan was to entrust the matter to those white Southern Unionists who could take the "iron-clad" oath of not having supported the Confederacy. He appointed Unionists as governors of a number of states, including Florida, Georgia, and Alabama, and the "iron-clad" whites elected constitutional conventions which repealed the ordinances of secession and ratified the Thirteenth Amendment.

Adopted by Congress in 1865, the Amendment states that: "Neither slavery nor involuntary servitude, except as a punishment for crime, whereof the person shall have been duly convicted, shall exist within the United States or any place subject to their jurisdiction."

It soon became obvious that the "iron-clad" allegiance of the Unionists to the United States was not based upon sympathy with the abolition of slavery, for in this respect most of them had all the iron-clad prejudices of "true Southerners." For example, Florida's provisional Governor, William Marvin, advised the Negroes "not to participate in politics and not to expect 40 acres and a mule." And the State's constitutional convention decided that "neither the white man nor the black is prepared for the radical change" of allowing Negroes to vote. In its ordinance to abolish slavery, moreover, Negroes were denied the right to testify in court when the personal or property interests of white people were involved.

David S. Walker, another Unionist, was elected governor by the iron-clad voters. At his inauguration he declared: "I think we are bound by every consideration of duty to make the Negroes as enlightened, prosperous, and happy as their new situation will admit. They have been faithful, and have remained at home and made provision for us. Not one instance of insult, outrage, or indignity has ever come to my knowledge. Much has been said about white labor from Germany, Ireland, and Italy. I am in favor of it, but let us remember that we have a white laboring class of our own which is entitled to the preference."

The iron-clad legislature, which convened in 1866 to carry out this promised New Deal for Negroes, enacted an elaborate system of regulations relegating the freedmen to a status very similar to that imposed up "free persons of color" before the war. A great many of these regulations are still operative, either as un-Constitutional laws or unwritten codes enforced by lynch law. Thus the present status of Negroes in the South is very much the same as that of "free" Negroes during slave days. The South may have lost the war on the battlefields, but she has been allowed to retain much of her institution of slavery.

26.........WOMAN TRANSPORTING GOODS.
This form of transporting things from place to place has had a venerable history all over the planet, but passed away in the Palmetto Country toward mid-century. From the Stetson Kennedy collection.

One of the first acts of the iron-clad legislature was to make the courts and legal processes available to Negroes; the courts had the power to substitute the whipping post for imprisonment, so this measure provided speedy punishment for Negroes so they would not be kept from their "employer's" work by prison sentences. Another law required the payment of a three dollar annual tax by every able-bodied citizen, with a penalty of forced labor for nonpayment; this virtually gave planters an opportunity to re-enslave penniless freedmen by paying their delinquent taxes.

If a Negro broke a labor contract he was arrested as a vagrant, whereas if a white broke a contract he was only liable to civil suit. Even today, however, it is practically "out of the question" for a Negro to sue a white person, though a Negro has little difficulty in suing a *large* corporation. In any case, Negroes must exercise extreme caution about offering testimony which conflicts with that given by a white man, lest the white man's lawyer win the case by asking the white jury, "Are you going to believe my client, or do you prefer to take the word of a lyin nigger?"

The iron-clad legislature made some provision for Negro schools, but white persons were forbidden to teach Negroes without a state license. Negroes were tactfully segregated by a statute forbidding whites to intrude on assemblies of Negroes, and vice versa. All Negroes living together as a man and wife were given nine months to separate or become legally married; otherwise they were charged with adultery. A fine of $1,000 and three months' imprisonment was provided for any white woman who had sexual relations with a Negro man; no mention was made of such relations between white men and Negro women.

These were but a few of the enactments under the Johnson Plan, which gave the Negroes certain limited civil rights they had not had as slaves— the right to assemble, attend school, and make labor contracts, but which denied them all political rights.

The manner in which labor contracts were made to serve the interests of the planters was described by Robert Meacham, who has already been mentioned for daring to teach his fellow slaves to read and write. "There is an understanding among the white employers to manage, in some way, to keep the colored people from having what they have justly earned," he told the Joint Congressional Committee investigating *"The Condition of Affairs in the Late Insurrectionary States"* in 1871. "There has been a great deal of difficulty in regard to labor contracts. The farmers draw up the contracts and read them to the colored people, but the colored people are generally uneducated and when a contract says this or that they hardly know what it means."

"When the farmers advance supplies, they get a lien on whatever portion of the crop is supposed to go to the workers. They also provide that if the colored people violate any of the articles of the agreement they are to be turned off and get nothing. The slightest insult, as the planters call it, is sufficient to turn the workers off. This takes place mostly in August and September, after the crops have been laid by. Many justices of the peace have their jails full of colored people for the most frivolous things. My advice to my people has been to get homes wherever they can; to go into contracts when they can do nothing else."

But the efforts of the Negroes to purchase land and homes were vigorously opposed by the white landowners. Emmanuel Fortune, a Negro from Jackson County (Florida) told the Congressional Committee: "They will not sell us land. We have to purchase it from the Government or the State, otherwise we cannot get it. They will sell our people a lot now and then, but nothing of any importance. I would have bought 40 acres if the man would have sold me less than a whole tract. There are only large tracts of not less than 100, 200, or 500 acres. Cultivable lands are worth from $10 to $15 an acre, and State lands are $1.25 an acre. A great many of our people take up homesteads, but homesteads in Jackson County are no account at all—very poor. I do not know that I have ever heard anything said against selling land to colored people, but that is the understanding."

The Negroes were not the only ones who were dissatisfied with developments under the Johnson Plan; so, too, were all the Southern whites who had been disenfranchised for having supported the Confederacy. When Florida Unionists elected Governor Marvin to the United States Senate, that body refused to seat him on the ground that he did not represent the people of the state. This paved the way for passage of the "radical" Congressional Reconstruction Acts of 1867, which provided for military occupation as the only effective means of guaranteeing the rights of freedmen. General John Pope, in charge of the Third Military District, declared that he expected trouble in Georgia and Alabama, but not in Florida.

Carpetbaggers and Scalawags

"They make no distinction about men who join the Republican Party, whether Northern men or Southern men," further testified Emanuel Fortune. "A Northern man is 'a damnyankee who came here to rule us'; and a Southern man who joins the Republicans is 'a damned scalawag, and there is no honesty about him; he is a traitor to his country and his race.' The crackers often say that we have plenty of men of our own to rule us, without having men come here and do it for us; they say, 'Those damned politicians should be got rid of.'"

27.........AFRICAN AMERICAN MAN AT HOME.
  This African American man sits on the front step of his modest Florida home in the early twentieth century. From the Stetson Kennedy collection.

The plantations of Florida had not been physically destroyed by the war, and by 1866 nine-tenths of the Negroes were back at work, and others were encouraged to come in from the bordering states. Most of this productive activity was arranged by the Freedmen's Bureau, an organization which has been maligned by Southern whites in proportion to the protection it afforded Negroes. In many parts of the South the Bureau found it necessary to conduct special courts for the trial of cases involving Negroes.

One of the Bureau's most important functions was to supervise the drafting of labor contracts, which stipulated the work to be performed, the amount of food to be advanced by the landlord, and the wages or share of the crop to be paid. The prescribed food per person per week was four pounds of bacon, one peck of meal, and one pint of syrup. Wages were usually in the neighborhood of fifteen dollars per month. Sharecroppers were promised, but seldom received, from one-third to two-fifths of the crop they raised.

The Bureau also served as a direct relief agency, issuing 25,000 rations to needy Florida freedmen from 1865 to 1867. In 1866, 1,000 of the state's Negro population of 44,000 depended on the Bureau for both food and clothing. It also established banks and schools for the freedmen.

As things quieted down after the war, the Palmetto Country was overrun with visitors from the North who wanted to have a look around. Though these visitors were not professional carpetbaggers, more than a few took the trouble to write books about what they saw, or what the planters or Negroes wanted them to see. It was simply a matter of where their sympathies lay.

Thus, strangely conflicting opinions appeared in print. For example, O. M. Crosby, in his *Florida Facts* (1869), misrepresented facts by saying: "Now that the negro is free he has no idea of working more than is barely necessary to keep him in pork and grits. His rations cost at most but a dollar a week, and he sees no reason in working six days out of seven, when three or four provide for all the wants of his family. Few colored men will agree to work faithfully by the month. Their sense of honor is low, and they cannot be trusted at the stores. The negro problem will assume a new form, to even the most rabid abolitionist, after a residence in Florida." The real fact of the matter was published the same year in *A Winter in Florida* by Ledyard Bill: "We suspect the chief reason why the negro is loth to labor is the uncertainty of his wages. Finding they received nothing but promises, the negroes naturally became idle."

Additional facts were provided by Emanuel Fortune: "At the outset after freedom they disturbed our schools a great deal until we raised a band to protect them. We complained to the United States marshal several times, but he didn't do anything. They were mistreating our children, stoning them, and talking about mobbing the teachers and all such as that. We never had any public schools, only private schools such as we could get up for ourselves. The Government had not done anything for us in the way of schools.

"They did not interfere with our churches at all, until recently I heard that one or two of our preachers have been shot or shot at." This growing hostility of the whites toward the Negro churches was caused by the leading role the churches were taking in demanding civil and political rights for Negroes. For example, in 1871 the African Methodist Episcopal (AME) Church resolved "that those steamers, railroad companies, and others who treat our people so disgraceful from sheer hatred, malice, and prejudice are not worthy of our support, and our people are advised not to cater to them more than is necessary, and to buy their produce from those who treat them fairest."

Still more information about Negro schools was provided by Robert Meacham: "In Jefferson County there are three young white men, born in the State, who are very poor and are teaching colored schools for a living. The other whites will hardly speak to them, and one of them has to board with a colored family because the whites will not board him."

Congressional Reconstruction called for a Florida election in November of 1867. This was to be the Negroes' first opportunity to vote, and strenuous efforts were made to organize and control their political strength. Colonel Thomas W. Osborne, Florida commissioner of the Freedmen's Bureau, organized a secret political society, the Lincoln Brotherhood, which soon had branches all over the State. The Brotherhood was a conservative Republican organization, favoring Negro suffrage but not the election of Negroes to high public offices.

The Brotherhood's monopoly was soon broken by the formation of the Loyal League, a radical Republican group advocating full political rights for Negroes. The League furthermore gave its members to understand that in time the Republican Party would divide up their ex-masters' land and distribute it most generously among League members. A final attraction was a ritual much more elaborate and secretive than that of the Brotherhood. Needless to say, the League became a formidable political force. Its organizers, who claimed to be members of the Republican National Committee, were William M. Saunders, a mulatto from Baltimore, and Daniel Richards, a white man from Illinois.

The planters naturally looked upon these secret Negro political organizations with grave apprehensions, regarding them in much the same light as they regard the Communist Party today, only more so. It is a significant fact that were these secret societies to be reorganized today—with the very same aims they had then—they would meet with precisely the same violent opposition.

At first the planters sought to persuade the Negroes to abandon their "carpetbagger" leaders. Typical of these efforts were the speeches of William Martin, a free Negro of Lake City (Florida), who toured his section urging: "Do not break with the Southern white man; do not be made tools to be used when wanted and then cast aside. I say to you to keep away from the secret societies. Let politics alone." Possibly his advice was well meant; more likely it was well paid for.

The planters also organized mass meetings in Pensacola and Tallahassee, where selected white and Negro speakers tried to sell the freedmen the same bill of goods. These meetings inspired numerous others throughout the Palmetto Country. The freedmen listened with respectful attention, then passed resolutions: "We cherish no ill-will against our former masters, but the loving people of the North deserve our thanks for our freedom; we resolve, therefore, to identify ourselves with the Republican Party."

The situation was reminiscent of the popular old Negro folktale about the fox who had his eye on a turkey perched in a treetop. "Hey, Brer Turkey," called Brer Fox, "is you heard about the new law?—Foxes can't eat no more turkeys, and hounds can't chase foxes. Come on down and we'll talk about it." "Nothin doin," said Brer Turkey, "we can talk about it right where we is." Just then some hounds were heard coming over the hill. "Guess I'll be runnin along," said Brer Fox. Brer Turkey said, "I thought you said the new law says no more fox hunts." And Brer Fox said, "Thas right—but them dogs will run right over that law."

The planters resorted to more forceful forms of persuasion by organizing a secret society of their own under the misnomer of the "Constitutional League." Its "Regulations and Bye-laws" required that applicants for membership answer affirmatively:

1. Will each and all of you give me your word of honor not to divulge what I am about to impart to you relative to the objects of this League?

2. Are you willing to support the Constitution of the United States?

3. Do you consider that whilst you are willing to concede to the negro all of his just rights that this should be a White Man's Government?

The principal object of the League was "to frustrate as far as lies in its power the attempts which are now being made to force into the Constitution of this State NEGRO SUFFRAGE, with its infallible result NEGRO SUPREMACY." The League appears to have been the forerunner of the Ku Klux Klan, and was soon absorbed by it.

Just Voters

In Florida's election of 1867 there were 16,094 Negroes registered, as compared to 11,040 whites. There were 14,300 votes cast in favor of a constitutional convention to undo the constitution of 1865, and nine-tenths of these favorable votes were cast by Negroes. Of the forty-six delegates elected to the convention, eighteen were Negroes, and seven of these were clergymen. A white observer at the convention reported, "Now I have never been known as a Negro-worshipper, but I must say I do not see any cause for alarm or want of intelligence in their faces or conversation. Fifteen of them are former slaves, well-bred gentlemen, and eloquent speakers."

Most of the funny stories still told by Southern whites about the capers of the Negro Reconstruction legislators are purely fictitious, but a few of them have factual basis. One true story is about Joe Oats, a Negro native of Leon County, who organized the first Negro political meeting in Florida. At one such meeting, held in a church in Tallahassee in 1866, Joe Oats was "elected" to Congress, and was given a large donation to cover his expenses. After a grand send-off, he traveled as far north as Savannah, where he lived in fine style until his funds were exhausted. He thereupon sent word to his "constituents" back home that he was returning from the nation's capitol. A huge celebration was arranged for his homecoming, and he shamelessly reported on "the doings of Congress."

Even before Florida's constitutional convention opened it was obvious that the issue was not one of party partisanship, but the question of what rights were to be granted the freedmen. The radicals were led by Jonathan Gibbs, a freeborn mulatto from Philadelphia, who had been educated at Dartmouth and Princeton Theological Seminary. Sent to Florida after the war by Northern philanthropists, he had dropped religion and taken up politics as a means of helping his people.

The conservative Republicans revealed just how conservative they were by voting against repeal of the three dollars per annum tax which worked such a hardship upon the freedmen to the advantage of the planters. And in various other ways they made it clear that they preferred compromising with the Democrat planters to collaborating with the radical Republicans.

For twenty-eight days the three factions struggled for the balance of power; then Daniel Richards (white) deserted the radicals and joined the conservative Republicans, giving them a majority. The constitution they drafted provided that the governor, lieutenant-governor, and members of the United States Congress must have been citizens for eight years and residents of Florida for three years, thus barring Negroes from these offices. The constitution further provided that after 1882 the legislature should establish qualifications for all voters who had not registered or voted in elections prior to 1867; and of course this was also directed against the Negroes. Though bitterly opposed by the radicals and AME Church, which declared that freedmen could expect more justice under the continued military rule, the constitution was adopted and remained in operation for nineteen years.

Both the conservative and radical Republicans submitted candidates in the election of 1868. The radicals depended entirely on the Negroes for support, whereas the conservatives, posing as bulwark against radicalism, also appealed to the white Democrats for votes. Through the desertion of another radical leader—the mulatto Sanders—Harrison Reed, the conservative candidate, was elected with 14,220 votes as compared to the 1,920 votes received by the radical, J. Walker. The conservative leader Osborne was elected to the United States Senate.

Reed asserted that his administration desired "peace, good government, and the respect of all classes of society." He refused to appoint a Negro to his cabinet, but placed two Democrats in the highest positions. Then Osborne and Reed split over the question of who was to hand out the political plums. Osborne's supporters tried to impeach Reed, and he, in order to get the support of the Negro legislators, was forced to appoint Gibbs as secretary of state.

The conservative carpetbagger Republicans began to display evidences of suddenly acquired wealth, which they obtained by outright theft of public funds, as gratuities for granting political jobs, and as bribes for passing legislation favorable to special individuals and companies. The radical Negro legislators took no part in this "plundering," and formed a "smelling committee" to locate the sources of the carpetbaggers' ill-gotten gains.

Though Reed continued to call for "peace, confidence, and equality," when the legislature passed a bill prohibiting segregation in public conveyances and public places, he vetoed it with the notation: "This act is unnecessary, for the common carrier must have power to defend themselves against intrusion of drunkards and dissolutes of whatever race or color, to regulate their affairs for comfort and safety."

By this time the Klan had become exceedingly active throughout the Palmetto Country, and violence was particularly widespread in counties where Negroes were in the majority. Of Florida's thirty-seven counties, six had a majority of Negroes in 1860. These counties—Jefferson, Gadsden, Leon, Madison, Marion, and Putnam—experienced a reign of Klan terror prior to the 1870 election.

Emanuel Fortune told the Congressional Committee, "I left Jackson County in May, 1869, because there got to be such a state of lawlessness and outrage that I expected that my life was in danger at all times; in fact I got, indirectly, information very often that would be missing some day and no one would know where I was, on account of my being a leading man in politics.

"I do not know anything personally about the Ku Klux, but I believe they are there as much as I believe anything. There is a man who saw two disguised men there eight feet high, in the moonlight, sitting in a place where they finally killed a colored man named Calvin Rogers. Besides Dr. Finlayson and Major Purman, three men were called out of their doors and shot. There were a great many cases of that kind before I left. I expected that my days were few, and I thought I would leave for a while."

M. L. Stearns, the white speaker of the house, told the Committee, "No one has been punished and no attempt has been made to punish anyone. I do not think there are any men who dare to take it up. The Klan can raise 150 of the best armed men of the country at any moment to resist any process."

When he was asked, "Why is it that, with the entire machinery of the State in the hands of the Republican Party, you do not indict these parties for these murders?" Stearns replied, "I do not think the State government, or the Republican Party, has any more control in Jackson County than if they did not exist. The county is entirely in the hands of a mob. They would shoot and kill any officers just as fast as they could be appointed."

"What was the feeling among the democratic part of the community, the masses of them, in respect to the killing of these men?" asked an investigator.

"The usual expression was one of approval. The press said it was done for money, and gave other excuses. The Quincy paper first stated that it was a political murder, but afterward stated most positively that it was not. It also said that some Negro had done the killing, or that a radical had done it for political effect. Some even asserted he was killed by a Negro man because of familiarity with his wife."

Stearns also related how, upon passing a cracker without speaking, the cracker had lifted Stearns' hat with a bowie knife "to teach him to recognize a gentleman when he passed one." Stearns replied, "I shall endeavor to do so—*when* I pass one." The cracker then threatened him with the knife, but when Stearns offered to meet him on even terms at any time, the cracker walked away. A dozen spectators did not interfere. Stearns was at length advised to leave Marianna by "a committee that represented a committee that represented the whole community."

The testimony given the Committee by Henry Reed, a Negro from Marianna, was typical. "The night assassins, or the Ku Klux, or something else, raided me so that I could not stay in Marianna. They knew my principles— that I was Republican, and always have been.

"One night about one o'clock I was sick; the doctor had given me medicine and told me to rest quietly. A crowd of men came to my door and knocked. They said Mr. Dickinson the Bureau agent, wanted to see me at the court-house. I said, 'Gentlemen, I am not able to go; tell Captain Dickinson please to wait until morning.' They said, 'You must go now.' I said, 'Gentlemen, I am not able to walk down there.' They said, 'Come out here! You've got to go now!'

"I was somewhat excited from the alarm, and being very feeble and sick, I said, 'Let me get my coat and hat.' They said, 'You won't need any coat and hat; come out!' My son, who is about 15, hoisted the window and jumped out. They shot at him as he ran. I cracked the door open a very small crack, and just as I could discern the men, I saw one standing at the corner of the house with a double-barreled shotgun pointed right at my head. I shut the door. They said, 'If you don't come out of that house, Goddamn you, we will tear your house down and blow your Goddamn brains out!'

"I did not know what to do. Nobody had anything against me on account of my behavior or character; I was apparently as square with the citizens as any man in the world. At that time my wife came out hollering, 'My son is dead, and they want to kill my husband!' The man at the gate got on his horse, and apparently went for the rest of his company. I jumped out of the window and went over to a neighbor's house. There I hid until some friends got me away with my wife and children. I had just bought a place, paid out a great deal of money for it, and had it fixed up nice and comfortable, everything growing nicely, and ready for good living. They deprived me of everything I owned there in the world, and I have not had five cents from it, and it seems I cannot hear from there.

"Matt Nichols, Maria Nichols, and young Matt were killed by Billy Coker and Peter Altman. The woman's throat was cut from ear to ear, her hair all torn up by the roots; the rest had their throats cut too. The same Peter Altman killed Oscar, Matt's brother. I saw that with my own two eyes. Altman went out hunting with Oscar, and when he came back his coat was spattered all over with brains, and I heard him say, 'Somebody had killed Oscar.' They said to him, 'What did they kill him for?' He said, 'I don't know.'

"Fifty or a hundred were mistreated by shooting at them and trying to cut their throats. In going to church at night they would stand behind a tree and shoot your brains out. They would take your property; and go to a minister's house and make him come out and preach. Caesar Ely was one preacher, and there was another named Reuben Wiggins. They went to his house, took all his family out, ate everything there and threw the rest away. Ah, Gentlemen, it was as terrible a place as ever there was in this world!

"Jimmy Coker, who keeps the store in Marianna, bitterly hates the Republicans. He would not give the Republicans any work, and would charge them double prices. He said the Democrats would carry the next election, or 'kill the last damn Republican in the place.' The head leading-men of the Democrats said that true Republicans could not live there in peace unless they came over to their side; that they intended to kill them or make them leave."

"They always speak very bitterly against Negroes voting," added Emanuel Fortune. "They say, 'The damned Republicans has put niggers to rule us an we will not suffer it'; 'intelligence shall rule the country instead of the majority' and all such as that. They always say this is 'a white man's government' and that 'the colored men have no rights that white men are bound to respect.' I hear such things both privately and in public speeches."

"The white people," said Robert Meacham, "say that a man ought not to vote except he can read and write nicely, and owns $250 or $500 worth of real estate. They say that the rule should apply to white as well as colored. That would exclude two-thirds of the colored people and a great many white people from the ballot."

The effectiveness of the Klan's program was revealed when Emanuel Fortune testified that, "Captain Dickinson said to me a year ago, 'Fortune, you could go back to Jackson County and live if you would; you would not be hurt.' I said, 'Could I go back there and be a free man, to use freedom of speech and act in politics as any man would want with his own people—could I do that?' He said, 'No, you could not—you would have to abandon all that if you went back.'"

And that is how matters still stand throughout the Palmetto Country.

28 AND 29 ....WALLACE RALLY.
Souvenir from the days when the "Solid South" was solidly Democratic. Party rules, with judicial sanction, barred blacks from the primary. The rally photographed here shows white men listening to Alabama Governor George Wallace, who "made history" on June 11, 1963, by standing in the doorway of the University of Alabama to bar a black from enrolling. From the Stetson Kennedy collection.

Conservative Radicals

The Negroes were beginning to tire of the perfidy, corruption, and conservatism of the carpetbagger Republicans, and in 1872 demanded that the Republican Convention nominate Negroes for some offices. As a result, Ossian B. Hart—a Florida Unionist thought to be sympathetic to the Negroes—was nominated and elected governor, while Joshua Walls, an Alachua County Negro, was elected to Congress. Hart, however, refused to appoint a Negro to his cabinet, until the Negro legislators threatened to combine with the Democrats; he then appointed Jonathan Gibbs as superintendent of public instruction. Walls—Florida's only Negro Congressman—proved to be capable, honest, and progressive. He took a keen interest in promoting educational facilities for freedmen, and presented many petitions for thousand-acre grants for Negro schools.

At a time when Florida's educational system was on the verge of collapse from lack of interest and funds, Gibbs toured the state and convinced both the whites and the Negroes of the need for improved facilities. He organized the system on a sound basis, and in 1873 was able to report to the National Educational Association: "The census of 1860 shows that Florida had 4,486 pupils in her schools at an expense of $75,412. Today Florida has 18,000 pupils in school at an expense of $101,820—fully four times as many pupils at an increase of only 33 per cent expense."

Gibbs' eminent career came to an untimely end in 1874. His brother has described his death as follows. "I found him in Tallahassee with his sleeping place in an attic which resembled an arsenal. He said that it had been his resting place for several months, as his life had been threatened by the Ku Klux Klan. It was the last time I saw my brother. After a three-hour speech in the legislature, he ate a heavy meal and died suddenly. The coroner's verdict was apoplexy, but I believe he was poisoned."

The first Klan warning received by Gibbs read:

> *K.K.K.*
> *No man e'er felt the halter draw,*
> *With good opinion of the law*
>
> *K.K.K.*

> *Twice the secret report was heard;*
> *When again you hear this voice,*
> *Your doom is sealed.*

The final warning read:

> *Dead men tell no tales.*
>   *K.K.K.*
> *Dead! Dead! Under the roses.*
>   *K.K.K.*
> *Our motto is, death to radicals!*
> *Beware!*
>   *K.K.K.*

The conservative Republicans began to lose the Negro vote in 1873, and a "moderate" Republican was elected to Osborne's seat in the Senate. Governor Hart died in the same year, and Marcus L. Stearns, the lieutenant-governor, took his place. Stearns was identified with the radicals, and appointed many Negroes to State and county offices.

30 .... KLAN RALLY.
This photograph of a Florida Ku Klux Klan rally was taken by author Stetson Kennedy during his infiltration of the group to expose their activities. From the Stetson Kennedy collection.

In 1876 he observed, "The newspapers tell that the Republican Party is now dead in Arkansas as in Mississippi, Alabama, and Georgia. The white Republicans have been forced to leave those states, and the Negro leaders are woefully different in self-reliance." In spite of this realization, his Florida convention of radical Republicans refused to send a Negro delegate to the Republican National Convention, and a race riot daily threatened to break up the meeting. This so disillusioned many Negroes that they either went over to the Democrats or abandoned politics altogether. Their radical white leaders had gone conservative on them.

The Rising Tide of Demockkkracy

The campaign of 1876 saw widespread violence on the part of whites, and Federal troops were requested for the election. At a Democratic-Republican debate in Lafayette County, a white judge declared, "I want Drew elected governor because it is to my interest to have his interests identified with my interests, and vice versa." To this the only Negro speaker, John R. Scott, replied, "I do not want you to vote for Mr. Hayes and Mr. Stearns because of my interest, but for the interest of the whole people."

For saying this he was struck by a Democrat named Chavis. "He struck me on the arm a half dozen times trying to strike my head," said Scott. "I found no one would touch him, and I did not want to hit him, as that would have been the end of me. Seeing that he was determined to knock me down, I deliberately let him strike my head. He hurt his hands, and yelled, 'Boys, come on and let's kill another nigger!' They all rushed me and the first that came had his knife opened. I stood still and looked them in the eye and I guess that saved my life."

On the same occasion a white Republican was assaulted for using the "Copperhead" argument that "the war was a failure as far as the poor whites are concerned—it was a rich man's war and a poor man's fight." His speech was denounced as an attack on Confederate soldiers, and he was almost killed.

In Leon County a Negro reported: "We were told that all colored people who voted the Republican ticket were going to starve the next year. We have got to go to the merchants and have advances of meat and corn. The newspapers stated that colored folks could not expect any further advances without voting the Democratic ticket." This tactic was highly effective, because the Freedmen's Bureau was gone.

Robert Meacham attended a Democratic rally at Madison, and that night he was called to his door and fired upon. The Democratic Club offered one hundred dollars reward for the would-be assassin. In Key West, the locations of many polls were suddenly changed on election day in an effort to confuse and discourage Negro voters.

Out of the turmoil came both a Republican and a Democratic claim of victory. In the resulting investigation evidences of fraud on the part of both parties were found all over the sate. The investigators awarded the radical Republicans the Senate seat, while the Democratic candidate became governor.

This was the beginning of the end of Negro influence in politics, and the whites were jubilant. Since the election had been hailed (by the whites) as marking the return of "democratic" home rule. For example, the State Information bureau wrote (1907), "In 1876 the conservative Democratic party, calling upon all liberty-loving people to assist in establishing a Government of, by, and for the people, elected George F. Drew Governor."

In 1877 a Negro convention at Tallahassee resolved: "We are aware that recently throughout the South a political revolution has taken place, and it is our hope that now the race issue in politics with all its accompanying evils will pass away and that intelligence and integrity will now dominate without regard to color and previous conditions."

"The Confederate cause is not lost, but is only sleeping."
—Jefferson Davis, 1882.

MEET THE FOLKS

Three centuries of effort by the Spanish and French to settle the Palmetto Country left virtually no ethnic strains and few cultural traces other than ruins and place names. The folks now living in Florida are comparative newcomers. They or their ancestors did not arrive until after Florida became a part of the United States in 1821, and newspapers still announce the deaths of "pioneer settlers." Thus Florida's folk culture, in so far as its local development is concerned, is less than 150 years old.

Florida folk hail from every state in the Union, but the bulk of non-natives in 1930 had come from the southeastern and northeastern states, in amounts of 443,000 and 172,000 respectively. Georgia contributed more than any other state: 220,000, while 75,000 came from Alabama and 50,000 from South Carolina. These folks who moved from the Deep South into the Deepest South have generally been seeking land or jobs, while non-Southern settlers have more often been in search of a congenial climate for convalescence or retirement.

The main current of life in the South is made up of Southern whites and Negroes. The crackers are descended from pioneer Anglo-Saxon stock, while the Negroes—who constitute a third of the region's population—include influential groups from the British West Indies and Cuba whose national cultural characteristics linger for several generations. The Spanish-speaking offspring of the Cuban Negroes are called "homemade foreigners" by native blacks, while those from the Bahamas and Jamaica—

who speak with a British accent—are indiscriminately lumped together as "Nassau niggers" by the crackers. Their behavior, carriage, and speech reflect the greater freedom and individual dignity accorded them in the islands of their origin, and they seldom display any of the traditional servility and deference of the "Southern darkey."

Yet even their individualism, like all such, borders on cannibalism—the freedom of anyone to acquire more than their share of essential commodities inevitably implies the freedom of others to starve. The fact is neatly expressed in this verse of the Nassau Negro children:

> *In all my mother's children,*
> *I loves myself the best;*
> *And when I gets my stomach full,*
> *God help the rest.*

"You can always tell a Nassau nigger by the way he will look you straight in the eye," a cracker has said. "You hire a hundred of em and you'll have to go right behind em and fire all but six. They'll work around boats, though; you put one in a boat and he'll work for nothin. I'll never forget the time me and my wife and another couple was out fishin. We had done cooked up a fine fish chowder, when the Nassau Nigger we had along picked up a stinkin conch in the bottom of the boat—all covered with flies—and began chewin off hunks and spittin em over the side to attract fish. The ladies just couldn't eat after that."

During World War I, thousands of Bahaman Negroes—by special treaty with Great Britain—were brought over to harvest crops in the 'Glades. After the war, many of them remained on the job, or took part in South Florida's boomtime construction. World War II again created an acute shortage of agricultural workers, and in 1942 the Duke of Windsor was consulted about the importation of 20,000 more Negroes under the treaty which was still in effect. Though few American Negroes were willing to pick beans at twenty-five cents per hamper, the Bahamans would welcome the opportunity, as they were being paid but eighty cents per day for unskilled labor in the islands.

Negroes from the sea islands of South Carolina speak Gullah dialect, and are called "blue-gummed Geechees." "His gums is blue as a jaybird," other Negroes say, "and he's a cross 'tween the Devil and a rattlesnake. If one ever bites you, it's a shore death! When a ordinary bad nigger dies, he turns to a mule and has to keep right on working through eternity, but when a blue-gum dies, he turns into a maggot and has to eat dead corpses."

SNOW JAMES

Snow James was a man of might,
He fought everbody both day and night;
He fought his mother and daddy too,
He would fight as long as his gums were blue;
His eyes was red and his love was true;
He was a nappy-head nigger right through and through.

Seasonally the Florida peninsula is invaded by a welcomed host of folk who can only be described as American tourists—a distinct type recognized the world over. Perhaps they have been most aptly described in Havana,

31.........TIN CAN TOURISTS.
   Before RVs, "tin can tourists" were. De Soto Park, Tampa. State Library and Archives of Florida.

119

where they are fondly referred to as ducks. Inclined on the whole to be stout or buxom, their habit of flocking together to toddle amiably wherever a guide leads them, quacking the while, is certainly enough to justify the appellation.

Palmetto Country crackers are wholly unable to understand why tourists ask so many "damn-fool" questions about things that have always been self-evident to local folk. This seeming stupidity and ignorance of the Yankees provides a perennial folklore theme. For example, there is the tale about the Yankee who approached a cracker's cart of covered wares, and sniffed suspiciously.

"What have you there?" he asked.

"Guavas," replied the cracker.

The Yankee sniffed again. "Ye gods!" he exclaimed. "how long have they been dead?"

Yet there is no lack of appreciation of the tourists' value in dollars and cents, and one hundred "Tourist Centers" worth $1,500,000 are only one manifestation of the public interest in giving them satisfaction. Just how much tourists mean to the life of the region is shown by the fact that the 2,600,000 of them who visited Florida during the 1939-40 season spent $291,000,000 in the state. There is, then, considerable truth in the popular tale about the tourist who asked, "What do you folks do for a living down here?" The cracker replied, "In the summer we lives on catfish, in the winter on Yankees."

Ever since the first tourist visited the region there has been an unceasing complaint that the natives charge tourists exorbitant prices for everything. This provides a favorite subject for tourist talk, as illustrated by the story of a cracker who offered to sell a jar of bugs to a Northern scientist.

"How much do you want for them?" asked the scientist.

"Well," said the cracker, "I went to a heap a trouble ketchin them critters, and I been neglectin my grubbin to feed em. But I reckon I better let you make me a offer—there's no tellin how much you Yankees will stand."

The economic factor behind such transactions was brought out by a tourist who wrote in 1876: "I don't know that the people of this section are more avaricious than in any other, but the temptation to bleed a man with money is irresistible where money is so scarce." The continued existence of two prices—one for local folks and a higher one for tourists—leads some establishments to advertise "One Price for Everybody." It is in the field of real estate, however, that the two-price system is most frequently encountered. The difference is often so great that non-resident buyers save money by paying a local person to handle their transactions.

Some property owners who are averse to disposing of property to Jews simply demand impossible prices of them. In the face of such opposition, it is all the more to the Jews' credit that they have recognized the advantages of Miami beach to such an extent that Gentiles accuse them of "taking it over." Numerous hotels and apartments there exhibit signs saying "Gentile Clientele Only."

But the Jews are not the only tourists who are unwanted in spots. Most particular community is Key West, which recently forestalled plans of Ma Baker (of Miami and New York) to convert the old Southernmost House of "the late respected Judge Vining Harris" into a gambling casino de luxe. The editorials in the Key West paper bore remarkable similarities to a leaflet published elsewhere in Florida in 1882, defining:

32.........."WHITES ONLY" JOOK JOINT.
"Whites Only" jook joint, Lake Okeechobee. After Stetson Kennedy filed a protest with highway officials, the signs came tumbling down. Photograph by author Stetson Kennedy.

WHO SHOULD NOT COME TO SUMTER COUNTY

1. We do not want those who expect to make a living conducting cheap dram shops, lotteries, and gambling saloons. We already have several of your class that could very well be spared. No increase desired.

2. We do not want those who expect plenty without labor. Some appear to be in search of a land where roaster turkeys walk the streets with carving knives sticking in their backs. This is not that land.

Statistics also reveal some interesting facts about Florida's tourists. Nearly half of them come from New York, New Jersey, Pennsylvania, and Massachusetts, while a fifth come from Illinois, Ohio, and Michigan. Almost half of them heard about "the best lied-about state in the Union" from other tourists. Two-thirds of them have been in Florida two or more times, and an eighth have visited the State eleven times or more.

Sixty percent come for vacations, twenty per cent for health, and the remainder for assorted reasons. About forty-three per cent stay in hotels, while thirty-six per cent stay in apartments or houses. They are most interested in water sports, beaches, sightseeing, fishing, shuffleboard, checkers, bowling, and horse-shoe pitching.

33 ....RECREATION FOR TOURISTS.
Northern vacationers in Florida enjoy a variety of activities including shuffleboard, played here in St. Petersburg. Burgert photograph, State Library and Archives of Florida.

Miami goes to considerable expense to encourage her visitors to "Stay Thru May." Figures for the State show that forty-three per cent remain two months or longer, one-third stay less than a month, and ten per cent remain more than five months. Their daily expenditures vary as follows: more than twenty dollars per day, twelve per cent; between twelve-fifty and twenty dollars, thirty-one per cent; between ten dollars and twelve-fifty, seven per cent; from five dollars to ten dollars, twenty per cent; from two-fifty to five dollars, twenty per cent; and less than two-fifty, ten per cent.

Those figures give only a rough idea of the wide variety of economic groups which make up Florida's tourist population. Their folkways are the folkways of America, and many foreign countries besides. In terms of personalities, they range from royalty and movie stars to the small-town Southern folk who come down as cut-rate summer visitors, and go home to ritz the stay-at-homes with, "We had a simply delightful stay at Miami Beach."

Some tourists are nocturnal, some are diurnal, and others are half and half. Prolonged exposure to sunshine has the effect of increasing libido, thus greatly accentuating the tourists' pre-occupation with whatever has sex-appeal. A cracker once rightly said, "By golly, you can see every kind of woman in the world right in Miami!" Not only that, Miami in the winter has more bottle-bleached blondes per acre than any other city in the world.

The resort areas have an air of brightness, cleanliness, and gay color that is otherwise lacking in the region, and the festive spirits of the vacationists also have a cheerful effect upon others who have a job to do. There is, moreover, a spirit of progressiveness, of partiality to innovation. This reaches its peak in Miami, which has pioneered in introducing super-modern things to the region and nation—including daring sunshine fashions, beautiful utilitarian architecture, and spectacular neon displays. All these things have a way of catching on in other parts of the Palmetto Country.

When the entry of the United States into World War II nipped the 1942 Florida tourist season in the bud, many hotel owners wondered if they would ever again have their rooms filled with guests paying twenty dollars or more a day for the privilege of waking at noon with a hangover. They clamored for Uncle Sam to send them some soldiers, so the Army Air Corps Technical Command took over many of Miami Beach's exclusive hotels and restaurants. Soon America's swankiest winter resort was echoing the tread of some fifty thousand Army-shod feet. The men marched to their training schools, marched to the golf course for calisthenics, marched to the beach for a swim, marched three times a day to a restaurant, and once each day for their regular drill. Mingled with the tramp of marching feet were the commands of the top-kicks and the singing of the men. They didn't know many marching songs, so they sang the popular stuff.

The KPs took over the big kitchens, and drying underclothes fluttered in the windows of all the best hotels. As the *Miami Herald's* Town Crier wrote, "Miami Beach on Saturday night? Well, she ain't what she used to be." Old businesses vanished overnight, and new ones sprang up, offering special rates to service men for everything from beer to taxi service. There was no more horse booking at the cigar stands, and not a garish light from the Pier to Surfside.

Large groups of non-American Anglo-Saxons have settled in Florida, where they have been readily absorbed into the dominant cultural pattern. They include 17,000 persons of Canadian birth or descent, 7,000 from

34 .... BOYDS MODERN TOURIST COTTAGES.
Fore-runner to the motel. Pensacola Florida. Marion Post photograph. State Library and Archives of Florida.

England, 5,000 "Conchs" from the Bahamas, 2,000 from Ireland, and 2,000 from Scotland. Florida's 40,000 Latins form a cultural pool that is still fairly intact, while 23,000 Germans are widely dispersed and thoroughly assimilated. In addition to these folks, there are 5,000 Swedes, 2,000 each of Poles, Czechs, Greeks, Russians, Norwegians, Danes, and smaller groups of Dutch, Belgians, Hungarians, Finns, and Turks.

In many cities and towns of the Palmetto Country the old saying that "When Greek meets Greek they start a restaurant" holds true. But at Tarpon Springs (Florida), Greek sponge divers and their families have established one of the most colorful colonies in America. Most of them came from southern Greece and Dodecanese Islands in 1820. At first they did their sponging along the Florida Keys, but in 1905 they moved up the west cost to Tarpon Springs. Four times each year they board their ships and sail to the deeper waters of the Gulf, where they gather sponges with the aid of diving equipment. There is great rejoicing when the fleet returns, and the sponges are stored in a co-operative warehouse where a million dollars' worth of them—most of America's supply—are sold each year.

Some of the 125 vessels of the picturesque fleet are named after such venerable, mythological, and modern Greek characters such as *Socrates, Venus, Apollo, Halki, Demokratia,* and *Bozzaris,* the latter being the doughty Greek patriot who "slew a thousand Turks before breakfast." Other boats bear such names as *Uncle Sam, President Roosevelt, American Girl, Dixie,* and *Katina of Tampa.* Before the fleet sails forth, a priest from the Orthodox Greek Catholic Church sprinkles the boats, engine rooms, bunks, and crew members with holy water. The womenfolk will not go to the dock to see the fleet depart, as this is thought to be bad luck. There is also a local witch, and no ship will set sail while she is in sight.

Life in the Greek colony is marked by many religious ceremonies and festivities, the most spectacular of which takes place on January 6, the Feast of Epiphany. Thousands of tourists and regional folk are on hand to watch the Greek congregation leave their church at noon, to be led by the priests and their resplendent acolytes through the gaily decorated streets. Slowly the procession winds toward Spring Bayou, where a priest on a barge sets free a white dove. He then tosses a small golden cross into the bayou, and a score of young Greek divers plunge after it. He who retrieves the cross receives a special blessing for the coming year. General feasting and merrymaking are then in order, and the Greek homes and waterfront cafés resound with music and laughter.

On their lonesome voyages the Greek spongers sing many ancient folk-songs, some of which were sung by their sponge-gathering ancestors in the Mediterranean. These songs show Turkish and Arabic influences, and occasionally lesser Italian, Spanish, and American traits. A few of them, of which the following is a sample, are typical pastoral songs of the Greek mountain country.

POVERTY

Poverty, you make the heart ache—
You can produce pain in a moment of time;
But you have charms that enslave
If you are accompanied by the virtue of honor.

Poverty, in this creation
You have in your clutches most of mankind;
Poverty, I do not envy riches
Because I have happiness in my heart.

Poverty, if I ever leave you
I shall lose a bosom friend;
If ever in palaces I dwell,
You I shall never forget.

Such sentimental attachment to poverty probably never envisaged the starvation which obtained in Axis-occupied Greece in 1942, when the exiled King George II told Americans that "The population of the villages on the islands are compelled to subsist on wild grass, which will wither and disappear in the summer."

The indomitable spirit of the Greeks is epitomized in "Old Demos," a folksong commemorating the liberation of Greece from Turkish domination in 1832. It is still sung by Florida Greeks, and translates like this:

I have fought for fifty years, and I am old;
I have had no sleep for fifty years, and I am tired;
I have had no good bread, no good water, no sleep;
My heart is always leaking blood, there is no blood left in my body.

35.........TARPON SPRINGS SPONGE DIVER.
Tarpon Springs, Florida, is the sponge capitol of the world. Greeks in diving suits harvested sponges from the bottom of the Gulf of Mexico. Their wooden ships were patterned after Mediterranean vessels dating back 3,000 years or more. P.K. Yonge Library,

Go cut blossoming green branches, fix my bed for sleep.
God knows what tree will grow over my grave;
I hope it will be a sycamore, so I can rest in the shade;
And I want my rifle to hang on the tree.

Run, soldiers, run up the mountainside and fire my rifle!
I want to hear my rifle for the last time.
Dig a well by my grave so soldiers may wash their wounds;
Have them fire a salute each morning over my grave;
Let them sing of my youth when I was a hero!

Old Demos will hear the sound of the salute
And the songs sung over his grave.
Run, soldiers, and fire my rifle over the mountain,
While I close my eyes and fold my arms in death.

Another interesting cultural pocket of the Palmetto Country is Slavia in Seminole County (Florida), established by a group of Slovaks who came from Cleveland in 1912. They organized a democratic Slavia Colony Company, purchased 1,200 acres of land, and by dint of hard labor and communal co-operation succeeded in building up a thrifty agricultural and poultry-raising community. They take a keen interesting in voting, send their sons to the State University, and subscribe to numerous American periodicals. Their social life centers around the Lutheran Church, and Reverend S. M. Tuhy teaches the children old Slovakian folksongs, such as:

THE MOSQUITO'S WEDDING DAY

On the skeeter's wedding day
Not a drop of wine had they. None!
Then flew in a nightingale
And filled their cups from his pail.

All the guests now drank until
The mosquito they did kill. Whack!
In the courtyard lies the groom,
While the fly weeps in her room.

"Dear fly, weep not in vain;
He'll come back to life again." Sure!
"Come to life again," said she,
"When they killed him mortally?"

All his fat they trimmed and sold,
For a hundred crowns of gold. Yes!
And his skin, forty brought;
That's the story I was taught.

A group of Czechs established a farming community near Tampa in 1924, naming it Masaryktown in honor of Thomas G. Masaryk, the revolutionary hero and first president of the Czechoslovakian Republic. The women operate a co-operative canning plant where they preserve their surplus farm products for their own use and local sale. They speak English well, and teach their children the Czech language after school hours. Their native Independence Day is celebrated with an historical pageant in the morning, special afternoon services in the Roman Catholic Church, and folk dancing in native costumes during the evening. One of the folksongs goes like this:

WHEN A SLOVAK LEFT HIS COUNTRY

When a Slovak left his country,
He sang on the slope of Mount Krivan;
Over the peak of Mount Krivan,
His voice was heard in the valley;

"O Krivan, you Krivan high,
I wonder if I shall see you again —
Whether in the next troublesome years
My eyes will see you.

"O Mother-soil, Slovakia, you are sad
Because you are always troubled by bad times;
Your children are wandering in the world
Because you could offer them no opportunities."

A real-estate promoter was responsible for getting a number of Poles from New York, Chicago, and Detroit to establish a colony called Korona on Florida's east coast. With native coquina rock they erected a shrine to St. Christopher, the patron saint of travelers, and hundreds of Polish tourists stop to see it each year. On Sunday afternoons, sacraments and benedictions are offered in the Catholic Church, and the travelers' cars are sprinkled with holy water.

The menfolk settle their grievances at a court they hold each Monday, and the women do likewise on Tuesdays. Another Salutary practice is their age-old custom of welcoming spring. Members of opposite sexes pour wine over each other's heads and administer half a dozen lashes on one another's backs, thus settling old scores and starting the season with a clean slate. These folk speak both Polish and English, and observe the Polish national holidays. Among their folksongs is one which goes:

> *From Cracow I am driving into far, strange countries;*
> *And the soul of my beloved Kasienka remembers me!*
> *On the way from Cracow I am driving in the forest;*
> *If she did not love me, I would stab myself with a knife!*
> *Why, Kasienka, are you angry that I have no possessions?*
> *We shall love and kiss from evening until dawn!*

A MAN IN FULL

Uncle Bud was a man, a man in full;
His back was strong like a Jersey bull.
Uncle Bud's got cotton, aint got no pears;
Uncle Bud's gotta gal aint got no hairs.
Uncle Bud! Uncle Bud! Uncle Bud!

The folk of the Palmetto Country have created their full share of legendary heroes of colossal proportions. Bullock County's nine-second man; Captain Charlie Coker, the Conch sponger who was "all man"; Quevedo, the artful Spanish rogue who had a way with women and kings; Big John the Conqueror, that wizard of slave days who could outsmart Old Massa, God, and the Devil, and who was probably the American Negro's first folk hero; Uncle Monday, the African medicine man who lives as a 'gator in Florida's Blue Sink; Daddy Mention, the Negro convict who can outrun the longest shotgun; Kerosene Charlie, the migrating Negro laborer personified; Old Pete, the herculean stevedore; and Roy Tyle, the ace mechanic—all these are cut from the same heroic cloth as America's number one lumberjack, Paul Bunyan, and that steel-drivin man, John Henry. All follow the same universal pattern for folk heroes which set the style for such immortals as Ulysses and Jack-the-Giant-Killer.

Many of these characters actually lived and breathed, performing exceptional feats which served to start their legendary counterparts on their astounding careers. Some of the heroes exemplify the urge of occupational groups to dramatize the work they perform, while others—particularly those of the Negroes—are also what psychologists call compensation mechanisms—the first step toward delusions of grandeur. They are wish-fulfillment projections of the poor and humble into the realms of the mighty. By brute strength, superhuman cunning, or incredible good luck, they utterly defeat or confound whoever their masters might be. In the case of Big John, his strength lives on in Big John the Conqueror Root, which is sold in conjure shops all over the region. Nothing can stand against it.

One thing stands out glaringly in Negro folk tales. The Negro is determined to laugh, even if he has to laugh at his own expense. His Bossman, his woman, his preacher, his jailer, his God, and himself must all be baptized in the stream of laughter—he tries to dissolve his whole world of troubles in laughter.

These folk tales are further proof that some of America's finest stories repose in the oral tradition of her folk. All that is needed to make them a permanent part of American literature is someone to record them.

Bullock County's Nine-Second Man

"I aint a-aimin to exaggerate none, but everybody in South Georgia knows I was the fastest runner in Bullock County, excusin none. Every year at the Kennedy reunion—when it seemed like half of Georgia showed up—I won all the foot races. It was the same at carnivals and County Fair; I taken all the prizes.

"When I was a boy me and my ten brothers used to go coon huntin a lots. We would start out at night and hunt in the hammocks and bayheads along the edge of the swamps. When the dogs struck trail I liked to have went crazy as a cross-eyed tadpole, I was fitten to be tied! To hear them hounds a-yowlin through the woods made me just rarin to take right out after them.

"My brothers would grab me, because they was afeared I'd run through the woods so fast I'd butt onto a tree, or maybe get rattlesnake bit. When they grabbed me I'd fight like a wildcat. 'Don't hold me, boys!' I'd beg. Sometimes I pulled the shirt off my back, and away I'd go after the dogs.

"When I got goin good I could leap over trees, pammetters, and briar bushes like a scairt buck deer. It didn't take me long to catch up with the dogs and pass em. Many a time I run ahead of the dogs and treed the coon myself. They'd skee-daddle up a tree, and I'd stand under it and holler.

"I'm gonna tell you a story you aint gonna believe, but anybody in Bullock County will tell you it's nothin but the Gospel Truth. When I was eighteen years old I was takin Pa's saddle horse out to the pasture one mornin about sun-up. Somehow or nother I left the gate open, and Lightnin—that was the horse's name—slipped through and lit out down the road tords Register.

"I knowed I was in for a good lickin if Lightnin got losted, so I taken a short cut that came out about a mile down the road. But when I come to the crossin Lightnin wasn't nowhere in sight, so I started to run down the road to Register to see if I could catch him. Register is thirty miles away, and I didn't get there until ten o'clock in the mornin. I asked Uncle Josh at the General Store if he'd seen Lightnin comin through town, but he said he hadn't.

"I went in a bar and had me a good shot of whiskey. Toreckly I heard a rumpus, and when I looked down Main Street there was Lightnin, sweatin and heavin like he was about to drop! I had passed him by takin the short cut, and had been runnin ahead of him all the way! That afternoon I backtracked to home, and Pa never could rightly understand how come Lightnin was so plumb tuckered out after a day in the pasture.

"I'm getting on in my forties now, and can't run like I used to could. But last summer our Men's Bible Class had a picnic at the beach, and when it come time to have the runnin races a young feller started braggin that he was a 'ten-second man' at college—meanin he could run a hundred yards in ten seconds.

"Nobody hadn't never held a clock to my runnin, so I didn't know how fast a ten-second man was. But I challenged him to a race, the gun fired, and off we went. I have to give that young feller credit—he could nachely-born run. I didn't pull ahead of him until just before we crossed the line. I could have beat him a heap sight more if it hadn't been for my arthritis."

Captain Charlie Coker, Brute

"I gad, Charlie Coker was one whale of a man. 'E was a *hellova* man! That yellow-headed, trench-mouthed sonofagun weighed all of 225 pounds and stood six feet two. I mean 'e was solid muscle, too. 'E didn't 'ave no belly to 'im. 'E was all man. 'E was there.

" 'Is bloody fingers was big aroun as my wrist. I shook 'ands with 'im once and 'e like to 'ave ruint me. I should've knew better—rot me if nobody could 'ave turned me to do it again. Oh, 'e was a powerful monaster, a brute!

"Coker was captain of the *Heron*, one of the old-time sailin spongers in the days when spongin was a big thing in Key West. 'E was the best in the trade. There are lots of stories told about 'im, and I know one to be a fact. 'E was caught in a 'eavy storm up at Bay Hundy [Bahia Honda] and the *Heron* couldn't live into it. Coker luffed 'er into the wind and lowered 'er sails to keep em from bein torn to shreds. The wind was drivin the *Heron* straight tord the reef, so 'e bellowed to the crew to 'eave over the anchor.

"The anchor weighed 500 pounds, and the whole crew of three mens was up there on the bow a-strainin their guts tryin to get it over the side. They was all three good men, and was putting out everything they 'ad, but they couldn't manage to get it over. The wind and the current was drivin the *Heron* a-hellin for the reef, and old Charlie was a-cussin the men for all 'e was woith! Finally he seen she was goin on the rocks for true if the anchor wasn't got over in a hurry. So 'e jumped up on the bow and nearbout knocked them other men overboard. Then 'e stooped over, picked up the anchor, and 'eaved it way out over the side, proper, without so much as a grunt!

"There's something else told on 'im I wouldn't swear to be true. It may just be Conch talk, but I'm heard people say it so much I'm kinda blieve it's so. They say one time Coker 'ad a nigger workin on the *Heron*, and the nigger said somethin that didn't suit Coker's 'umor, after Coker 'ad done told the nigger to close 'is trap. So Coker 'auled off and 'it the nigger on the jaw and killed 'im perfectly dead with one punch! By Jiminies, 'e could've done it, too! People say if 'e'd started out to be a prize fighter 'e woulda been famous that way!

"My God, could Coker drink! 'E would kill one quart right after another. It didn't make no matteration what it was—rum, gin, whiskey, awgydent [*Agua Diente*—"Fiery Water"]— any blamed thing 'e could get 'old of. One night 'e was whoppin up a jimboree in No Name Bar up on No Name Key. 'E 'ad done drunk a coupla quarts and 'is money was run out. So Coker picked up one of them bottles of red-hot tabasco sauce and swore up and down 'e'd drink the whole damn thing if anybody'd buy 'im a drink! There was some stranger at the bar, and 'e said, "Ell man, if you can drink that bottle of sauce I'll do better than buy you a drink—I'll buy you a quart of whatever you want, and give you two bucks besides!'

"'Open a quart of awgydent,' says Coker. Then 'e took a full bottle of tabasco sauce, knocked the top off on the edge of the counter, and poured it all out in a glass. 'E drank that tabasco in one swallow, and chased it with the quart of awgydent!

"You can bet you ass Charlie Coker was a brute! Nobody can dispute that!"

Quevedo

The most renowned legendary folk character among Spanish-speaking peoples is Quevedo. The real Quevedo, whose name was Francisco Gómez de Quevedo y Villegas, was born near Madrid in 1580. The Quevedo family was one of the most influential in Spain; Francisco's father was royal secretary to King Felipe II, and his mother was the Queen's maid, whom his father married with the blessing of the court.

Quevedo studied under the outstanding cultural leaders in Spain, but as he grew older he left the court and lived among the common people. He became a prolific writer of satiric essays and verse, which were critical of the regime and the nobility. For this he was frequently thrown into prison, where he produced some of his best works. Today Quevedo is credited with giving literary dignity to the Castilian language, and with having been comparable with Seneca as the instigator of a cultural renaissance.

Quevedo, the folk character, has been vulgarized, but is still recognizable as a hero of the common people who dared to criticize the rulers of Spain. The innumerable tales which perpetuate his memory after three and a half centuries are to be heard in Spanish-speaking communities the world over.

Small pornographic booklets of these tales have been published illegally in Cuba and smuggled into the Florida Latin colonies, giving new life to the Quevedo tradition. At the University of Florida, Latin American exchange students and students of Spanish have organized a fraternal group, Los Pícaros de Quevedo—The Rascals of Quevedo.

Most tales portray Quevedo as a cunning rogue who took great pleasure in outwitting the King and Queen, doing impossible deeds, displaying his prowess with women, and artfully escaping from any predicament. The following stories are illustrative of these themes:

Once upon a time the King ordered that Quevedo be executed. So Quevedo was thrown into prison, and as the last day set for his execution arrived, Quevedo asked that the King allow him to choose the manner in which he should die, and the King replied that since he was to die one way or another, he would grant him his wish. So Quevedo requested that he be allowed to die of old age. The King had given his word, so he had to let Quevedo go free.

Another time Quevedo happened to see the Princess driving past in her carriage. He immediately fell in love with her, and resolved to meet her. Having heard that she was very fond of eating black beans, Quevedo, with customary cunning, went to the palace and was introduced to her. He told her that his name was Frijolito (black bean).

Then one night he invited her to have some *frijolitos*, which he said were exceptionally good, and she accepted. So Quevedo, who was a natural-born rascal, entered her room, which adjoined that of the Queen. Without a moment's hesitation he made advances to the Princess, and she began to cry for her mother.

"Mama!" she called. "Frijolito is hurting me! Frijolito is hurting me terribly!" But the Queen, not realizing what was taking place, replied, "You certainly deserve it! I've told you many times not to eat *frijolitos*."

The only time that Quevedo was ever fooled was when he made love to two girls who slept on the second floor of their father's house. They promised Quevedo that at midnight, when everyone else was asleep, they would lower a large basket on a rope, and thereby hoist him to their room.

Promptly at midnight Quevedo was under the window. The girls let down the basket, and Quevedo climbed in. Then the girls hauled him up until the basket was midway between their window and the ground; then they tied the rope and left him hanging there. In the morning all the passersby mocked Quevedo, and when one of them asked him what he was doing, Quevedo replied:

> "Que ni subo ni bajo;
> Siempre estoy quedo."
> (I neither go up nor down;
> Always I am motionless.)

Big John the Conqueror

"Every night Big John used to go up to the Big House and stand in the chimney corner and listen to what Old Massa talked about. That way he learned a lot about what was goin to happen. If he heard Old Massa say he was gonna kill hogs the next day, Big John would slip back to the quarters and tell the other niggers, 'Tomorrow we kills hogs.'

" 'How you know that?' they asked him.

" 'I can tell fortunes, that's how,' said Big John. 'Aint nothin hid from me.'

"And the next mornin when Old Massa come out and told all the niggers to get ready for a big hog-killin, they decided Big John was a fortune teller for true. From then on they believed anything he told em.

"One day when Big John was hanging around the back door of the Big House, he seen his Mistress throw the water out of her wash basin, and in it he saw her diamond ring. But before he could pick it up, a turkey gobbler gobbled it down.

"Soon the whole house was raisin a ruckus lookin for the lost ring, so Big John went to Old Massa and told him he knew where it was. Old Massa promised him if he could find the ring he would make him a present of a fine fat shoat. So Big John told him to kill the gobbler and he would find the ring. At first Old Massa didn't want to kill his prize gobbler, and he told Big John that if he was foolin him he would kill him for sure. But when he killed the gobbler, there was the ring. From then on Old Massa thought Big John was a fortune teller too.

"One day Old Massa was braggin to some white folks that he had a nigger who could tell fortunes. One man disputed his word, so Old Massa said, 'I'll bet you forty acres of a good bottomland my nigger can tell fortunes!'

" 'If you are so sure, what you spuddin for?' asked the man. 'Why don't you make a real bet? I'll bet you my whole plantation.'

" 'Since you really wants me to make a bettin thing outa my statement,' said Old Massa, 'let's make it worth my time. I'm a fightin dog, and my hide is worth money. We'll bet our whole plantations and every horse and mule and hog and nigger on the place!'

"So they agreed on it, and decided to prove the thing out a week from that day. Old Massa took Big John aside and told him about the bet, and said, 'I bet everything I got in this world on you, and if you make me lose I'll kill you!'

"The provin day came and Old Massa was up bright and early. He was up so early he had to saddle his own horse and then go wake up Big John. Big John climbed on a mule, and off they rode to the provin ground. When they got there it looked like everybody and their brother was on hand to see the sight. The other bettin man had the privilege of fixin the proof, so Big John was led away a little piece. Then they brought him back and showed him a great big old black iron washpot turned upside down, and they asked him what was under it.

"Everybody knew but Big John. Old Massa told him he better think good if he wanted to live. Everybody kept quiet waitin to hear what Big John would say. He looked hard at the pot and walked around it three or four times, but he didn't have the least idea what was under it. He began to sweat and scratch his head and Old Massa looked at him and began to sweat too. At last Big John decided he might just as well give up and get the killin over with.

" 'You got the old coon,' he said.

"When he said that Old Massa throwed his hat up in the air and let out a whoop, and everybody else was yellin with surprise, cause that's what was under the pot—a big old coon. So Old Massa went off to Philadelphia to celebrate, but before he left he gave Big John his freedom and a hundred dollars and left him in charge of the plantation.

"Old Massa and Old Miss had no sooner got on the train than Big John sent word to the niggers on all the plantations, "Massa is gone to Philamayork and won't be back for three weeks. He done left me in charge of everything. Come on over to the Big House for a big time.' While the invite was bein carried round, he told some of the hands to go into Massa's lot and kill hogs till you could walk on em.

"That night Big John really spread a scrumptious table. Everybody that could get hold of white folks' clothes had em on. Big John, he opened up the whole house and took Old Massa's big rockin chair and put it on top of Massa's bed. Then he climbed up and sat down in it to call the figures for the dance. He was sittin in his high seat with a box of Massa's cigars under his arm and two in his mouth when he seen a couple of poor-lookin white folks come in.

" 'Take them poor folks out of here and carry them back to the kitchen where they belongs,' Big John said. 'Don't allow em back up front again.— Nothin but quality up here.'

"He didn't know that they was Old Massa and Miss, who had slipped back to see how he would behave while they was gone. They washed the dirt off their faces and came back up front where Big John was still sittin.

" 'John,' said Old Massa, 'after I trusted you with my place you done smoked up all my fine cigars and killed all my hogs and let all these niggers in my house to act like they was crazy. Now I'm gon take you out to the persimmon tree and hang you. You is entitled to a good hangin, and that's what you gon get.'

"While Old Massa was gone to fetch a rope, Big John called his friend Ike to one side and said, 'Ike, Old Massa is gonna take me out and hang me to the persimmon tree. Now I want you to hurry out to that tree and climb up in it. Take a box of matches with you, and every time you hear me ask God for a sign, you strike a match.'

"After a while here come Old Massa with a rope, and he led Big John out to the tree. He tied a noose in the rope and put it around Big John's neck and then threw the other end of the rope over a limb.

" 'I just have one favor to ask of you, Old Massa,' said Big John. "—Let me pray before I die.'

" 'All right,' said Old Massa, 'but hurry up and get it over with, cause I never been so anxious to hang a nigger in my life.'

"So Big John kneeled down under the tree and prayed, 'O Lord, if you mean for Massa not to hang me, give me a sign.'

"When he said that, Ike struck a match and Old Massa seen it and began to shake. Big John kept prayin, 'O Lord, if you mean to strike Massa dead if he hangs me, give me a sign.' Ike struck another match and Old Massa said, 'Never mind, John, you done prayed enough—the hangin's off!'

36.........STORYTELLER ANNIE TOMLIN.
Storytellers like Annie Tomlin, photographed here at the Florida Folk Festival, May 5, 1956, keep the folktale tradition alive. State Library and Archives of Florida.

But Big John prayed right on, 'O Lord, if you means to put Old Massa and all his family to death unless he turns us niggers loose, give me a sign.' This time Ike struck a whole handful of matches, and Old Massa lit out from there as fast as he could run.

"And that's how the slaves was freed."

Uncle Monday

"In his native Africa, Uncle Monday was a big-time medicine man—a leader in the powerful crocodile cult of men who claimed brotherhood with the savage saurians. Captured and brought to American as a slave, Uncle Monday soon escaped and made his way from South Carolina and Georgia down into the Indian territory of Florida. There he made medicine among the Seminoles and their Negro allies, the Maroons.

"When the white men drove the tribes deeper and deeper into the peninsula, Uncle Monday rallied the warriors on the shores of Lake Maitland. Again they were defeated by superior arms and numbers, and Uncle Monday was forced to retreat with his men to the dense woods around Blue Sink Lake. He told them the gods had revealed to him that further resistance would be useless. But Uncle Monday swore that he would never submit to slavery or death at the hands of the whites. He said he would change himself into an alligator, and join his brother saurians in the Blue Sink until the wars were over. Then he would come forth from the lake and walk the land in peace.

"So the tribe held a ceremony on the banks of the Blue Sink. As the men beat savage rhythms on their drums, Uncle Monday danced. As he danced his face grew long and terrible, his arms and legs grew shorter, his skin grew thick and scaly, and his voice changed to thunder. From the Blue Sink came an answering roar of deep-throated bellows, and a thousand 'gators swept up from the lake in a double column. Uncle Monday was the biggest 'gator of them all, and he marched majestically between their ranks and slid into the Blue Sink. With a mighty roar all the other 'gators plunged after him.

"That's how Uncle Monday changed himself into an alligator. He still lives in the Blue Sink, but every now and then he changes himself back into a man and walks through the land casting all sorts of good and bad spells on folks.

"Not long ago old Judy Bronson of Maitland was braggin around that Uncle Monday wasn't no better hoodoo doctor than what she was. She said she could not only undo any spell he cast, but she could throw it right back at him. When Uncle Monday heard about her braggin, all he said was, 'The foolishness of tongues is higher than mountains.'

"One day Judy asked her grandson to rig up a pole and dig her a can of worms; she was goin fishin down at the Blue Sink, even if the mosquitoes and red-bugs did eat her old carcass up. Folks tried to get her not to go, because Blue Sink is bottomless a few feet from shore; but Judy said she just *had* to go, and that's all there was to it. She was there at sundown, and had no sooner got her hook baited and in the water than she felt the dark slippin up and grabbin hold of her like a varmint.

"Judy wanted to get up and run off through the brush, but her legs were paralyzed. Then she heard a big wind come rushin across the brush, and the next thing she knew she had fallen into the Blue Sink. Of all things on earth, Judy was most afraid of the dark and the water, and now they both had her in their claws. She was afraid to move for fear she might slip off into the deep. Finally she found strength enough to scream. At the sound of her voice a bright beam of light fell across the Blue Sink like a flaming sword, pointing straight at her.

"Then Judy saw Uncle Monday. He was clad in flowing robes and marched across the water toward her. Behind him swam an army of 'gators.

" 'I brought you here,' said Uncle Monday, 'and here you will stay till you own up that you can't do no such magic as me.' The light faded, and Uncle Monday and the 'gators sank beneath the water. But one big 'gator remained, and sidled up so close to Judy she couldn't help touching him when she breathed.

"Judy hated like everything to give in to Uncle Monday, but she was too scared to let pride stand in her way. First she admitted it inside, then she said it out loud. When she did, the 'gator swam off into the darkness, and she heard her grandson calling to her. Soon she was lifted out of the Blue Sink and carried home. Folks still try to tell Judy that she only suffered a stroke and fell in the lake, but she knows better. She threw away all her voodoo stuff, and says she has Uncle Monday to thank for being able to walk again.

"Uncle Monday still walks through the countryside as a man, but he always changes to a 'gator again and returns to the Blue Sink. When he does all the other 'gators in the lake keep up an all-night bellowing, and folks in the village hear them and say with a sigh of relief, 'Uncle Monday has gone back.' "

Daddy Mention

"Daddy Mention didn't have nothin in particular against the Polk County jails, exceptin the dirty little jug outside of Lakeland. He told em when they locked him up in there he didn't think he'd be able to stay with em so very long. They had him locked up for vagrancy. He tried to tell em he'd be glad to go to work if only he could find a job, but you know a colored man can't say much in Polk County.

"They gave him ninety days straight up—no time off for good behavior. After he had stayed in the Lakeland Jail awhile they sent him out to the County Farm and put him on the stump-grubbing gang. It was afternoon when he got there and started to work, and he made the day all right. But when supper-time came and he seen what we had to eat I could hear him grumble under his breath.

"The next morning we et grits with bacon grease for breakfast, and Daddy Mention grumbled some more. At sun-up we went out to the woods and started to work. Before it was ten o'clock Cap'm Higgenbotham had done cussed out Daddy Mention four times; Daddy didn't work fast anuff to suit him. When we took time out for lunch I heered Daddy growl, 'They ain't treatin me right.'

"After lunch we lined up to go back to the woods and Cap'm Higgenbotham walked over to Daddy. 'Boy,' he hollered. 'You gonna work this afternoon or would you rather go back to the sweat-box?'

"Daddy Mention didn't say nothin at first, then kinda slow he said, 'Whatever you want me to do, Cap'm.'

"Cap'm Higgenbotham didn't know what to make of that, so he slapped Daddy into the box in a hurry. He didn't go back to look at him that day, neither. He didn't go back till the nex day. 'Hey, boy,' he called. 'You feel like workin today?'

" 'Whatever you want me to do, Cap'm,' answered Daddy Mention.

"I didn't see Cap'm Higgenbotham then, but they tell me he got so hot you could fry eggs on him. He spit in the box and walked off and didn't come back all that day. Every mornin after that he would come to the box and ask Daddy Mention the same thing, and every mornin Daddy answered him the same way.

"Finally Cap'm Higgenbotham got to thinkin that maybe Daddy Mention wasn't tryin to be smart-aleck or sassy, but was just plain dumb. So he let Daddy out of the box and put him on the tree-choppin gang that was workin just ahead of us.

"Daddy Mention was glad to get outa the box, cause he had done set his mind on goin to Tampa. He told some of his gang about it when the Cap'm wadn't listenin. But Daddy knew bettern to try to run away; you can't get away with that in Polk County. They'd sooner shoot you than go to all the trouble of tryin to ketch you. Even if you got away the hounds would ketch up with you before you could even get to Mulberry.

"Daddy Mention knew he had to have a better plan. He got busy and thought one up. None of us knew much about it cause he didn't talk about it. But we began to notice he was doin more work than anybody else in his gang; he would chop a tree down all by hisself, and it didn't take but one more man to help him tote it to the pile. Then one day when he was sure Cap'm was watchin him, he picked up a tree all by hisself and carried it all the way to the pile before he put it down.

"The Cap'm couldn't hardly blieve his own eyes. He didn't see how any man could lift one of them big pines all by hisself, much less carry one around. So he made Daddy Mention do it again, just to be sure. Then he called the other guards to see Daddy do it again.

"It wasn't long before the Cap'm and some of the other guards was pickin up a little easy money bettin folks that Daddy Mention could pick up any tree they could cut. And the Cap'm didn't fuss so very much when Daddy won a coupla bumpers [nickels] at it hisself.

"It got to be a regular sight to see Daddy Mention walkin around the jail-yard carryin a big tree in his arms. Everybody was used to seein it by then. That was just what Daddy Mention wanted. One afternoon when we come in from the woods Daddy Mention brought a tree-butt with him. The Cap'm thought one of the other guards musta asked him to bring it in to do tricks with, so he didn't say nothin about it.

"Daddy Mention took his tree-butt in the dinin-hall with him and stood it up by the wall, then went on to the table the rest of us and et his supper. He didn't seem to be in no hurry or nothin, but I noticed he didn't have much to say to nobody.

"After supper he waited till nearly everbody got finished, then he got up and went back to his log. Most of the Cap'ms and guards was around the yard, and they watched while Daddy picked up that big log. Daddy clowned around in front of the guards for a while, then he started walkin tords the gate with the log still on his shoulder. None of the guards didn't bother him, cause they never thought a man would try to escape with a log on his shoulder.

"You know you have to pass the guards' quarters before you get to the gate in the Lakeland Blue Jay. But Daddy Mention didn't even turn around when he passed, and nobody didn't say nothin to him. The guards at the gate musta thought one of the Cap'ms had sent Daddy to take the log somewheres, or was makin a bet or sumpum. Right on out the gate Daddy Mention went, and onto the road that goes to Tampa. Off he walked down that road with the log on his shoulder, and he kept right on walkin till he was plumb out of sight. . .

"I never saw Daddy Mention again until a long time after, in Tampa. I had never been able to figger out how he got to Tampa after he left the Lakeland Blue Jay, so I asked him.

" 'Why, I didn't have no trouble a-tall,' Daddy Mention said. 'I jus kept that log on my shoulder, and everbody I passed thought it musta fallen offa truck and I was carryin it back. They knew nobody would have the nerve to steal a good pine log like that and walk along the highway with it. Soon's I got to Plant City I took the log to a woodyard and sold it. Then I had me enough money to ride to Tampa. —Ain't nobody ever gonna ketch me in Polk County nomore.'"

"Once there was lotsa folks workin on the Cross-State Canal near Ocala, and they was all makin good money. Daddy Mention, he was there, and makin more money than anybody else. But he wadn't exactly workin on the canal; he was sellin shine to them what was. They wouldn't let Ocala police arrest nobody at the canal, and the county cops didn't bother you much neither. There was some special Government men could get you, but they didn't bother you none unless you raised a ruckus of some kind.

"When Daddy Mention sold out all his shine he useta hafta go into Ocala to get more. He didn't want none of them Ocala policemens to get him, so he always rode into town with one of the white men at the camp. It useta make them cops mad as stunned gopher to see Daddy come ridin into town with that white feller, and then go ridin back out to camp again where they couldn't get him.

"But one time Daddy Mention had just got his load of likker into the car when the white feller spied somebody he knew. So he climbed outa the truck and told Daddy to wait, he'd be back in a minute. Bout that time a policeman came up and seen Daddy Menion sittin there all by hisself. He had been waitin a long time for a chance to ketch Daddy alone so he could lock him up. But first he thought he'd have a little fun. So he walked over and started to joke with Daddy, kiddin him bout always ridin into town with that white man.

" 'You must think you're as good as white folks.' He told Daddy, and laughed.

"Daddy Mention thought maybe the policeman really was just playin with him, so he started kiddin back and tellin stories. He told bout how when the Lord was makin folks he put all the dough in the oven.

" 'The Lord taken out the first dough,' said Daddy, 'and it wadn't but half baked. It was still white, so he made it into white folks. A little later he taken out some more dough, and it wadn't nowhere near brown; it was just yeller. So he use it to make Chinks and foreigners. Then he taken out the last batch of dough. It was good and brown, well-done and seasoned just right. Thas what he used to make us colored folks.'

"Daddy Mention laughed, and the policeman laughed too.

" 'Wadn't there no dough left over," asked the policeman.

" 'Oh,' said Daddy, 'the Lord taken them measly little scrapins and made policemen out of them.'

"Then Daddy laughed hard as he could, and the policeman laughed too. But I don't know if the Judge laughed or no, cause the very nex day he sent Daddy to the Big Rock at Raiford for two years. It taken Daddy a long time to figger out why he done got sent to the Big Rock for so long, but when he finally got it through his head he said he just couldn't stay there, and that was all there was to it.

" 'You can't beat Jinny, Cap'm Hysler's mule,' the other men tried to tell him.

"But Daddy Mention just laugh. 'I done drownded blood-hounds in the creek and dodged guards with double-barreled Winchesters—how you think no mule gon stop me?'

"The other prisoners tried to argue with him, but Daddy wouldn't have it no other way but he must try to escape and make it to the Okefenokee Swamp way up the other side of Olustee. So one mornin, soon's they let us out in the yard, Daddy Mention ups and runs. He was in good shape, too; he beat them shot-guns a mile.

"When he got a chance to look back over his shoulder he seen one of the guards put his fingers to his mouth and whistle. But didn't no dogs come; out trotted a little jack-ass-lookin mule, and she backed into a drop-bottom cart without nobody havin to say nothin to her. It didn't take the guards but a minute to hitch that Jinny in the cart, and by the time the harness was on her all of the dogs was in the bottom of the cart and it was flyin down the road after Daddy Mention.

"Daddy Mention was plenty smart; he had stole one of the other prisoner's shoes before he left, so when he got to the woods he taken off his shoes and put the other ones on. Then he throwed his shoes in the ditch to fool the dogs. It sho nuff fool em, too. Daddy, he had time to find hisself a good big oak tree and hide hisself in it before the dogs came and lost his trail. He was doin a lot of laughin when they run across the ditch and kept on goin farther and farther away.

"Daddy Mention was so busy watchin the dogs and figgerin when he could come down and head for the swamp that he was might surprised when he felt sumpum grab him by the pants. Before he can figger out what it is, it had done tore out the whole seat and a little of Daddy Mention too. They he seen it was Jinny. She had two feets on the bottom of the tree and was reachin up for another piece of Daddy Mention's pants. He tried to hurry up a little higher, and one of his feets slip down a little. That's when Jinny showed him she et shoe-leather too.

"Daddy, he didn't know what to do. He clumb round to the other side of the tree, and jump down to run. Jinny, she come right on behind him. He had to keep goin straight ahead, cause the dogs was off the other way.

"Before Daddy knowed it Jinny had done chased him right back to the prison fence. But he decided even getting back inside would be bettern getting et up by that mule, so he grabbed for the top of the fence. Just as he was climbin over Jinny caught up with him and bit him again. This time there wadn't no pants for her to bite, so she just grabbed a mouthful of Daddy Mention.

"And he hung right there till Cap'm Hysler come; right there with a good hunk of him in Jinny's mouth. It was a long time before Daddy Mention could sit down to eat. But that didn't worry him none, cause in the box where he was you don't set down or eat much, anyway."

It is interesting to note that, according to F. Adeuyi Ajaye, a native of Sierra Leone, Daddy Mention's story about the origin of the races is a variant of a West African folk tale.

Kerosene Charley

These tales about Kerosene Charley were obtained from Cull Stacy, an old turpentine Negro. He preceded the stories with the following rather incoherent explanation of their origin, which is presented here for its face value.

"I'm goin to tell you about Kerosene Charlie. I bought a whole book of those stories. I bought them at the Western Union Telegraph Office, where they sell them at the lunch counter. I can't remember the author's name—his name was Thomas H. Dickerson. I believe he was a colored man. He was afraid of being sold, and he made a confession. He had a good education. He sold the book and went around the world. They say he started around the world with twenty-five cents, and when he got back he still had ten cents left. I don't believe that, but I read it. You know a man can't walk around the world.

"One time Kerosene Charley got a job diggin potatoes. Before he start work in the mornin his Bossman give him a breakfast of fried potatoes.

Kerosene Charley didn't much like potatoes, but he didn't say nothin cause he was might glad to get the job.

"He dig potatoes all mornin and when lunch time come round he go to the back door of his Bossman's house and the Bossman's wife hand him a big plate of boiled potatoes. This made Kerosene Charley pretty mad, but he didn't say nothin cause he figgered they'd at least give him a good supper after feedin him on potatoes all day.

"So he finished up his day's work and when it come supper time he could hardly wait to see what they gon give him to eat. It turned out to be baked potatoes this time, with a piece of potato pie for dessert. Kerosene Charley made up his mind to quit that job right then, but he decided to spend the night and the leave before it got daylight.

"Way in the middle of the night the Bossman heard Kerosene Charley moanin with a bellyache.

" 'That nigger is ailin with a bellyache,' he say to his wife. 'I guess we gotta do sumpum for him. I kain't git no sleep with him moanin like that.'

" 'All right,' his wife say, 'I'll git up and make him some potato tea.'

"Another time Kerosene Charley was on the road lookin for a job. Come nightfall he went to a colored farmer's house and asked him could he give him a place to sleep until mornin.

" 'I only got two beds,' the farmer say. 'Me and my wife sleeps in one, and my grown daughter sleeps in the other.'

"They didn't know what to do, so the farmer's wife say, 'I know; I'll fix you a pallet to sleep on.'

" 'I be might proud to sleep anywheres tonight,' said Kerosene Charley.

"So the farmer's wife spread him a pallet in the dark and Kerosene Charley lay down on it and fell asleep in no time. Way in the middle of the night he woke up sudden, feelin sumpum wet hittin him in the face.

" 'Sumpum wet hittin me in the face,' he say. 'It must be rainin and the house leakin.'

" 'That ain't rain,' said the farmer. 'Don't you know you sleepin under a chicken roost?'

"Then there was the time Kerosene Charley was travellin through the state of Texas, and while he was walkin down the road he come to a farm.

Back at the loft he seen a man with a mule, and the man had the mule hitched up to a winch and was winchin that mule up to the loft.

"Kerosene Charley stood there and watched while the man kept winchin the mule up and up, till finally he had got the mule up level with the loft window. Then the mule stick out his neck and start eatin the corn in the loft.

" 'What you got that mule winched way up in the air like that for?' Kerosene Charley asked the man.

" 'Kain't you see I'm feedin him corn?' the man say.

" "But how come you didn't go up in the loft and throw down some corn for the mule?' ask Kerosene Charley.

" ' By golly,' the man say, 'I never thought of that.'

"So Kerosene Charley shake his head and walk on down the road. 'I often heard that people in Texas was fools,' he said."

Old Pete

"You never heard tell of Old Pete? I thought most everbody had heard of him. Those what knowed him ain't likely to forget him. He was the biggest, strongest, blackest man what ever lived in these parts.

"Old Pete aint been dead so very long. As I reckleck it was 1934 when he died, and he said he was 87 years old then. He never did get sickly; the day before he died he was straight as a stick and as spry as he ever was.

"His real name was Henry Peterson, and he was born a slave somewhere or other. He worked off and on as a plantation hand, dock laborer, railroad worker, sawmill hand, and when he died he was a general roustabout at the Atlantic Coast Line railroad yard at Port Tampa. I guess he had worked all over.

"To hear him tell it, he had been married nine times and had fifty-six chillun—thirty-seven by his wives and nineteen on the outside.—You know what I mean: nineteen in the woods. I know for a fact that when he died he had some kids what wadn't moren 10 years old.

"Old Pete had a skull an inch thick, hard as iron. Many a time I've seen him break one-by-ten-inch boards in two by buttin em with his head. He used to get in buttin matches with goats for fifty cents, and he always win. Old Pete would get down on his hands and knees and meet them goats head-on. You never heard such a whackin when their heads come together. Them goats would shake their heads and back off and come at him full tilt again. But Old Pete allus got the best of em, and they'd walk off with their heads hangin low.

"Old Pete used to help unload the coconut boats that came into Port Tampa from Honduras, and for a nickel he'd let anybody crack a coconut on his head.

"But that wadn't nothin. One time he lay down beside the railroad tracks with his head restin on a rail for a pillow, and fell fast asleep. A switch engine kicked a loaded freight car over the track, and it ran right smack over Old Pete's head and turned over. Some of us run to get Old Pete's body, but when we got there he was still sound asleep and snorin. When we got him woke up and told him what happened, and all he done was scratch his head and say, 'Dawgone! My head do feel kinda funny,' [This event appeared in Robert Ripley's *Believe It Or Not* in 1938.]

"One of the best things Old Pete ever done was when he stopped a runaway freight train. A cut of six cars got loose in the railroad yard and rolled down the mile-long grade to the dock over the bay. Old Pete happened to be standin on the dock, and seen the cars comin. He got right out in the middle of the track and braced hisself to wait for em. Pretty soon they run right into him and pushed him back, but he kept on pushin and bracin. Finally, when the cars was just three feet from the end of the dock, he got em stopped. Then he give em a good shove and they rolled back up in the yard again.

"He done lots of things like that. Once a locomotive run off the tracks and he picked it up all by hisself and put it back again. Another time a ship got grounded out on the bar, and Old Pete swam out and towed it off and into the dock. They say he used to use a anchor to pick his teeth with. With my own eyes I see him pull up a tree by the roots, tote it home, and cut it into three cords of wood.

"Old Pete had religion, too. He couldn't read or write, but he could quote the Scripture by the hour and tell you the exact book, chapter, and verse he was quotin. He was a deacon at the church and never missed a Sunday. When it thundered I remember he allus took of his hat and said, 'Thas the Lawd talkin; he's scoldin us sinners.'

"One time Old Pete was workin for a farmer who lived 'bout ten miles from Fort Myers, and the farmer sent him into town to fetch back a horse he had bought. Pete set out to walk to Fort Myers, carryin a saddle and bridle for the horse.

"On the way he took a short cut through a swamp and saw a great big alligator. Old Pete wrastled that 'gator, saddled and bridled him, jumped on his back and rode on a gallup for Fort Myers. They came to the Caloosahatchee River, and Old Pete made the 'gator swim right across with him still on his back. When they got to Fort Myers Old Pete sold the 'gator to a circus for ten dollars, saddled the horse he had come for, and rode back to the farm.

"Another time Old Pete was ridin on the old stern-wheel steamboat on the St. Johns River, goin to Jacksonville to see a gal. On the way the crank shaft broke and the capm of the boat told everbody it would take a whole day to get fixed. But Old Pete was in a powerful hurry to get to Jacksonville, so he grabbed the crank and began turnin the paddlewheel himself. He turned it so fast the boat got to Jacksonville three hours ahead of time.

"Old Pete was all the time telling jokes. I can't remember all of em, but I can tell you some of 'em.

"Pete once had a cabin in the clearing, he useta tell, and a old turkey gobbler, a guinea, a rooster, and a hen that all scratched around in the dirt.

"One day the gobbler flew up to the top of the cabin to have a look around. All of a sudden he straightened up and gobbled, 'Preacher comin, preacher comin, preacher comin!'

"All the other fowls look down on the highway and sho nuff there was the preacher's buggy and old gray mule. They all knew what that meant—one of em would be popped in the boilin pot. So they all run for the woods with the hen-a-cacklin, 'Cut-cut-cut-cut your head off, cut your head off, cut your head off!'

"They all hid in the woods till it was near-bout dinner time, and the turkey gobbler and the guinea flew up in a tree to have a look at the cabin. The rooster looked up at em and crowed, 'Has-e-gaw-n-n-yet?'

" 'Not yet—not yet—not yet!' clacked the guinea. Then suddenly the gobbler gobbled, 'Lord-a-mighty! There's a couple-of-em, couple-of-em, couple-of-em!'

"So they all ran deeper into the woods and stayed there till they heard the buggy drive away. The preachers had to eat fat pork and grits instead of a nice fowl like they expected.

"Once a friend of Pete's was ridin to town on a mule. The mule stopped in the middle of the road and tried to scratch his side with his hind leg. But the mule knocked the man's foot out of the stirrup and got his own foot caught in the stirrup instead.

" 'Look here, mule,' said the man, 'if you gonna ride I gon get off and walk.'

"I remembers one more story Old Pete useta tell, One time a colored woman called to her little boy who had done gone out in the street to play with some white chillun, and taken his lunch with him.

" 'You, Willie,' she call him, 'you stop playin with them white chillun. You know they'll jus lick all the syrup offen your bread and then call you nigger!' "

Roy Sold His Car to God

"Roy Tyle runs the Maitland Garage down in Orange County, Florida. Everybody knows he's the best mechanic that ever lived. He never could find a ready-made car that would nowhere suit him, so one day he said he was goin to make one of his own. He said he was goin to make a collision-proof car.

"So he went in his garage and got out all his tools and went to work. After a while he was ready to demonstrate his super de luxe, free-wheelin, supercharged, floatin power, synchromesh, wizard control, auto-clutch, no-draft, knee-action, turret top, golden ply, self-startin, collision-proof car. One after another, people tried to run in to him, but Roy would just press a button and his car would squat down and run right under the other cars. You just couldn't hit him. They even tried big old Mack trucks, but Roy ran under them too. Then somebody went and got a Buick and bet Roy he couldn't run under no under-slung Buick. But Roy showed him.

Finally he drove his car up North and sold it for a lot of money and came on back home.

"Well, after a while Roy got tired of just sittin around his garage, so he said he was goin to make hisself another car. This time he made one with wings folded on top so he could take off and fly over the top of any car that tried to run into him. It wasn't long before he got so he like flyin better than drivin. And that's how he came to get rid of the thing. One day he was way up there loopin-the-loop and God was watchin him. God like Roy's car so much he bought it off him—paid cash, too—and started creatin models just like it for the angels. Ever since then the angels aint flew a lick with their own wings.

"Now Roy's back at his garage and workin at sumpum else. Lord knows what it will be this time. There aint no tellin what Roy's gonna make next."

STUFF AND SUCH

You gotta cook vegetables so they won't loose their sumption," say the colored cooks of the Palmetto Country, meaning that food values should not be destroyed by overcooking. So, too, with folklore, which is the boiled-down juice or "pot-likker" of human living. It must be handled with care and recorded with fidelity.

No people are so primitive or so civilized that they are not continuously adding to their fund of lore. Lore comes into being whenever the group mind looks into the whys and wherefores of daily existence. The more right answers the group finds, the more civilized it becomes. This inquisitive process is variously inspired by practical considerations, to satisfy intellectual curiosity, to find religious or esthetic expression, or to escape boredom.

Some people have the idea that folklore is dead or phony stuff. But if they would look more closely they would see that folklore is more often wise than foolish. Its rare integrity and profundity springs from the fact that the folk artist is identified with, and speaks for, a group. Thus it necessarily has a democratic point of view. Perhaps more than anything else, folklore is of the people, by the people, and for the people. People create, improve, preserve, and use it. No one can say it is "mine," because it is "ours."

The functional approach to folk culture is predicated upon an understanding of the determining influence of economics, and requires that culture be projected against the background from which it springs or in which it has taken root. Furthermore, like the society it reflects, it must be regarded as vital and dynamic. This is especially true of folkways, which are nothing less than the ways of people: ways of working, eating, loving, thinking, learning, playing, worshiping.

A growing appreciation of the wealth and significance of folk culture is leading to its encouragement in many lands. The strength of this movement is always in proportion to the democracy obtaining in the country where it occurs, and is integrally bound up with the right of all folks to full freedom and self-determination-political and cultural alike.

America's general attitude toward folk culture is by no means ideal. Not only has our native American lore been discouraged to a point approaching extermination, but we also make the mistake of running our citizens-by-choice through a naturalization mill which seeks to supplant their exotic culture with our native brand. If we had sense enough to preserve the good in all these imported cultures we would be so much the richer. To continue to stress integration at the expense of diversity will lead to standardization-which would be admirably suited to the regimentation of fascism. The path of democratic progress lies midway between cultural integration and diversity.

Palmetto Country lore is exceptionally lush because, comparatively speaking, "book larnin" has made lesser inroads on oral tradition. The attractions of diverse industries and resorts have made the region a culture delta over which has been deposited rich sediment from many states and nations. In the inland agricultural communities, provincial isolation has made for a minimum of disintegration of the indigenous culture, whereas the industrial, commercial, and port cities and resorts manifest a considerable degree of cosmopolitanism. All this has contributed to the complexity of the regional folkway pattern.

The abundance of folksongs in the Palmetto Country is reflected in the Archive of American Folksong at the Library of Congress. Begun in 1937 under the supervision of John A. Lomax and his son Alan (authors of *Our Singing Country*), the Archive in 1942 contained more than ten thousand phonograph discs on which were recorded many times that number of American folksongs.

The moderate climate of the southernmost region-one of its most fully exploited resources-has brought Florida in particular a disproportionately large number of oldsters in search of better health and prolonged life. "Folk hardly ever die down here," a story goes. "One time I was walkin through the piney woods and seen a gray-headed old man settin on a fence cryin his eyes out.

"'What you cryin for? I asked him.

"''Cause my daddy done whupped me,' he said.

"''What did he do that for?'

"''For chunkin rocks at my grand-daddy.'"

Many stories spring up about specific locales in the region and the following is a good example of these.

The Sea Serpent of Cape Sable

"What about the legend of the big snake of Cape Sable?" ninety-two-year-old Uncle Steve Roberts of Homestead, Florida, was asked in 1942.

"Hell," said Uncle Steve, "that aint no legend-it's a fact. One of the Simmons boys told me that in 1892 a Seminole named Buster Ferrell killed that big snake out in the 'Glades around Pahokee. Buster was huntin and come across a trail where the grass was all beat down in a wide path. Thinkin it was done by a 'gator, he decided to follow it.

"Then in the distance he saw that big snake. It was a long rifle shot from him, but he was afraid to go any closer, so he fired from where he was. The snake went threshin off tord a lake, but Buster didn't go to find out whether he'd hit or missed, cause he remembered stories about that snake swallowin Indians whole. So he made tracks in the opposite direction.

"Some days later he noticed a flock of buzzards flyin around that same lake, and he went to see what they was after. The big snake was dead. The buzzards had scattered the carcass so bad Buster couldn't tell how long it was, but it looked to be all of sixty feet. The Simmons boy claims to have handled its jawbones, which Buster cut out and kept. He said they were so big he could open them up and drop them over his body."

So goes Uncle Steve's version of the Cape Sable sea-serpent legend. So many fishermen have sworn to having seen the serpent that many folk firmly believe in its existence. Most eyewitnesses have agreed that it is more than fifty feet long and is banded with red and white stripes. It is said that the Seminoles never visited the Cape Sable area because the serpent once swallowed one of their braves. But the dozen or so families of fishermen who now live there are inclined to think that the presence of mosquitoes and absence of fresh water kept the Indians away.

But whenever visitors ask these fishermen about the big snake, they get a kick out of confirming the story and adding, "One day that snake caught a man by the foot and started to swallow him. But the man got stuck in the snake's throat, and the snake couldn't get him in or out. For days and days that snake wallowed around in the water, almost chokin to death."

Then the storyteller pauses, until the listener asks impatiently, "But what finally became of them?"

"Well," is the answer, "a bigger snake came along and swallowed the two of them."

By way of getting better acquainted with Cape Sable folk, consider this story which appeared in the *Key West Citizen* in 1941:

"David Lopez and Ellis Tomlinson, who admit they beat up an old man at Flamingo, Cape Sable, 'because we wanted to lick the biggest man in town,' today are in county jail awaiting trial before Judge William V. Albury.

"First prisoners to be brought here from Cape Sable section in more than five years, they were arrested by Constable Cleve Johnson on the complaint of Clayton Brown, the elderly fisherman who was beaten.

"Flamingo, an isolated fishing village on the Florida mainland, is described by officers here as a rendition of the old frontier law. Peace officers seldom go there and the population makes up its own laws more or less to suit the occasion."

The way this impromptu law functions was demonstrated in 1930 when some Negro fishermen got in a shooting scrape on the Cape and one of them was killed. The Roberts boys and a man called Judge Lowe "tried" the guilty Negro and sentenced him to be hanged. Bull Roberts was sent for the only rope on the Cape, but instead of delivering it for the hanging he "took-off" through the swamp with it. "Aint gonna hang nobody on the Cape just for killin a man if I can help it," he said.

"Oh, well," said the other men, "let the nigger go."

The Cape Sable region and Ten Thousand Islands have long been notorious as a refuge for all sorts of tough characters and fugitives from the law. Whenever the sheriff at Key West boards a boat to hunt a man through those uncharted waterways, speculation is rife as to whether he will ever return, either with or without a prisoner.

South Florida folk often tell about the tough-looking individual who rode up to the Homestead drugstore astride a huge panther. In his hand the man swung a live ten foot rattlesnake which he used as a whip. He entered the drugstore and ordered a pint of carbolic acid, which he drank thirstily.

As he wiped his lips, an amazed bystander asked cautiously, "If I aint too bold, stranger, would you mind tellin me where on earth you hail from?"

"Not a-tall," said the man. "I been down around Cape Sable and right now I'm leavin these parts as fast as I know how. Them sons-of-b—down there are too tough for me."

The families at Cape Sable live in shacks which stand high on stilts to escape tidal waves. Their life is extremely primitive, and they have never had a church. For four years, beginning in 1915, they had a small school, but it was impossible to get a teacher to remain more than a year. The last of the teachers was a Mr. Fry, a man who stood six and a half feet tall, weighed 250 pounds, and wore a long black beard. But he was no match for Cape Sable's children; when they barricaded the school door and refused to admit him, he gave up in despair and became a farmer.

Whenever Mr. Fry went to Homestead or Miami he told folks about the rich Cape Sable soil. He told them he raised sweet potatoes weighing sixty to seventy pounds each, with six to the bunch. He said that when he planted pumpkins the vines grew so fast they jerked all the blossoms off.

One time the Government sent a soil specialist down to Cape Sable. "He didn't think the soil was so good just to look at it," said Uncle Steve. "After you dig down six inches through the black dirt you come to soil as white as cotton, and once in awhile you'll find a patch as blue as the sky. It's so fine when you put it in water it looks like milk. A man told me that soil is worth millions of dollars. He said it could be used for beauty clay, talcum powder, and to make fine china. When the government soil expert got around to testing, he said it wasn't even soil-it's pure fertilizer."

Until 1910 the Cape Sable settlers were engaged in sugar-cane raising and the manufacture of syrup, but in that year a hurricane destroyed their mill and carried off three thousand cans of syrup. Since then they have made a living by catching fish and shipping them to market. Other fishermen do not dare to horn in on their territory.

Two years before the hurricane put an end to their syrup making, the Cape folk were beset by a horde of rats which destroyed their cane and brought the mill to a standstill. During this sad period, Gene Roberts sat and watched the Cape's several sleek cats idly maul a dead rat. That gave him an idea, and he called a meeting of all the men.

"Boys," he said, "we've done everything we could think of to get rid of the rats, but it aint done no good. No use in us spending any more money on poison-them rats would rather eat our sugar cane. These few cats we got here has done the best they can, but they can't eat but so many rats. So I say we ought to chip in and run down to Key West and buy up a whole bunch of cats and bring em here."

At first the men all laughed, but the more they thought about it, the more they began to take the idea seriously. Finally they decided to give it a trial, and Gene set sail for Key West. When he got there he stuck up a sign saying "Will Pay 10¢ Apiece for Every Cat Delivered to this Dock." Soon there was a steady stream of children with cats to sell. When Gene had purchased four hundred of them-all his boat would hold-he cast off for Cape Sable. "That ninety-mile trip was the worst I ever made," he said. "Them durn cats fought and yowled all the way."

At last he reached Cape Sable and put the cats ashore. They scampered off in every direction, and soon became so wild that people said they were breeding with the wildcats. But Cape Sable hasn't been bothered with rats since, and after a few years the mosquitoes killed all the cats.

West Hell

West Hell, Heaven, Diddy-Wah-Diddy, Ginny-Gall, Beluthahatchee, and Zar have a very real place in the fertile imagination of the Palmetto Country's Negro folk.

West Hell-situated some distance west of Regular Hell-is the hottest and toughest suburb in that torrid resort. Only the most wicked sinners are consigned there, and their souls are first transferred to rubber caskets so they can bounce to their destinations without having to be toted. West Hell is celebrated as the scene of the fight between the Devil and Big John the Conqueror. Big John flew into Hell on the back of an eagle, just to have a look around. But he fell in love with the Devil's youngest daughter, and they eloped on the Devil's favorite steeds, Hallowed-Be-Thy-Name and Thy-Kingdom-Come.

The Devil got on his jumping bull and caught up with them in West Hell, and he and Big John fought it out all over the place. Finally Big John tore off one of the Devil's arms and almost beat the hell out of him with it. Then Big John married the girl and got ready to take her away. But before he left he handed out ice water to everybody and turned down the dampers. He said he and his wife might want to come back and visit her folks some day, and he didn't want the house kept so hot. He said if he came back and found the Devil had opened those dampers up again he would tear down the whole works and turn West Hell into an ice house.

Heaven is a different sort of place, featuring a sea of glass where the angels go sliding every afternoon. All heavenly streets are a pleasure to walk on, but the two main thoroughfares-Amen Street and Hallelujah Avenue, which intersect in front of the Throne-play tunes when strutted upon. Rumor has it that Negroes are currently banned from Heaven. Quite a few of them used to get in, but then one came along who was too impatient to wait for Old Gabriel to teach him to fly. Soon as he got his wings at the commissary he took off on his own hook and flew all over Heaven. He got so cocky he tried to fly across God's nose, but he fell and tore down a lot of God's big gold lamps and knocked over some of those golded-up vases. God got mighty mad, and told Gabriel to rip off the flier's wings. "You is grounded till further notice," Gabriel told the Negro, "and it'll be a powerful long time 'fore you get your wings back."

"I don't care if I never get em back," said the Negro. "I sure was a flyin fool while I had em!"

Negroes don't worry much about not being admitted to Heaven, because they'd just as soon go to Diddy-Wah-Diddy. This is a place way off somewhere, where even the curbstones make good sitting chairs, and all food is ready-cooked. Baked chickens and deep sweet-potato pies come along with knives and forks stuck in their middle, and the more you eat the bigger they get. Everything is on a grand scale. Even the dogs can stand flat-footed and lick the crumbs off Heaven's tables. The biggest man there is the Moon Regulator, who starts and stops it when he feels like it. That's why on some nights there's no moon at all-the Moon Regulator didn't feel like putting it out.

Everybody would live in Diddy-Wah-Diddy if it wasn't so hard to find and so hard to get to even after you know the way. The road leading to it is so crooked that a mule pulling a load of fodder along it can eat off the back of the wagon as he walks. The Diddy-Wah-Diddy barbecue-on U.S.1 north of St. Augustine-is much easier to find and claims its barbecued pig and goat is just as good as that in the real place.

Ginny-Gall is just the opposite of Diddy-Wah-Diddy. It is a place of tremendous want, where folks have to eat whatever they can get. Thus when a Negro finds himself in such a bad fix that he can't think of anything worse, he says:

"I just as soon be in Ginny-Gall,
Where the folks eat cowbelly, skin and all."

Beluthahatchee is a blissful state where all unpleasant doings and sayings are forgiven ande forgotten. If a Negro woman brings up something distasteful in her man's past, he tries to change the subject by saying, "I thought that was in Beluthahatchee."

As for Zar, very little is known about it, because no one who has been there has ever come back. It's way on the other side of Far.

Variants of many of the Palmetto Country's Negro tales-especially those of Uncle Remus animal story type-are to be found in French among the Negroes of Haiti, in Spanish among the Negroes of Cuba, and in English among the Negroes of the British West Indies. This is usually conclusive evidence that they had a common African origin. Though most of the fol-

37 .... ZORA NEALE HURSTON.
Zora Neale Hurston recording folksongs and folktales in her adopted home town, Eatonville, in 1935. Alan Lomax photo, Library of Congress.

lowing stories feature Protestant Christian elements, it is quite possible that they also embody episodes of African creation.

How Folks Got Their Colors

"God didn't make people all of a sudden. He made them by degrees whenever He could take time off from the other creatin He was doin. To start with he took a big chunk of clay and stomped it out till it was nice and smooth. Then he cut out all the human shapes and stood them up against His long gold fence to dry. When they was all dried He blowed the breath of life into em and they walked on off. Altogether the job took God two or three workin days.

"Later on He called everybody to come up and get their eyes. So they all came up and got their eyes. Another day when He had some time to spare He told everybody to come and get their nose and mouth and they all come and got em. Then one day he give out toe-nails, and so on till the people was practically finished. For the last thing He called everybody and said, "Tomorrow mornin at seven o'clock sharp I am going to give out color, and I want all you folks to he here on time.'

"Next mornin at seven God was sittin on His throne with his high gold crown on. He looked North, and He looked South; He looked East, and He looked Australia; and blazin worlds was fallin off His teeth. The great multitude was standin before Him, so He looked over to His left and says, 'You is yellow folks.' They said, 'Much obliged, Lord,' and walked off. Then He looked to His right and said, 'You is red people,' They thanked Him too and went on off. 'You's white people,' He told another big squaddle of folks, and they went on their way. Then God looked around to hand out some more color, but there wasn't nobody left.

"'Looks like I miss some of my multitudes,' God said to Gabriel.

"Gabriel looked all around and said, "Yes Sir, there is some multitudes missin, all right. I reckon they'll be along toreckly.' So God sat there and sat there, but didn't nobody else show up. After God had done wasted a whole hour and a half He said, 'Look here, Gabriel, I don't intend to wait for them missin multitudes much longer. You go hunt em up and tell em I say they better come on and get their color, cause when I gets up from here today I aint never gonna give out color no more.'

"Gabriel went out lookin for the missin crowd, and when he found em he told em what God said, They all jumped up from where they was and went runnin up to the throne hollerin, 'Give us our color! We want our color! We got as much right to have color as anybody else!'

"The first ones that got to the throne couldn't stop because all those in behind kept pushin and shovin until the throne was knocked clear over to one side. This made God so mad He hollered, 'Get back! Get back!'

"But the crowd was makin so much noise they thought He said, 'Get black!' So they got black and been keepin the thing up ever since."

Why Folks Aint Got Tails

"Long time ago-long before the War, the good Lawd made the world, and then He rested a day. The next mornin He decided to plant a garden in the world He'd done made, so He set out the Garden of Eden. Then He say to Heself that a garden such as that needed somebody to live in it, so He made Adam, the first man. Adam, he was kinda lonesome, so the good Lawd took pity on him and made him a wife-Eve was her name, and she was the first woman. She and Adam was just like folks is today, except they had big long tails like cows.

"The Lawd, He says to Adam and Eve, says he, 'Adam, this here garden is for you and Eve. Stay here, keep good care of it, eat any of these fruits and berries and yarbs, all 'cept this one tree with the yallar fruits on it. Yeah, that's the one. Don't you touch that fruit. That there's my tree, and you mustn't touch it.' Then God left the garden. Adam knowed He was gone, cause he heard the gate click.

"Adam walked around awhile, and pretty soon he found hisself lookin at that forbidden fruit. He couldn't seem to take his eyes off it. It looked bettern all the other fruit in the garden. When he couldn't stand it no longer he whirled in and ate every fruit-thing on that tree. That night he slept hard, right on through till late the next mornin.

When the day break, the Lawd came back to have a look around His garden. When He seen what Adam had done He didn't even take time to open the garden gate-He put His hand on top of the fence and jumped right over it. Such a sight He never saw-where last night had been a tree full of ripe fruit, this mornin there wasn't a scrap left-it had all been et. He looked this-a-way, and he looked that-a-way, but Adam and Eve was clear out of sight.

"The Lawd called, 'Adam!' but there wasn't no answer, 'Adam!" the Lawd called agin. Still Adam lay low and didn't say nothin. Then the Lawd called a third time, 'Hey, Adam-you come here right *now!*" And so Adam come a-inchin up to God to take his chastisin.

"'How come you eat up all my fruits after I done told you not to?' asked the Lawd.

"'It musta been Eve done it," said Adam.

"'That won't do, Adam,' said the Lawd. 'Just look at them big footprints around that tree. Eve aint got no sucha foot as that.'

"Then Adam got scared and took out for the bushes, with the Lawd right in behind him. Adam couldn't run so fast on account of havin eaten so many of them 'simmon things, and also because of havin to drag that big long tail of his. He run and he run, but he couldn't outrun God. After they had made two or three turns around the garden, God caught up with Adam enough to grab hold of that tail of his. He set His heels in the ground, and fetched up. Zook! Out come Adam's tail, clear by the roots! And ever since then folks aint had no tails."

Why the World is so Wicked

"One Day when Adam was out workin in the fields the Devil turned his-self into a good-lookin man and came to call on Eve. He had been wantin to get up to her for a long time. He showed her the deep point about every-thing and got her all excited. So they went out under the apple tree and Eve parted with what she didn't know she had. It happened under the tree and that's why people still make love under trees today.

"The Devil knowed there would be some hereafter to the thing, so he put Eve up to get Adam into it too. Soon as Adam come home Eve started in on him and kept on till he got mixed up in it.

"The next day Eve put on a pretty calico dress, and Adam put on some clothes too. Then when God came and saw em He drove em off. After that, Adam and Eve often fussed about how she come to know what she knowed. Eve would say, 'Satan just told me about it, and I told you just as he told me."

"'If that's the case,' Adam said, "I don't see why you didn't call me to talk with him, instead of you lyin around with him all the afternoon like you did.'

"That's the way they fussed about Satan, and when Cain was born Adam saw he looked just like Satan, and not a bit like him, so they fussed some more. But Eve stuck to her point and Adam couldn't do nothin about it.

"When Abel was born, Adam compared the two children, and there wasn't no comparison between them. That's why Cain hated Abel-they was not whole brothers. And that's why God wouldn't accept Cain's sacrifice-because he was the son of the Devil.

"Cain finally flew away and married a gorilla, and all the people in the world come from him and that she-gorilla. That's how the animal got into us, and why those old patriarchs used to live so long. They was close to the gorilla and strong. Old Methusaleh lived nine hundred and sixty-nine years because he was just full of that old gorilla blood. As time goes on that old animal blood works out, leavin the human blood, and that's why we are growin weaker and wiser.

"And the reason we is so wicked is that Cain, the first child born in the world, was a bastard.

Why Solomon Said, "Vanity of Vanities-"

"Do you know why Solomon said, Vanity of vanities; all is vanity and vexation of spirit? 'Well, it was this way. Solomon married-up thousands of women, He had a special room in his palace and whenever he was considerin takin on a new wife he would take her into that room and sit and talk with her awhile. He picked out thousands of women, but after awhile he began to get old and tired.

"Then one day the Queen of Sheba came to visit him. She was very beautiful and everything, but he had to admit to himself.

> "When I was younger and in my prime,
> The Devil in Hell couldn't beat my time;
> Now I'm old and getting gray,
> My constitution's wore away."

"And he took off his crown and throwed it against the wall and cried, 'Vanity of vanities; all is vanity and a vexation of spirit!'

"Accordin to another story, King Solomon didn't do so bad with the Queen of Sheba. He fell in love with her as soon as he saw her, but she acted so indifferent he didn't know how to get up to her. But he was the wisest man in the world, and he thought up a scheme.

"'Now Queen of Sheba,' he said to her, 'you mustn't take nothin while you are here in my kingdom, cause if you do I'll have to punish you by makin you do whatever I want.'

'You don't need to fret,' the Queen of Sheba said. 'I aint no thief.'

So King Solomon gave her a banquet. All of the food was salty, and there wasn't no water or nothin else to drink with it. The only water to be found anywhere around the palace was in the fountain out in the courtyard. Right after the banquet was over, King Solomon run out in the bushes close to the fountain. Pretty soon the Queen of Sheba come tiptoein out to the fountain and got a drink of water.

Then King Solomon rose up out of the bushes and said, "Uh-huh, Queen of Sheba, I caught you takin some of my water in spite of my warnin for you not to take nothin. Now I got to punish you.

"She was in his power then, and he took her into the palace."

Why Women Talk so Much

"When God made Adam and Eve, Eve was plumb dumb. So Adam said to God, 'God this here woman is dumb as they make em. She can't talk none. I can't get no pleasure out of bein with her, cause she got no tonuge.'

"Just then a rabbit come hoppin by. God reached down and snatched off the rabbit's tail and stuck it in Eve's mouth. The hair on the tail made her spit and ever since then women been waggin their tongues tryin to spit the hair out."

God and Moses

"Moses was prayin to God to take him out of the world. While he was prayin he heard somebody say, 'Who's there?'

"'Moses,' answered Moses. 'Who's there?'

"'God,' answers God.

"'What you want God?'

"'Want Moses.'

"'Who?'

"'Moses aint here, but his wife is. Won't she do as well?'

"'Come on. Moses, and go with God.'

"'Wait a minute. I can't go nowhere without my shoes. Where my shoes?'

"'You know good and well where they's at. They's under the bed there.'

"'Where's my hat?'

"'You know where your hat is. Go get it!'

"Moses finally got his shoes and hat on, then he say, 'O God, you so high I can't go over you. You so wide I can't go around you. You'll hafta stand to one side.'

"God stood to one side-and then what a race he and Moses had! Moses jumped over a high rail fence, and a rail fell on him.

"'Get off me God-get off me,' begged Moses.

"But God never did get off."

Samson versus Satan

"Satan said to Samson, They tell me you're the strongest man in the world.'

"'Yeah, I spose I am,' drawled Samson. 'Wanna make sumpum of it?'

"'There's no use in us fightin,' said Satan, 'but let's see who can throw this anvil hammer the highest.' So he threw it first, and threw it seventy-five miles.

"Shucks,' said Samson, 'you aint half a man! Gimme one of them hammers.'

"'How far you think you can throw it?' asked Satan.

"'The sky's the limit,' said Samson. He took up the hammer and said, "Michael and Rafael and all the holy angels, stand back, cause here comes the anvil!'

"Samson swung the anvil twice, and was bout to heave it when Satan cried, 'Don't do it! Save heaven and the host! If you knock em outa existence, what we gonna do for a livin?'"

BLACK MAGIC

Congo Talk

In the realm of black magic, Darkest Africa has very little on the Deepest South. Transplanted African cults and practices thrive in the Palmetto Country as in no other part of the United States; besides the Southern Negro stuff variously known as hoodoo, voodoo, and *cunjervation*, there is the *brujeria* and *ñañiguismo* brought in by the Afro-Cubans, and the obeah of the Bahaman blacks.

A modern student of Africa has written, "Even today western Africa is the land of idols. The visitor encounters them on every road, near all the river fords, over every house door, and tied around every neck. The idols ward off sickness, or produce it if neglected. They cause the rains to come; they fill the sea with fishes which rush to be caught in the fishermen's nets; they discover and punish thieves; they make brave their worshipers, and fight against their enemies. There is nothing which the idol cannot do or undo—provided it is convenient with the idol."

The foregoing also applies very well to the Palmetto Country, except that idols are generally supplanted by various voodoo charms. Beneath the outward cloak of Christianity which lends an air of conformity to the region's Negroes there is an underlying mass of inherited superstitious belief, much of it pagan (non Christian) in character. Conditions, actually exist which should raise the eyebrows of the Committee for Metaphysical Research. Consider, for example, some of these recent works of voodoo:

In 1941 a Key West Negro named Eugene "Chucker" Edwards rode by on his bicycle and threw a bottle of liquid at a white woman as she sat rocking on her front porch. The bottle missed her, but the liquid ate away the wood near her chair. A complaint was made, and the police said, "Old Chucker's gone haywire again—let's go round him up." Constable Bienvenido (Welcome) Perez went to Chucker's home to make the arrest. Chucker drew a gun, and Bienvenido shot him dead. Among Chucker's personal effects Bienvenido found a wooden voodoo idol, which Chucker had often boasted "ate steel wool for breakfast." At the inquest, Chucker's relatives revealed that he had thrown the bottle of voodoo mixture in an effort to break a spell he believed the white woman had cast over him.

Miami has an equal strange story to tell. Since its founding, the city has been plagued by chicken thieves, but nothing extraordinary about this was noted until an entire coop of prize black leghorn hens disappeared. A study of police records then revealed that black hens were most often among those missing. The mystery was solved recently when a Negro woman was arrested for stealing a black hen. When questioned about her choice of chickens she tearfully protested that she was an expectant mother, and to reveal the secret of the black hen might cause her death or the death of her child. But at last she trembling confessed that it is a common practice for voodoo doctors to slowly cut to pieces a live black hen in the presence of a woman in labor. The suffering of the hen is believed to alleviate the suffering of the woman!

No less gruesome is the fact that Bahaman Negroes in the region, having blamed a particular black cat for their misfortunes, toss the living feline into a tub of boiling water and cook it until the flesh falls away. The bones are then strung and worn as a necklace to ward off all manner of evil.

In the Palmetto Country when Negro women fail to report for work their employers do not always lay it to ill health. As likely as not the servant has been incapacitated by a voodoo spell, and nothing short of twenty-five dollars will be required to hire a voodoo doctor to set things aright. It is not at all uncommon for police to have to lock up Negro women who have been frightened out of their wits by the "Congo talk" of a voodoo doctor—some of them actually require hospital treatment for acute shock, or become permanently insane. The weirdly assorted bags, bones, and other voodoo charms found in the pocket of Negroes are another source of continual amazement to the region's police.

Why do some Palmetto Country Negroes behave so? Only Africa can answer.

The primitive man of all races tend to anthropomorphize such inanimate things as wind, water, fire and stone, giving them a mind like his own, conceiving them as being capable of good and evil, and of being accessible by ordinary means of communication. Death, dreams, sickness, breathing, sneezing, procreation, echoes, shadows, reflected images—these are some of the things which comprise the basic stuff of superstition and religion.

Voodooism—one of the names given to the remnants of African tribal religion in America—constitutes a shield which protects the uneducated Negro from that forger of gods—the Unknown. Voodooism is seldom an organized religious ideology, but, as an initial attempt to understand phenomena, it is religion in one of its most primitive forms. By no means static, it is an example of animistic and anthropomorphic fetichism evolving into polytheism. The Negro chastises his idols and charms when they fail to render satisfaction, and, like all religious groups, continually alters his ritual in an effort to get better results.

When the slaves arrived in the New World their minds were saturated with fetichistic notions, and the degree to which these notions have survived has depended in large measure upon the sort of society into which they were thrust. In the United States, the Negro slave was kept in fairly close touch with the Big House—its medicines, culture, and religion. Not so in the British West Indies and Cuba, where absentee ownership and the preponderance of Negroes required much greater self—reliance of them and tended to perpetuate their African ways and culture.

Environmental factors not only operated to destroy or maintain Africanisms, but also made for the natural selection of the fittest customs. Those with the largest number of followers and the greatest utility (real or fancied) won out in the struggle for existence. Each tribal pantheon and rite underwent this process, with the survivors generally taking on some of the attributes of the vanquished. All this, together with the varied national and religious acculturation of the United States, Cuba, and the Bahamas, accounts for the highly bastardized form of voodooism as it exists in the Palmetto Country.

The vast influence of the Palmetto Country voodoo doctor is also a heritage from Africa, where the tribal houngan combined spiritual and temporal leadership (just as the British ruler includes among his titles "King, Emperor, Defender of the Faith"). Besides his duties as priest, herb doctor, alchemist, psychiatrist, astrologer, physicist, augurer, rainmaker, and interpreter of the supernatural, the houngan had to prescribe laws and apprehend and punish offenders. Many of these functions were incompatible with the Negro's position in America society, where the houngan's work is largely performed by specialized scientists. The voodoo doctor retains, therefore, only his curative and augurative roles, inseparably bound up with his religious character. In all his doings he relies more or less on the supernatural.

Cunjure Shop

Through the Days of Labor and Nights of Rest,
The Charms of Fairy Stones Will Keep You Blest.

That sign hangs over the entrance of The Eureka Store, one of the typical Palmetto Country's cunjure shops which deal in the *materia medica* of voodooism. The sign refers to a legend of Patrick County, Virginia, which says that some fairies were playing there when the news of Christ's crucifixion arrived. When they wept their tears struck the earth and formed perfect crosses. These Fairy Stones—available at the Eureka—are worn as good luck charms. It is said that Theodore Roosevelt and Woodrow Wilson never went without one.

A mere hole-in-the-wall, the Eureka is located in Jacksonville, just two blocks from the largest Negro high school in Florida. Apart from its sign, its presence may be detected by the inescapable odor of burning incense which drifts out to the sidewalk.

The white proprietor asserts, "Some of the leading business men and bankers, both white and colored, come here regularly for their secret desires." Many voodoo doctors refer their clients to the Eureka Store to have their prescriptions filled. Almost half of its patrons are white, and they come from every walk of life. In telling of a typical transaction, the proprietor said, "A colored woman came to me with the news that the doctor had said that her breasts would have to be amputated. But I sold her a special flour, and told her to make pancakes out of it and apply them to the affected parts. Two days later the woman returned full of joy and happiness—she had been completely cured."

The Eureka Store publishes a leaflet entitled *Myths and Legends of Root, Herb, Bark, and Seed Magic, as used through the ages by various people in various lands*. Among the items listed for sale are "Queen Elizabeth Root—a very special root. To answer questions, tie a piece of white thread, 13 inches long, to the root with the opposite end of the thread held between the thumb and forefinger. Medium addresses root: 'Will the person standing before men have his wish fulfilled?' If the answers is 'yes,' the root will circle to the right. If not, the root remains motionless. Full form roots, $3.50; half female form, $2 each; small and broken roots, 50¢ each.

"Queen's Root. There is a legend of a queen who wished to become a mother, and she made a tea from this root and drank it; 50¢. Lesser Periwinkle—Dr Culpeper says that if the leaves are eaten by man and wife together it will cause love between them; 25¢. Grains of Paradise—one drop taken in hot water before retiring for stimulation; 25¢. Smellage Root—make tea and rub on person who has been a bad influence; 25¢. Waahoo Bark—to uncross a person, make a tea of it, and while rubbing it on head of person, call Waahoo seven times; 25¢.

"Oriental Gum—chew it as a gum to attract opposite sex; 25¢. Dragon's Blood—to uncross a person, burn for seven nights, at midnight, near window; per reed, 50¢. European John the Conqueror—carried in pocket for good luck; 50¢. High John the Conqueror—carried in pocket to offset melancholy moods; 50¢. Frankincense—mentioned in the Bible; whosoever prays while this incense is burning will have their prayers listened to and answered; 50¢."

Perhaps the most remarkable thing about this leaflet is that it contains this notice in fine italics; "These articles are sold for their historical and medicinal value and as curiosities and are not recommended for their evidently impossible magic properties. Although we do not believe in magic of this brand, many people believe in it." So much credit is due the postal regulations which prevent the use of the mails to defraud—but it is highly improbable that the wordy paragraph deters many of the Eureka's prospective customers.

Such conjure shops are to be found in most of the region's Negro towns, and many drugstores also cater to the trade. One of the most popular materials is Graveyard Dirt, often used by Negro rooming-house proprietors to get rid of non-paying guests. The mere threat of leaving a can of Graveyard Dirt under a window is usually sufficient. Anyone who digs the dirt personally must do the job at exactly twelve o'clock noon or midnight. Thirteen cents must be left on the grave to pay for the dirt, thus removing the dirt's curse from the digger. If he should later return and find the money gone, it is a good sign that the Spirits have found it acceptable—but woe to the digger who retrieves the money!

Voodooism's behavior is followed even unto death. Like the Indians, some Palmetto Country Negroes think they can take it with them when they die. At Ocilla, Georgia, Negro graves are littered with old knives, medicine bottles, tools, jugs, plates, shoes, sewing baskets, and similar personal paraphernalia of the deceased. One grave is even covered with a bedstead, and a walking cane protrudes from another.

Who's Who in Hoodoo

The Palmetto Country is literally overrun with practitioners of the occult. Florida, in particular, is plagued with almost as many as that other haven for all things other-worldly, California. Leaving aside the more respectable and accepted sects like the Christian Scientists, Seventh Day Adventists, Jehovah's Witnesses, Holy Rollers, and so on, the region is a seventh heaven for everything from fortune-tellers with a deck of cards to palmists, astrologers, crystal-gazers, soothsayers, spiritualists, root doctors, and other voodoo groups.

It should not be assumed that those who cater to these quacks are always impoverished and illiterate, for such is by no means the case. Some of the most exclusive hotels and night clubs in the region find it profitable to engage the services of cultured and expensive fortune-tellers of all kinds. There appears to be a preponderance of the very rich and the very poor among the devotees, which suggest that unemployment of itself—whether due to lack of opportunity or superfluous wealth—is a favorable condition for the growth of illogical speculation of the sorts fostered and catered to by the occultists.

The Palmetto Country has its share of voodooists whose fame has expanded beyond regional borders—some of the following are as widely known as The Frizzly Rooster of New Orleans, Doctor Buzzard of Beaufort, South Carolina, and Doctor Wade of Coosawitchie.

Father Abraham

Father Abraham's fame as a master of Black magic is known from the Atlantic to the Pacific. He could heal, it is said, any kind of infirmity, remove the worst spells, give winning bolita numbers, and ward off any ill luck that a human might fall heir to.

A tall, copper-colored Negro, Henry N. Abraham was born in Manning, South Carolina, about 1872. His parents were poor and he worked on a plantation. After a little schooling, Abraham went to work in a sawmill. Then one day a Negro came to Manning looking for men to work at the turpentine camp of Russ Edwards in Lawtey, Florida. He offered higher wages, and Abraham went along. That was about 1900, and Abraham worked hard in the turpentine camp for the next twenty years.

Then his boss sent him with a truck to recruit some more Negro workers in Georgia. He succeeded in enlisting a truckload, but at the last minute the Negroes balked and jumped down from the truck. Abraham pleaded and argued with them to no avail. Suddenly he had an inspiration. "Niggers," he said, "you see these two stones I got in my hand? If you don't get back in that truck in a hurry I'm gon rub these stones together and throw the worst spell on you you ever heard about." The Negroes clambered quickly aboard the truck, and Abraham brought them to Florida.

From that day on, Father Abraham become conscious of powers he had known nothing of, and his fame began to spread as a man who could "fix you." Having saved a little money, he bought a small farm. But his health was poor, and doctors told him he had Bright's disease and heart trouble. One day when he was plowing under the hot sun he suddenly stopped and called his wife.

"Honey," he said, wiping the perspiration from his face, "the Lord has called this chile for higher things. Ever since I was a boy I had this feelin but I didn't obey. 'Quench not the Spirit,' sayeth the Lord." Throwing aside his plow, he left the field never to return as a laborer.

Father Abraham entered at once upon his Holy Work. People flocked to him with divers diseases to be healed and spells to be removed. At first he set no specific fee. "Give whatever the Spirit moves you to give" was his motto. But as his services became more in demand his motto changed to "The laborer is worthy of his hire." He always said, "If you give something you get something; if you give nothing you get nothing."

As his wealth increased he purchased two hundred acres of land, built cottages for a dozen families of Negro tenant farmers, and soon became one of Bradford County's biggest strawberry growers and wealthiest men. He discarded the horse and buggy with which he had traveled about the countryside, and bought a custom-built $3,000 Cadillac and a de luxe Hudson.

White and colored folks came to Father Abraham from places as distant as California and Connecticut. His usual treatment began with collecting his fee and placing it in a large Bible which he kept on a table. He would then massage the afflicted organs, mumbling the while an intelligible jargon in which the only understandable words were the names of Biblical prophets. At the end of each treatment he looked his patient in the eye and assured him that he would be completely recovered after a few more treatments.

One of his patients was Estella Barber, a Negro resident of Lawtey. She said, "In 1936 I was sufferin sumpum terrible from indigestion; had been sufferin with it for two years. I went to Father Abraham, and I had no sooner gotten on his front porch than I began to feel better. After three treatments I was cured, and ever since then I been able to eat anything. It cost me three dollars for each treatment. Father Abraham said I had high blood pressure too, but I never did go back to let him cure me of that cause I didn't have no money and I had heard he talked mighty rough if you didn't have money."

Eventually Father Abraham's own illnesses began to catch up with him, and in 1937 he was stricken. At first he refused to let a doctor be called, for fear of the effect upon his own reputation, but at length two of Starke's best physicians were consulted. Nevertheless, Father Abraham passed away. Funeral services were conducted in Lawtey's Mount Zion African Method-

38 .... AUNT MEMORY ADAMS.
Aunt Memory was born into slavery. At 24 years of age she was purchased for $800 by Mr. Argyle in Tallahassee. In 1893, Aunt Memory attended the 1893 World Fair, selling photographs of herself to pay for expenses. State Library and Archives of Florida.

ist Episcopal Church, which was filled to capacity with weeping whites and blacks. His body was laid at rest in a $400 mahogany casket and a $700 monument was erected to his memory. Father Abraham had healed others, but could not heal himself.

Aunt Memory

One of the first Palmetto Country voodoo doctors of whom there is any record was Aunt Memory, who at the age of four was walked with a drove of slaves from Virginia to Tallahassee, where she was sold for $800. In her old age she became widely respected by colored folk for her voodoo powers. As she walked the streets of Tallahassee she always carried a small broom and water sprinkler with which to efface any witch-tracks she encountered—and small boys made it a point to keep her path well supplied with mysterious markings. Aunt Memory hurriedly swept them away and then sprinkled the ground.

So great was Aunt Memory's fear of voodoo that she had a well dug inside her house "to keep them niggers from witchin my water." In 1893 she went to Chicago World's Fair "to see what the white folks had made in all their wisdom."

Aunt Memory has not been forgotten around Tallahassee. When a historical parade was held there in 1924, Aunt Memory—complete with broom and sprinkler—was depicted by one of the city's most prominent citizens.

"Deliverer to Satan"

Mary Collis, a Bahaman Negress living in Miami, had such a reputation as an obeah woman that it was said she could cast spells that would "deliver you to Satan." At the peak of her career in 1910 she was much in demand as a contraceptionist, abortionist, and "bringer"—one who could bring on pregnancy.

For many years Mary Collis was in charge of one of Miami's hotel kitchens, where her obeah powers were of great value in managing the other Negro servants. On numerous occasions she correctly foretold that certain groceries being purchased for the hotel would be found unsatisfactory upon delivery, and in various other ways continually astounded her employers and fellow workers.

Once she became angry with the wife of the hotel manager and proceeded to cast a spell on her. Taking two matches from the woman's waste basket, and some hair from the woman's comb, she twisted the hair about the heads of the matches. Thus binding them together. Then she clothed the effigy with a scrap of cloth from the woman's sewing machine, and finally hid it in the woman's bed so she would sleep with it "and put life into it." Mary then carried it about with her and frequently stuck it with pins and spat on it while muttering, "*Goo-la-mu-antu-mu-la!*" The spell, she said, was good for many years of bad luck.

Mary's services were finally dispensed with when it was learned that she was spiriting away large quantities of the hotel provisions.

The Prophet of Maaii

"Get out of here! Go! Go! What do you want here anyway? Flee!" Such is the customary greeting which Brundus Hartwell, a Negro voodoo doctor of Chester, Florida, gives to his callers. But before the prospective customer can depart, Doctor Hartwell explains that he was merely driving out the evil spirits which accompanied the customer into his shack.

Brundus Hartwell came to the Palmetto Country from New Orleans, where he, his mother, and his brother practiced black magic as "Prophets of Maaii." His one-room shack is situated near a creek and is surrounded by deep underbrush. Around the shack he has erected a barbed-wire fence, and whenever two or more callers appear at the same time, Doctor Hartwell always admits them in the order that they touch the fence. It is said that he can always tell the exact order, even though he is completely out of sight.

A small man weighing not more than 110 pounds, Doctor Hartwell explains that for days he neither eats nor sleeps, as a full stomach interferes with his powers. It is his belief that food, drink, and sleep are necessary but once a week.

A person who took Doctor Hartwell's cure for evil spells in 1935 told this story of his experiences. On the first visit, Doctor Hartwell inquired into the patient's financial status and then quoted him a price for undoing the spell. A down payment of five dollars was required and the patient was asked to return at an appointed hour, bringing a change of clothes with him.

Upon his return the patient found the shack darkened by heavy cloth bagging over the door. In the center of the room was a small table, and on it a white candle was burning in a cup of blue liquid. Doctor Hartwell sat at the table, and the patient stood before him. First the patient was told to face the east, then the west, then the north, and as he made the final turn, the Doctor pinched out the white candle and lit a larger black one. Then he consulted a large black book, which he said was a combination of the sixth and seventh *Books of Moses* and *White and Black Magic*. To find the appropriate remedy for his patient's case, he consulted a Zodiac chart.

The patient was then marched behind Doctor Hartwell to the near-by creek, and there told to strip nude. With much cursing and unintelligible jargon, the Doctor cast all of the garments, including the shoes, into the water. Only running water will destroy demons, he said. The patient was then thoroughly sprinkled with a mysterious powder to take home and sprinkle on all of the clothes he owned. Then the patient was marched in front of the Doctor back to the shack.

There the patient was again told to strip nude, while the Doctor retired to consult his black book by the light of the black candle. The patient asked why the Doctor took the book away to read it, but was told to mind his own business. One portion of the book is for his eyes alone, the Doctor said, and went on to say that there was still another portion of the book which he would read at midnight in the woods near the creek, where he would have a pit of boiling water containing potash to destroy any evil spirits which might have escaped from the clothes thrown in the creek. "Devils are smart beings," he said.

Now nude again, the patient was approached by the blindfolded Doctor, who carried a small basin containing a clear yellow liquid and in the center of which were standing a blue, a green, and a red candle. He lit the candles, and, still blindfolded, completely anointed the patient's body from head to foot. Taking a strip of red silk, he dipped it into the liquid, passed it over the light of the candles; then, directly over the lower terminus of the patient's spine, he formed a cross with the silk. The cross was formed three times, to the accompaniment of incantations.

During the anointment and cross-making the patient stood with his back to the Doctor; now he was told to face the Doctor, and the cross was again formed three times over the navel. This done, Doctor Hartwell told the patient to dress, and as this was going on he kept up a monotonous chant.

Before departing, the patient was given "a few rules to live by." Primarily, it was recommended that he follow the zodiac in every respect and read a Psalm every day. He was also given a small packet to be kept among clothing at home, and a larger packet to be worn next to the skin over the navel. The patient was told that he would be free of evil spirits for a period of three years, after which another treatment would be advisable. And there was a final warning that the balance of the fee be paid as agreed, or the evil spell would return twofold.

Doctor Hartwell also urged his patient to return whenever he might need a cure for some physical ailment such as TB, but added that he might soon have to leave the village of Chester. As Prophets of Maaii, he, his mother, and brother had to travel through all the world before their mission was fulfilled. Doctor Hartwell said he could never die until his work was finished.

The Gods of Yoruba

The variant of voodooism which the Afro-Cubans brought to the Palmetto Country is called brujeria, and the men and women who practice it are known as *brujos* and *brujas*. According to Doctor Fernando Ortiz in his *Negros Brujos*, the African word *brujo* was in use in Cuba before the Portuguese word *fetichero*. This cult of the Yoruba Negroes has predominated in Cuba and Brazil because of their numerical superiority and the fact that their language is understood by some three million blacks.

Brujeria is monotheistic to the extent of worshipping a Jupiter Optimus maximus named Olorun, alias other African names meaning the Señor of the Heaven, Glorious and Elevated Being, the Ever-Just, King of Glory, and so on. A pre-eminent god without an idol, Olorun is far above communicating with men. He is the common property of a number of African tribes and cults.

Olorun can only be reached through secondary divinities called Orishas, which are divided into three categories. First, like the Christian god-head, there is a trinity; Obatalá, Changó, and Ifá. The second group consists of anthropomorphic gods of lesser power; and finally there are the generally unnamed idols, amulets, and various *gris-gris*.

Obatalá is bisexual, symbolizing the productive energies of nature, and his prestige is so great that *brujeria* is often called the Obatalá religion. He is also known as the One of Good Clay, because, like Jehovah, he made men out of clay. Changó is the God of Thunder, the Storm-Thrower. When he is angry he hurls meteors against the earth—and consequently meteoric stones are highly prized by his worshippers. He is also the God of War, in token of which his followers carry symbolic booty bags. Whenever a house is destroyed by lightning (Changó), his faithful think they have a right to loot it.

Elements of Catholicism are commonly incorporated in *brujeria*. On the *brujo* altar, Obatalá is often represented by the image of Christ on the crucifix. However, the real image of Obatalá-a crude wooden idol clothed in semi-feminine vestments and with its face tattooed after the manner of the Carabali Negroes—is sometimes found in the Palmetto Country. Numerous Christian saints are also included in the rites of *brujeria*, and likewise the belief in the transubstantiation of divinities into bread and wine.

The traditional emblem of the *brujo* consists of three ears of corn nailed over the entrance to his house; if there is any persecution of his profession, he nails the corn inside the door. The *brujos* are most noted for their skill in casting spells, usually by means of a potion or charm. The best explanation for the existence of zombies—walking dead—is that the voodooists of Haiti administer a drug causing a cataleptic trance which appears to be death, then surreptitiously exhume their victims after they have been buried, revive them partially with another drug, and put them to work as slaves on inland plantations. So far as is known, no zombie has yet made his way to the Palmetto Country.

In Cuba the *brujos* sometimes went so far as to kidnap a white infant, cut out its heart, and prepare a broth with it to be administered to an ill member of the cult. Such acts led the Spanish authorities to make periodic attempts to suppress *brujeria*, but nothing effective was done until the inauguration of the Cuban Republic.

One of *brujeria's* most potent spell-casters is prepared by removing the entrails of a black cat or white chicken, and stuffing it with human excrement, roasted corn, fruit peels, buttons, black beans, herbs, the feet and comb of a rooster, coins, nails, tacks, shells, fishhooks, blood, grated coconut, lard, and Guinea pepper. The thing is then secretly deposited as near as possible to the victim, preferably under his house.

Professional *brujos* and *brujas* do a thriving business at Key West and Tampa, but greater influence is wielded by the much more numerous and equally adept amateurs. Thousands of Afro-Cubans, as well and many Hispanic—Cubans, live in mortal fear of having a *brujo* spell cast over them. As is generally the case in voodoo, women predominate among the believers, and their spells almost always have to do with marital and other amorous relations—serving to initiate, maintain, improve, or serve them.

Most powerful and elite of the *brujeria* cults is *ñáñigo*, an African society imported bodily to Cuba and thence to the Palmetto Country. Besides its religious functions, *ñáñigo* is something of a fraternal and mutual-aid society. Each group consists of thirteen members; four big chiefs are elected, and the remaining nine also have titles and particular duties. The four best dancers are selected as *diablos*, or devils. Only the most fearless and virile of men are admitted, though some groups initiate one unmarried woman.

The principal *ñáñigo* ceremonials and street dances customarily take place around Epiphany and during the carnival season. Not infrequently, street dances were performed to distract public attention so that a *ñáñigo* could murder one of his enemies. Needless to say, the dances created considerable apprehension whenever they occurred. Eventually *ñáñigo* was banned in Cuba, but it continues to exist in many of the island's urban and rural slums.

In Cuba there are Negro, Creole, and white *ñáñigos*, both in the same and separate organizations. The secretiveness of the society lent itself well to the plotting of revolutionary activities, and the *ñáñigos* contributed substantially to the overthrow of Spain's control. With the founding of the Republic, many of the island's most prominent white citizens joined the *ñáñigos* in a vote-getting maneuver.

The *ñáñigo* ceremonies and dances are probably closer to Africa than anything else performed in the region. Incantations are intoned in the "words of *ñáñigo*," a jargon combining highly corrupted African and Spanish dialects. One of the most primitive aspects of the rites is the manner in which the ceremonial rooster is killed. Some *diablos* grasp the cock by the legs and repeatedly strike its head against the floor as they perform their grotesque contortionist dance. Other *diablos* prefer to grasp the cock's neck between the first and second toes of the right foot and decapitate it with a jerk on its legs. The blood is deposited in a basin called a *chumba*, and sprinkled over the altar, idols, and floor.

Another dramatic ceremony is the symbolic burial held whenever a member is to be expelled or murdered for revealing the cult's secrets—it is their "death from *ñáñigo*."

Ñáñigos among the Cuban patriots were driven to Key West and Tampa and they were later joined by other "notorious *ñáñigos*" who were wanted in connection with *ñáñigo* killings in Cuba. Some became respected citizens in their Palmetto Country communities.

A *ñáñigo* group was organized in Key West, and enjoyed its greatest popularity between 1880 and 1890. Street dances were given from time to time, and dance parties on New Year's However, a Cuban resident was mysteriously murdered during one of their street dances, and although the police could find no evidence, the belief is general in Key West that it was an act of the *ñáñigos*. After that the society gradually disbanded. In 1923 the last *ñáñigo* street dance to be held in Key West was performed "for fun" by Cuban young people attired in makeshift costumes.

The greatest living influence of *ñáñigo* in the region is in the Cuban popular musical compositions which feature the characteristic *ñáñigo bongó* drum rhythms, and the "words of *ñáñigo*" addressed to the Gods of Yoruba.

The Fire Dance

Bahama voodoo is known as obeah, an African word of Ashanti origin. Like *ñáñigo*, obeah is more purely African than the Southern Negro's voodoo. It's drum rhythms in particular have been preserved more or less intact, whereas *ñáñigo* music has been considerably affected by Latin rhythms. The small primitive drums used by both groups are made of wood and covered at one end with goatskin. Before being played, these drums must be tuned over fire, which tightens the skin by expanding the wood. In the Palmetto Country, canned Sterno heat is sometimes used for drum tuning.

The Bahamans can readily identify rhythms—and individuals—according to their African tribal origin. Even the old tribal status is maintained; the proud Yoruba still exclaims, "What! A Congo talk back to a Yoruba? Don't you check me, Congo!"

The belief in the power of graveyard dirt is also to be found among obeahs, probably attesting to its African origin. In the Bahamas, however, a sixpence takes the place of the American thirteen cents. The dirt is bottled, water is added from the ebb tide, and a blue lizard is dropped inside to swell. Tightly corked, the bottle is then hung in a tree or stuck neck down in the ground. The belief is that anyone who steals from the grave or home where one of these bottles exists will swell until they burst.

One of the most colorful of obeah's introductions to American soil is the Fire Dance, which to a large extent has assumed a social character. But in Africa, where it originated, the Fire Dance was full of significance. When a certain tree began to bud in the spring, it was taken as a sign that the new year had come. The houngan thereupon kindled a ceremonial fire in the temple, and everyone came and got a torch and carried it to the dancing place, where the brands were heaped together to form a new fire.

The Fire Dance consists of three phases: the Jumping Dance, Ring Play, and Crow Dance. Everyone is supposed to be costumed as some animal or tree, and the very movements of the dance symbolize the procreative urge of spring. In Africa the climactic dance was a tribute to a sacred bird similar to the American crow—a custom which may have been related to Egyptian hawk-worship.

With fingers and palm-heels the drummer starts the dance by beating out a grand flourish—or "hot break," as it is known in American jazz parlance. A circle of dancers forms and the drummer swings into a vibrant, sensuous rhythm. Someone starts singing, and everyone joins in and also claps hands in tempo with the drum. Then someone "cuts port"—introduces a step—to shouts of "Lime-oh, lime! Juice and all! Two banana, two! Two banana, two!"

The dancer leaps into the ring where he exhausts his stock of moves or steps, chooses a partner, and retires to the circle. Each dancer takes great pride in his original step creations, and fights occur when anyone tries to appropriate them. As the dancer dances he sings this song, and those in the circle join in on the refrain:

> *Bimini gal is a hell of a trouble.*
> *Never get a lickin, you go down to Bimini!*
> *Bimini gal is a rocker and a roller.*
> *Never get a lickin, you go down to Bimini!*
> *East-southeast take you to the lighthouse.*
> *Never get a lickin, you go down to Bimini!*
> *Jim Curry, Joe Curry, Bully for Skelton.*
> *Never get a lickin, you go down to Bimini!*
> *Eh, lemme go down to Bimini.*
> *Never get a lickin, you go down to Bimini!*

To introduce the Ring Dance, the dancer begins circling the ring to look for a partner, and as he circles he sings:

> *Good morning, Father Fisher,*
> *Good morning, Father Brown;*
> *Have you any sea crabs?*
> *Sell me one or two.*
> *Bonefish is bitin;*
> *I got no bait to catch em;*
> *Every married man got his own bonefish.*
>
> *Emma Dee's mad with me,*
> *For what, I don't know....*
> *Jacob burned the kitchen for bread,*
> *For what, I don't know....*
> *Peas and rice, loggerhead fin,*
> *For what, I don't know....*

Sometimes substituted for the above song is the verse:

> *Mama I saw a sailboat*
> *A-sailin in the harbor;*
> *I saw a yaller gal aboard it,*
> *And I took her to be my lover!*

As he finishes this verse—or the first verse of the bonefish song—he selects his partner, who dances out to meet him. They execute steps together, while the others shout:

Down the road, Baby!
Two shillings in the cooker!
Roll it, Roland-but save me some!
It's killing me, Mama! Killing, Mama!

In time the original dancer rejoins the circle, while his partner carries on the process by selecting someone else. Eventually, when all have danced, the rhythm changes and the Crow Dance begins. Everyone in the circle begins singing the crow song and looking for the crow to make his entrance. The crow enters the ring, giving a startling imitation of the bird flapping about looking for food. As he looks he sings, and the others chant the refrain:

The crow, the crow, the crow!
   See how he fly!
This crow, this crow goin fly tonight!
   See how he fly!
Run your Mama, come see the crow!
   See how he fly!
Oh, Ma-ma-ma, come see the crow!
   See how he fly!

When the crow finds his food (partner), they exit amid the shouts of the crowd.

JOOK TOUR

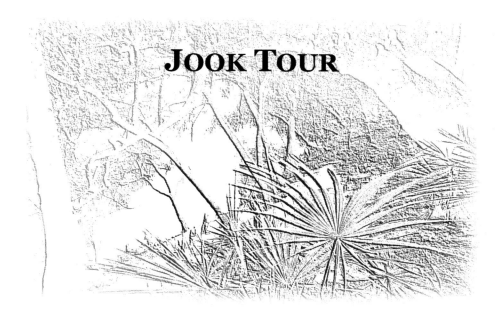

There's something about jooking that gets in your blood—the soothing smell of spilled beer, the whine of boogie-woogie from the resplendent jook organ, the sight of superwomen catering to lusty men. No cocktail lounge can equal it. Of course, there may be some degree of lust, hunger, and thirst in the cocktail lounge, but it is usually expressed according to the dictates of Emily Post, and not instinctively as in the jook. In a cocktail lounge, events and conversation can be predicted with dreadful certainty; but in a jook anything can happen, and often does.

The vital importance of jooks in America's war effort has been widely recognized. Although the Army's southeastern morale officer has said that service men prefer wholesome recreation to jooking, the Army and Navy have found it necessary to blacklist hundreds of jooks all over the South. As a private from New York City stationed at Florida's Camp Blanding said, "These jooks are tough joints. They'll murder you, caress you, and bless you. Not long ago I was in one and just because I'm a Yankee a cracker pulled a knife on me. He reached around my ribs and I was in the hospital three weeks."

Just last year that notoriously American organization, the Ku Klux Klan, burned a fiery cross alongside Joe's Place, Miami, while a Kluxer with amplifier informed spectators, "We haven't been doing this sort of thing lately, but if the citizens call on us again we will act!" Shortly afterward a much more reputable group, the Florida Educational Association, representing 12,000 teachers, declared that jooks are a serious menace to public morals, and asked that the State Legislature ban them.

But the jook is too firmly rooted in American life to be disposed of by blacklists, fiery crosses, or legislation. A one hundred per cent American institution, it is one of the strongest holds of the laissez-faire system, where anarchy (not to mention the bouncer) rules supreme. Altogether the jook is a democratizing influence-a place where the "best people" and "reliefers" can drink away their inhibitions in neighboring booths.

All of which sounds contradictory; but the jook as such couldn't exist in a society without contradictions, anyway. Rank weeds springing from a corroded culture, jooks are a life-sized commentary on the region's (and America's) economics, recreational facilities, and home life. As the *North Georgia Review* has pointed out, the jook is but a symptom of physical and psychic malnutrition. After all, how can Sister be expected to entertain her boy-friend in a two-room shack? The jook naturally wins out over the time-honored bush. We shall crave less "rot-gut" liquor and jook-jive when we have more eggs-butter-cheese-fruit-vegetables in the diet, and more security and gaiety in the home.

As Southern as jazz, fried chicken, corn bread, channel cats, chewing tobacco, and lynching, the jook has a universal appeal which has carried it far beyond the Mason-Dixon Line. Also like jazz, it is a Negro contribution to Americana. Fittingly enough, Florida, "The Nation's Playground," is the home of the jook. Some years ago when they made their phenomenal appearance throughout the Deep South, a Florida newspaper made an abortive attempt to explain them.

"Back yonder," said the editorial, "a jook was a shack somewhere off the road where a negro could go for a snort of moonshine or maybe a bottle of bootleg beer. After repeal of prohibition many jooks for white folks appeared along the main highways, and plenty of them are a far cry from the negro shacks which gave them their name. From a beer joint with a skimpy place for dancing, they range to establishments which put on a country-club dog."

An insight into the original nature of the jook is given by the following editorial from the Savannah *Journal and Courier*, September 29, 1855:

"By reference to the recent homicide of a negro, in another column, some facts will be seen suggestive of a state of things, in this part of our popula-

39 .... WHITE JOOK JOINT.
   Jook joints were created by African Americans, but after the repeal of of Prohibition, many white jooks appeared in Florida. Charles Foster photo, State Library and Archives of Florida.

tion, which should not exist, and which cannot endure without danger, both to them and to us. The collision, which terminated thus fatally, occurred at an hour past midnight-a time when none but the evil-disposed are stirring.

"To the impunity thus given the negroes by the darkness of midnight, was added the incitement to crime drawn from the abuse of liquor. They had just left one of those resorts where the negro is supplied with the most villainously-poisonous compounds, fit only to excite him to deeds of blood and violence. Indeed, we have the declaration of the slayer that the blow, by which he was exasperated so as to return it by the fatal stab, was inflicted by a bottle of brandy!"

The deviation of the word "jook" is still obscure. In "A Note on Jook," Will McGuire has reported that nothing like it is to be found in the English language as far back a Chaucer. He believes "jook" to be a corruption of "dzug," a word in the African Wolof dialect meaning "to lead a disorderly life."

A different explanation is offered by Henry "Britches" Young, a century-old Negro resident of Lake Butler, Florida. Says centenarian Young: "A long time ago Negroes danced the jubilee, the predecessor to jitterbugging. The jubilee consisted of two steps, the Walkin Jawbone and the Jumpin Jim Josey. The men and women lined up opposite each other, and the two at the head of the lines approached each other, with jaws extended, in cake-walk fashion; then when they met they cut the lively Jumpin Jim Josey, a buck-wing step. At this point the other dancers shouted, "Go on, jubilee!" As time went on, says Young, this cry was shortened to Go on, jube!" and then to "Jook it."

Another idea is advanced by Webster's *International Dictionary*. It spells the work "juke" or "juck," and says that it came to be a designation for joints because of the notoriety given the Juke family as an example of the inheritance of criminal and immoral tendencies. Still another source maintains that jook is an Irish word which was first applied to San Francisco bawdy houses many years ago.

The spelling of the word (which is usually pronounced to rhyme with "took") once posed a problem for the Florida Supreme Court, as related in the following news story:

"Tallahassee, Nov. 3. (AP)-A case involving the so-called 'jook' tax law caused a Supreme Court discussion today on the spelling of the word. Justice Rivers Buford, who spent his boyhood in the Apalachicola timberlands, suggested 'j-o-o-k' and explained; 'Before white folks started using the word, there were negro jook-joints as far back as I can remember.'"

The Court was hearing a case in which Bessie Pellicer of Jacksonville protested having to pay the $150 annual jook license on her small hotel. Attorney John E. Mathews, representing her, pointed out that large hotels are not required to pay the tax, and said the law "taxes this woman's jook and lets go free those other jooks with 300 rooms."

But it should never be said that a jook is worthy of the name if it lacks any of the following characteristics. A jook is an establishment that is usually crude but sometimes sumptuous; it is commonly equipped with tables

40 .... JOOKING, MOORE HAVEN.
The term "jook joint," referring oft-times to primitive shacks where beer and wine were dispensed, originated in Palmetto Country turpentine camps and other areas where black labor was concentrated. By the end of the centry the institution of "jooking" had spread to France and perhaps elsewhere. Marion Post Wolcott photograph. State Library and Archives of Florida.

or booths and space for dancing; beer, wine, and perhaps liquor are sold; edibles if any are apt to be barbecued ribs or sandwiches; music is provided by a jook organ (called piccolo by Negroes) or jook band (ensemble of rhythm instruments); girls, as waitresses or hangers-around, are available for dancing without charge.

Most jooks are called somebody's Place, although some have more imaginative names like The Golden Slipper (Hotel Upstairs), The Ship A-hoy (on the fish docks), and Black Bottom (a white jook in Negro town). Black Bottom, incidentally, is graced by a work of art showing a debonair darkey in checked trousers and derby hat emerging from an outhouse, and is also noted for a large black goat that wanders about under the tables eating lighted cigarettes, etc.

The major role of the jook is catering to the great masses of common people who can ill afford to pay admission, cover, or minimum charges. Offering a maximum of attractions at minimum cost, the jook is the answer to their problem of nocturnal entertainment; even the most underpaid wage-slave can go jooking on Saturday night (opponents of jooks, please note). Beer is ten cents per bottle, wine ten cents per glass, and a shot of whiskey costs fifteen cents. Mixed drinks are considered to be unfit for human consumption, besides being wasteful of time and money. In addition to their cash customers, jooks attract many "look customers" as a jook girl has called them; "all they do is look in to see what they can see."

It is not to be denied that the jook has its less wholesome aspects, particularly that of serving as a clearing house for prostitution, both mercenary and eleemosynary. This may be accomplished either independently or by arrangement with the management. In the former case, the jook merely serves as a meeting- or market-place, and the couples depart on foot or in a taxi or automobile. But in the latter case, the jooks maintain adjoining rooms or "Cabins for Tourists" (Innerspring Mattresses; Running Ice-water). This leads respectable tourists camps to erect signs which read Out-of-State Travellers Only.

Some jook operators contribute to the delinquency of minors, and are guilty of other law violations, as related in the following news dispatch.

"*Tallahassee, Feb. 1.* (AP)-Federal and State officials arrested four persons here today and charged them with transporting women across State lines for immoral purposes. Three others were charged with operating houses of prostitution. Sheriff Stoutamire said he started an investigation into a 'general situation all over the area.'

"'We found,' he said, 'that people have been renting jooks, then getting girls from 16 years on up to work for $3 a week and their room, board, and washing. Their duties were to serve drinks, dance with the men, and fill dates with the men. They had to pay the operators one dollar for the time they had off to fill dates. The dates were filled either in cottages on the place or in cars.'"

Another periodic complaint against jooks is embodied in the following news story.

"It was something they put in those drinks I had at a jook-joint, Judge."

Thus J. W. S.-, 38, Jacksonville insurance salesman, explained to Judge Himes yesterday why he crashed his car into a parked truck and filling station, and didn't come to his senses until 24 hours later.

"I just had two drinks, Judge," he insisted, "and that amount of liquor wouldn't hit me like that. They must have put some knockout drops in them. The girl told me it was a special kind of drink. She called it a velvet."

"You ought to have better sense than to go in those jook-joints," Judge Himes told him. "As it is, you're lucky not to be facing a manslaughter charge."

Not only the press and police records bear evidence that jooks are centers of illegal activity; there are also signs like this one, posted in the company-owned jook of a turpentine camp near Lakeland, Florida.

To whom it may concern

Effective this date anyone shooting a gun in these Quarters will be charged $5 and required to forfeit the gun, or go to JAIL. I will pay $2.50 for proof of anyone shooting a gun.

The notice bears the signature of a company official.

At Benny's Place near Brooksville, Florida, this warning appears over the bar:

YOU CAN DRINK IN HEAR
BUT GO OUTSIDE TO GET DRUNK

Some signs are characteristic of cracker modes of expression, like the laconic pronouncement at Don's Place, Billygoat Hill, Jacksonville:

WE TAKE NO ADVISE FROM NOBODY

This spirit of pronounced individualism again crops up ferociously in an Alabama jook:

DON'T ASK US, NEITHER
BECAUSE WE DON'T KNOW, NEITHER
AND IF WE DID WE WOULDN'T TELL YOU, NEITHER

In the same jook, painted in red on the ceiling, is the question: WHAT IN HELL ARE YOU LOOKING UP HERE FOR?

41 .... "SKIN" GAME, MOORE HAVEN JOOK JOINT.
Games of chance, such as this "Skin" game, were popular Jook Joint activities along with drinking and listening to music. Marion Post Wolcott photograph. State Library and Archives of Florida.

In Baker Bryan's, on U.S. 1 just south of the Florida border, this cryptic notice hangs over the gambling room door:

NO WEMEN ALOUD IN HEAR
THIS DON'T MEAN BOB;
IT MEANS YOU

At near-by Mabel's Place, however, girls operate the gambling tables. One table is equipped with a novel rig: an ordinary scrub-board stands on a slant at one end, and the dice are rolled down it to display their spots on the table. The girl whines interminably:

"The more you put down the more you pick up!
Watch your pile grow like a Georgia pine!"

Popular demand requires that the music provided by jook organs be corn and jazz. Much of the corn is produced in Jacksonville, Tampa, and other Southern cities, usually by a vocalist with a guitar. Two of the best-liked singers among Negroes are Tampa Red and Tampa Slim, and favorite titles include:

"I Wonder Who's Booging My Woogie Now," "No-Good Woman," "Rattlesnake Daddy," "Mistreatin-Mama," "No-Good Woman," "Teenincie Mama," "Jesse James Blues," "Bad Blood Blues," "B&O Busline Blues," "Drinkin My Blues Away." One remarkable lament declares:

From the ankles up you sho is sweet,
But from the ankles down, you's too much meat!
Oh, your feet too big, feet too big,
Papa can't love you cause your feet too big!

Another hit sings praises of:

Lou-u-ise, sweetest gal I know,
She made me walk from Chicago,
To the Gulf of Mexico.
I had a dozen women,
I had em big and small;

But when I met this Mama, Right then I quit em all.

Somebody's been a-fishin,
Where I fished before;
If I can ever catch em,
They aint gonna fish no more.

Jook girls are deeply moved by jook music, and it is not the least of the attractions that lure them away from home. They seem perfectly contented while their favorite records are playing. Sometimes there is a mercenary reason for this: the management allots certain records to each girl, and pays them a percentage of all the nickels they can cajole out of customers to play their "favorite." Jook organs are seldom quiet; bleary-eyed customers who take a fancy to a particular tune have been known to keep it playing continuously until dawn-to the apparent enjoyment of all listeners.

Often the recorded songs become integrated with the lore of the region, and when this happens there are usually some changes made, like when a jook girl paraphrased "Blue Eyes": "I'm thinking tonight of my brew-eyes-I wonder if he's thinking of me..."

In the jook, profanity has degenerated into a mere manner of speaking, without which statements seem lacking in conviction. Sincere cursing, though occasionally indulged in, takes the form of a dog fight, with much growling and little fighting. Indeed, advanced intoxication often renders fighting impractical if not impossible. The man or woman who attempts a hay-maker often passes out before landing the blow.

With the jook girls consistently outnumbered by male customers, it is not surprising that a democratic spirit of share-the-gals has developed. The men, who are either unmarried or have left their wives at home, are out for a jook, and when jook girls see fit to hand out kisses to all and sundry with each bottle of beer it is seldom that anyone objects.

Jook girls have been known to object to such straightforward approaches, but the men have little patience with non-essential preliminaries. For example, a Yankee jook girl once declared, "You damn crackers can only think of one thing-you don't know how to have a good time!" To which her cracker companion replied, "The roads back North aint crowded."

Men seldom show any sympathy for jook girls, as was demonstrated by a cracker who sat down beside a girl who was in the throes of a crying jag.

"Who jerked your chain?" he asked unconcernedly.

"I guess I got the jitters," she replied. "I get that way after four A.M. Must be an inferiority complex-knew I'd get one sooner or later."

Most girls, however, are extreme extroverts. Their well-developed individualism was exemplified by the girl who informed her loud-mouthed companion, "you may yell at your wife, but you can't yell at me."

Probably jook bartenders are in the most advantageous position to probe the verities of jook life. "Little Bit and Garnet drink too much on the job," Black Bottom's bartender once sagely observed. "No girl can do that and spect to last. Too much drinkin makes girls end up with the horrers and they goes queer and has to quit."

Yet there's always something about a jook that is beyond all understanding, and therein lies much of the their inexplicable charm. Once upon a time, for example, there was a little jook girl sitting all alone at a table, drinking beer and not bothering anybody. Then in stalked a big overalled cracker. He looked around, walked over to the girl, and stood staring down at her. After a minute she looked up.

"See anything green?" she asked.

"Yeah," he answered, and brined her with a beer bottle.

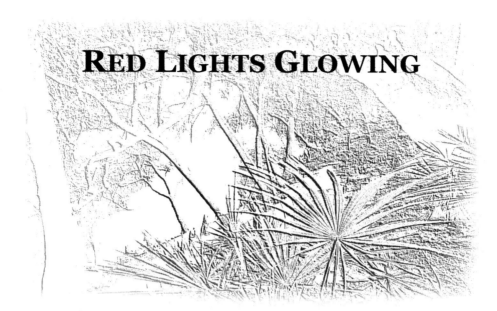

RED LIGHTS GLOWING

All over the Palmetto Country menfolk tell about the farmer who went to the city for a two-week vacation. When he got back home his neighbors wanted to know all about it.

"Reckon it cost a heap a money to live in one a them hotels for two solid weeks," one of them ventured.

"Didn't stay in no hotel," replied the farmer.

"Then where did you stay at?"

"In a whorehouse."

"In a whorehouse for two weeks! That must of cost, sure enough!"

"Nary a cent," said the farmer. "I was visitin kinfolks."

It's a story which tends to show that prostitution is a member of the regional family in comparatively good standing.

Prostitution in the Deepest South has all the earmarks of the profession as practiced elsewhere, according to informed sources. The red light, ancient badge of houses of prostitution, burns brightly in most of the region's self-respecting towns and cities. Usually these lights are in the hallway or parlor, with only a suffused glow visible from the street.

Poverty is probably the chief reason why girls take up the comparatively lucrative profession, but there are often contributing factors. Perhaps indicative of a trend is the bitter complaint made recently by a madam on Jacksonville's famed Houston Street, that "the streets are full of hungry girls who would rather starve than work." She says she "can't understand it."

Though many prostitutes die early in poor houses or asylums, a goodly number achieve success in their own modest way. Typical success sagas of the red-light district tell of girls who have accumulated comfortable nest eggs and then retired, of girls who gave birth to children and then reformed, and of others who became happily married.

Small-town whores are usually local girls who have gone bad, and their life stories are as much a part of common knowledge as the careers of other prominent citizens. About half of the city prostitutes are of regional origin, while the other half hail from various parts of the country. There is considerable interstate migration.

Resort areas experience a noticeable influx of prostitutes during the tourist season. This breed produces such individuals as the artist who in 1935 executed her self-portrait with an eyebrow pencil on the back of a Paddock Bar & Grill (Miami) poster, and inscribed it, *To Bernie with lust. Always, Marie.* These arch-sophisticates are generally distinguished from the natives by mascara, artificial eyelashes, expensive clothes, luxurious quarters, more civilized techniques, and higher prices. Instead of bluntly demanding. "D'ya wanta fill a date?" they ask, "Do you have the time?"

An encouraging reply to the first question is said to lead to an expenditure of about two dollars, whereas the same answer to the other more often involves the outlay of about twenty-five dollars. Payable in advance, these rates do not include transportation, entertainment, or beverages. Besides the popular price of two dollars, rates of three dollars and five dollars are commonly encountered where circumstances warrant. Many houses offer a special "student rate" of one dollar to youths of high-school age.

Negro houses, where rates are lower, enjoy a considerable amount of white trade. A cracker who has collected furniture bills among Negroes from more than forty years declares that most Negro women are delighted to be approached by white men, and that the husband of a Negro woman who gives birth to a mulatto child is usually proud of the child and flattered to think that some white man found his wife so attractive. Though this cracker's statements must be discounted, they are significant because innumerable other *crackers* would endorse them.

A Jacksonville taxi driver says he has driven prostitutes (personally known to him) to the homes of well-to-do Negro men. If this is true-and there seems to be no reason for doubting it-a considerable sum of money probably changes hands in the transactions. On the other hand are incidents like that which occurred in Jacksonville in 1939. Two Negro men

42 .... CORA CRANE.
Cora Cane, once married to author Stephen Crane, was the owner of The Court, a popular house of prostitution in Jacksonville. circa 1902. State Library and Archives of Florida.

tried to pick up two white prostitutes on Houston Street and were shot by outraged crackers who, happening on the scene, sprang to the defense of Southern Womanhood.

From time to time, large construction projects cause local increases in the incidence of prostitutes. This problem, with its corollary, the menace of venereal disease, comes in for much attention in local church circles and similar places. If public officials fail to act then the Ku Klux Klan is apt to appear dramatically on the scene. If warnings and fiery crosses do not have the desired effect of driving out the undesirables, the Klansmen proceed to more violent action.

An example of this took place in Miami in 1940 and brought the Klan much publicity. The occasion was the raiding and wrecking of La Paloma Club. Later, the operators of the club were charged with white slavery. The sensational trials, which resulted in convictions, brought out testimony that transportation from Georgia was provided for girls who became prostitutes in the club; that managers made a practice of living with various girls in the cottages in the walled courtyard of the club, where they often walked together in the nude; and that certain city officials had been "fixed" by being allowed to spend a night with the girls.

The Klan's favorite method of dealing with such establishments, however, is to commit arson. Indeed, the folkway of burning out undesirables seems to date back to pioneer days when the woodsmen learned the trick from the Indians. It has been widely used since then against whorehouses, gambling dens, jook joints, and Negroes who tried to establish themselves on the "wrong side" of town. Following the Civil War, it was often employed against carpetbaggers, and has since been used against damn-yankee farmers who have had the nerve to fence land that was formerly open range.

A few years ago in Gainesville, site of the University of Florida, Blondie's combination jook de luxe and whorehouse was rumored to be the source of an epidemic of venereal disease which was taxing the facilities of the university infirmary. So one fine night the Klan burnt Blondie's to the ground. Blondie, incidentally, who was known as the Queen of the Jooks, married a wealthy college youth who was known as the King of the Jooks. They soon parted on grounds of incompatibility.

An interesting demonstration that prostitutes are made, not born, took place in 1940 when Harry Silver, a Jacksonville attorney, was disbarred after hearings at which witnesses testified he had arranged for the operators of houses of prostitution to pay the fines of girls in jail, provided the girls would enter the houses to repay them. It was charged that Silver was paid a fee for each new recruit. In 1942 he was sentenced to five years' imprisonment for wiring ten dollars to Albany (Georgia) for the transportation of a woman to his Jacksonville night club "for purposes of prostitution or debauchery." Jean Brennen, who testified that she was a "prostitute who used to work for Silver," said, "Dates were priced at $3-we got $1, Silver got $1, and the cab driver got $1."

There is ample evidence that prostitution is a major source of graft for public officials. Municipal Judge Manucy Anderson and the Rev. James E. Barbee (Jacksonville's anti-vice clergyman) have long been feuding on this subject. Following is a report typical encounter between them:

"JUDGE ANDERSON: It had been reported to me that Mrs. Soloman [wife of the editor of the *Florida Baptist Witness*] was putting out propaganda linking me with alleged collection of protection money from the poor, downtrodden prostitutes. I called on her, and asked Mr. Barbee to sit in on our conversation. I told her the story being circulated about prostitutes paying $10 a week for protection and said I did not know anything about such a situation.

"Mr. Barbee said he knew about the situation, and he blessed me out for not knowing about it. I told Dr. Barbee I would discuss the situation with the city attorney's office-not the mayor. Mr. Barbee said that would do no good. He said some of us had to run for mayor or go to Governor Holland. I have considered Mr. Barbee my friend. But Mr. Barbee has embarrassed me-terribly.

"REV. BARBEE: The conversation opened on gambling, and I said it was handled through protection and payoff. Judge Anderson said he didn't know there was any gambling going on in Jacksonville. To show him there was-and is-gambling, I took Judge to visit several gambling houses. Gambling in Jacksonville exists under graft and payoff. Otherwise it could not continue 24 hours.

"JUDGE ANDERSON: I was never so humiliated! He intimated right there in front of all those people that I knew who was getting graft! Why, I was embarrassed to tears!

REV. BARBEE: "I didn't say who was getting the graft. I said you must be very ignorant if you didn't know about the vice and gambling in Jacksonville, and still say so.

"JUDGE ANDERSON: Those poor, underprivileged prostitutes! I think I would help string up any city official who took graft from those poor unfortunates!"

Needless to say, there is an intimate relationship between prostitution and venereal disease. In 1941 Surgeon General Thomas Parran announced that 63,000 of the first million selectees and volunteers for the Army were found to have venereal disease-48,000 had syphilis and 15,000 had gonorrhea. One-fourth of the Negro men had syphilis. As was the case in World War I, the incidence of venereal disease was highest among the men from Florida.

The announcement of this fact caused no little apprehension in "The Ante-Room to Heaven." The *Miami Herald* editorialized: "The national report is bad enough, but Florida's is even worse. Florida's shame can be turned into Florida's victory if every one of us realizes the tremendous importance of united effort in the battle." But on the following day the *Herald* printed a story, "Syphilis Rate Here Defended," which said that Dade County's syphilis rate is "lower than those of Detroit, Cleveland, Memphis, Chattanooga, Nashville, and Knoxville."

A frank opinion about the role of recreation in the life of service men was voiced by a representative of the Federal Security Administration, who said, "Everybody knows that 999 out of 1,000 service men come to town with the principal idea of meeting girls. I don't look at organized recreation as a substitute for sex life; I think normal men require both." A draftee supported this with the observation, "Trying to repress sex is like trying to repress the tide. Maybe those who are trying to repress it don't feel any need for it, but what about us soldiers? Somebody ought to ask us what we think about it." And a seaman added bluntly, "Everybody knows that ever so often we have to go ashore and—the ship. We all get tattooed, stewed, and—. In Honolulu the Navy has regular inspection of prostitutes by Government doctors—if you ask me that ought to be done everywhere."

Jacksonville, recreation center for more than 150,000 service men, has an interesting record of attempts to suppress vice and venereal disease, though these evils are by no means localized. The city has required the registration, examination, photographing, and fingerprinting of prostitutes since 1940.

In March, 1941, red-light houses were declared "out of bounds" for service men, and MP's and SP's were assigned to enforce the ruling. Public opinion was satisfied for a time, until a U.S. public health officer toured the district and reported that the only difference since the ban went into effect was that the shades had been drawn. He added that in the preceding week the city-county clinic had treated 2,000 cases of venereal disease, and that an average of four new patients with primary syphilis were reporting daily.

43 .... MAIN STAIRWAY, THE COURT.
The main stairway for **The Court**, a popular house of prostitution in Jacksonville, Florida. circa 1902. State Library and Archives of Florida.

Florida health officers then launched a quarantine campaign against prostitution. Dr. Gilbert S. Osincup, in charge of the campaign, declared: "It is impossible to eliminate prostitution entirely, but we can cut down the number of contacts and in that way greatly curtail the spread of venereal disease. The policy of segregation, advocated by some as the best means of control, is directly opposed to the policy of repression laid down by the Army, Navy, U.S. Health Service, and the American Hygiene Association. It would seem that the total result of the quarantine will be that prostitutes will fan out from cities and counties adjacent to defense centers into other counties. However, the squeeze campaign will gradually spread, and we can make it uncomfortable enough for the prostitutes to force them to leave the State."

Many of the quarantine signs were torn down as fast as they were put up. After four more months of the out-of-bounds and quarantine edicts, a

44 .... BEDROOM, THE COURT.
An elaborately decorated bedroom at Jacksonville's The Court. Prostitutes worked in this room in the early 1900's. State Library and Archives of Florida.

squad of police was sent out with these instructions: "We want every prostitute notified that this is the final permanent warning. The Government is behind us this time." The officers told the operators of houses: "Your business is closed up. This is no fly-by-night warning. No more prostitutes in Jacksonville. There will be no use for you to hole up in another part of town to wait until the blow is over. We are going to run this business into the ground wherever it crops up."

The madams were suspicious. "We were told to close up before and it didn't mean a thing," they said. One of them wept. "I don't know what I'm going to do," she said. "I've just spent $10,000 refinishing this place, with air-conditioned bed-rooms and everything." Many of the houses are expensively furnished, with paneled walls and thick carpets. In one house all carpets are monogrammed with the madam's initials.

A *Jacksonville Journal* reporter, Gardner Botsford, who was on hand at the closing, wrote: "I got the whiff of an enormous grafting business going on. The rents in the district were way out of sight according to their true value. One landlady was paying $150 a month, and they averaged $100. Fourteen houses were notified, and the officers then started a canvass of some hotels. The hotel proprietors were warned not to take in any known street-walkers, and to clean out any undesirable women already registered. It seemed to me that the hotels were more jammed with prostitutes than the regular houses. At one hotel I found eleven girls who frankly admitted they were prostitutes; and another hotel had eight. The police were careful to explain that the old dodge of hanging up 'Rooming House' signs would do no good."

The most conspicuous houses were actually closed, with interesting results, chief among which was a decentralization to other neighborhoods. As was expected, the prostitutes established themselves in small hotels and rooming houses, where their detection and conviction was extremely difficult. One such place displayed a neon sign reading: *Tea Room, Chicken & Beer, Sailors Welcome*. Another sign of the times, appearing on the best tourist cabin camps of the region read: *Tourists Only*. Some prostitutes rented bungalows in "respectable" sections, and, with great discretion, managed to operate quite profitably until detected by irate neighbors. The lack of a permanent and well-known location also required that the girls make contacts by street solicitation, in jook joints, and as waitresses.

Another significant development has been the appearance of mechanized prostitution. The prostitutes cruise about in taxicabs and look for opportunities to attract men, and many taxi drivers have an arrangement with the girls whereby they are given a percentage of all money spent by the men they deliver. In cars and trailers the girls also ride about in the neighborhood of the army camps.

By such devious devices the most ancient of professions adapts itself to the exigencies of our time.

45 .... THE COURT.
Exterior view of The Court, one of many houses of prostitution in Florida in the early 1900's. State Library and Archives of Florida.

WAITIN ON TIME

Little corn, UGH!
Yellow corn, UGH!
Little fight, UGH!
Lotta time, UGH!

The maintenance of law and order in the Palmetto Country has always been beset with special problems because of the remoteness of the region, its comparatively recent settlement, the survival of pioneer concepts of conduct, and conflicts between whites and Negroes. The crackers in particular have a traditional dislike for legal proceedings, preferring to settle their disputes without benefit of attorney.

Thus the Palmetto Country has been and continues to be wild in its own peculiar way. As the saying goes, when a cracker says he'll do you a favor, he'll most likely do it- and of course if he says he'll kill you, he'll do that too.

Got my knapsack on my back,
And my rifle on my shoulder;
Gon' kill me a nigger fore Saturday night,
If I have to hunt Florida over.

The Negro is seldom a deliberate man-hunter, but often kills in the heat of anger or desperation of fear. Afterward he will probably say, "I didn't know what I was doin. I didn't mean to kill." On the other hand, the cracker is more apt to be unrepentant and say, "By God, he had it comin to him. I'd do it agin if I had to."

Since colonial days the region has been a haven for all manner of lawless elements. Contemporarily, the socio-economic jungle which created Bigger Thomas (in Richard Wright's *Native Son*) reaches its rankest growth in the Palmetto Country. Jacksonville, for example, has had the highest homicide rate of any city in the world.

The region is also noted for the production of moonshine, an illicit industry that continues to thrive because of the high cost of tax-paid liquors. The product of the moonshiners' art ranges in quality from good corn whiskey to "rot-gut" and "white lightning." The following song pays tribute to the power of moonshine.

46 .... REVENUERS DESTROY A STILL.
Revenuers destroying a moonshine still near Miami. During Prohibition days, moonshining and rum-running were major Florida occupations. State Library and Archives of Florida.

COME ALL YOU ROUNDERS

Come all you rounders, if you want to hear
What kind of moonshine they make around here,
It's made way back in the swamps and hills,
Where there's plenty of moonshine still.

A drop will make a rabbit whip a bulldog;
A taste will make a rat whip a wild hog;
Make a mice bite off a tomcat's tail;
Make a tadpole raise the mud with a whale.

Make a fice bite off a elephant's snout;
Make a poodle dog put a tiger to his rout;
Make a toad spit in a blacksnake's face;
Make a Hardshell preacher call for grace.

Florida's early penal system has been characterized as one of "aimless experimentation, followed by about thirty years of the lease system." Under that system, private contractors hired convict labor from the state at the rate of about one dollar a day. The contract went to the highest bidder, and the convicts were then hired out to sub-lessees—usually turpentine, lumber, phosphate, and railroad companies—for about two dollars a day.

The State's Prison Bureau was established under the Department of Agriculture in 1868. In 1912 the Bureau reported, "The State has received $2,722,620.14 from the hire of prisoners since the first convict lease in 1880 until 1912 inclusive. That is what the convict has done for the State. WHAT HAS THE STATE DONE FOR THE CONVICT? Nothing. We have taken the money from his labour and have used same for every known purpose except the betterment of his unfortunate condition.

"The prisoners remain at the concentration camp until distributed to their labor camps. The lessee is required to provide one guard for every five prisoners, and one mounted guard for every twenty-five. One trained bloodhound is requested for every squad at work. The State furnishes a punishment book, and the date, reason for punishment, number of licks and by whom administered must be entered. I found some camps where there is entirely too much punishment. I think it is a wise and just ruling that no prisoner should be whipped on the bare skin. The guard proposition is the worst thing we have to contend with. It is hard to get men that will stick to the rules.

"The County prison camp convicts are confined in iron vans holding from twelve to twenty-two prisoners. This does not appeal to me as being conducive to health, as they necessarily breath the same air over and over gain. The vans are very unsanitary and are hard to keep free of vermin, as they are not fixed with water tanks, bath tubs, or flush sinks. They stand in the hot sun all day and when you put it full of dirty men on very narrow bunks I call it cruel treatment."

In the same report, the prison physician stated, "The great majority of prisoners are physical wrecks when they come from the various jails of the State. At least seventy-five per cent of the colored prisoners have syphilis."

A Survey of Florida Jails, published by B.C. Riley in 1921, said, "At Ft. Lauderdale we find the worst jail in the State. The prisoners work on the sheriff's own farm and are frequently deprived of food and severely whipped or beaten. The Arcadia jail, in response to our query about odor, reports 'Good enough for a jail.'"

Georgia abolished the lease system in 1908, but Florida did not follow suit until 1919. Both states outlawed the lash in 1923, and Florida "abolished" the sweat-box at the same time. As a matter of fact, however, Florida law in 1942 still prescribed solitary confinement on bread and water in a seven-by-seven foot sweat-box which may be divided vertically in half during the daytime. In Georgia, Governor Eugene Talmadge said in 1941 that "Sweat-boxes are injurious to health at best. Stocks are too, but you have to control convicts, and you have to have discipline."

Talmadge also advocated the installation and use of whipping posts as the most effective method of punishing habitual drunkards. He defended two wardens charged with cruelty, saying, "If you want to get somebody who knows how to treat convicts, get somebody who has et the cake." The wardens were ex-convicts who had been sentenced for murder and later pardoned. The Georgia artist who decorated the state penitentiary with a bas-relief of a powerful man instead of the traditional blindfolded Goddess of Justice must have known what he was doing.

The sweat-box—which becomes an ice-box in winter—has brought great notoriety to the Palmetto Country. It was a favorite method of punishment with the region's aboriginals, who dug pits, lined the bottom with hot stones, covered the stones with wet green boughs, and then dumped in the culprit to bake and steam until he was unconscious.

In 1941 this same savage spirit must have inspired the warden who confined twenty-two Negro convicts in a seven-by-seven sweat-box for ten hours. By that time several of them were unconscious, and the remainder were shouting, "We're dyin!" One of the unconscious Negroes did die. His was the fourth violent death among Georgia convicts in less than three months. When brought to trial, the warden pointed out that the sweat-box was an official approved method of punishment, and said, "I'm awfully sorry the man died." He was sentenced to three years for "involuntary manslaughter."

Earlier in the same year, the *Atlanta Constitution* published an uncensored photograph showing three convicts in stripes, sitting in a barbed-wire enclosure at Georgia's "Little Alcatraz," breaking rocks with iron bars. Their legs were bandaged, and it was revealed that the convicts had deliberately broken them in an effort to keep off the work gangs. Conditions were so bad that a number of other prisoners had done the same thing in the several preceding years. In explaining why he put the men back to work before their legs had healed, the warden said, "I did it to convince them and others who might harbor similar intentions that the fracturing of legs isn't the profitable thing to do."

Until 1939 the county and city "Blue Jay" prison farms at Jacksonville employed a novel method of plowing. Trios of Negro women prisoners were harnessed to plows, which were also guided by Negro women. Unless it has been disposed of, the human harness still hangs in the prison warehouses.

The use of striped convict uniforms was still optional in the Palmetto Country in 1942, when some counties were using them. A modern chain gang innovation is a small armored trailer which is pulled behind the truck carrying the convicts. A guard sits in the trailer with a shotgun or .38 "riot gun." Though Palmetto Country convicts take their lives in their hands when they attempt to escape, escapes are nevertheless fairly frequent. In 1938 when a Negro convict fled from the Jacksonville Blue Jay, pursuing bloodhounds forced him to swim the river on a freezing night. The next morning, officers found the Negro had sold the hounds to a farmer as "the best coon dogs in the country."

Another unusual jail-break took place in Jacksonville in 1940. The Negro prisoners asked for permission to get together and hold an old-fashioned revival meeting. Permission was granted and the prisoners were ushered into a large room and left to their singing. Up front the jailer marveled at their loud shouts of "hallelujah" and "glory-glory," never dreaming that they were covering up the sound of saws and files cutting the prison bars.

It is a common practice in the Palmetto Country to incarcerate persons without due process of law, the chief victims being Negroes, strike leaders, and indigents. A typical example took place in 1941. When a Negro witness was called for in court, the defendant happened to know that the Negro was in the county jail on a charge of "using an automobile without the owner's permission." The sheriff's office was consulted, but it knew nothing about the alleged prisoner. Actual search nevertheless showed that the Negro was in jail and had been for the past sixty-eight days, "due to an oversight." Commented the *Miami Herald*: "Oversight? That's too soft a word for gross carelessness or negligence. This Negro had a right to a speedy trial. Conceivably, he might have languished behind the bars from now until the jail house collapsed or until weight of years carried him off, waiting to find out what 'the law' was going to do with him."

Police brutality, especially in dealing with Negroes, is another commonplace in the region. As a case in point, in 1941 two seventeen-year-old white boys testified that they were blackjacked by detectives. This brought on a probe and much publicity. One policeman admitted slugging an intoxicated prisoner, and a police lieutenant denied that his electrified "hotseat" was ever used.

The municipal judge told investigators, "Unnecessary roughness, if allowed to continue, will reach out into the citizenry until no one is safe. But in its usual impotence the public may be content to forget all about this as soon as the last article is published in the newspapers, and next year we will have to start all over again."

The murder of a white man in Pompano, Florida, in 1933 resulted in a chain of events which have attracted nationwide attention. Following the murder, from twenty-five to forty Negroes were rounded up without warrants, and held for questioning. Four of these Negroes—Jack Williamson, Charlie Davis, Walter Woodward, and Izell Chambers—were indicted, convicted, and sentenced to death. In the past nine years their case has been in state and federal courts ten times. Three times the Florida Supreme Court reversed their sentence, and then upheld it. Meanwhile Izell Chambers, due to his prolonged residence in the death cell, became insane and was sent to the asylum. The case reached the U. S. Supreme Court in 1940 and when the Negroes testified that their confessions had been forced from them by beatings and torture, their sentences were set aside.

The Supreme Court's decision, written by Justice Hugo L. Black, created a sensation in the Palmetto Country. It said in part, "The record develops a

47 .... CHAIN GANG.
Chain gang, Temple Terrace. Toward the end of the century, after several decades of disfavor, the chain gang was revived in the hope that it would stem the rising crime rate. State Library and Archives of Florida.

sharp conflict—the dragnet methods of arrest on suspicion without warrant, and the protracted questioning and cross—questioning of these ignorant young colored tenant farmers by state officers and other white citizens, in a fourth-floor jail room, where as prisoners they were without friends, advisers, or counselors, and under circumstances calculated to break the strongest nerves and stoutest resistance.

"For five days they were subjected to interrogations culminating in Saturday's all-night examination. Over a period of five days they steadily refused to confess and disclaimed any guilt. The very circumstances surrounding their questioning, without any formal charges having been brought, were such as to fill them with terror and frightful misgivings.

"To permit human lives to be forfeited upon confessions thus obtained would make of the Constitutional requirement of due process of law a meaningless symbol. No higher duty, no more solemn responsibility rests upon this court than that of translating into living law and maintaining this Constitutional shield, deliberately planned and inscribed for the benefit of every human being subject to our Constitution—of whatever race, creed, or persuasion."

But new indictments were obtained and hearings held. The first of the new indictments was dismissed because no Negroes served on the grand jury. A second grand jury was drawn from a panel which included the names of three Negroes; two of them were excused "for cause," and the eighteen-man jury was completed before the name of the third Negro was reached. In 1942 local lynch law still seemed determined to find a way.

Just as the Daddy Mention tales lighten the monotony of life in a cell, so do the convicts' songs relieve the drudgery of work on the chain gang. Reflecting many aspects of prison like in the region, these songs afford convicts their sole expression of protest.

The following selections from the convicts' songbag are to be heard all over the Palmetto Country, and doubtless in other regions of America. The verses of the first song have the familiar "Lord, Lord" refrain common to the John Henry classics and other Negro work songs. If the whole song has a name, no two singers will agree upon it. One convict declares simply that it is their

CHAIN GANG THEME SONG

Wha'd you do, Boy, to get so long?
Wha'd you do, Boy, to get so long?
I was highway robbin, Lord, I know I was wrong.
Lord, Lord, know I was wrong.

I asked Mister Police to turn me loose,
I asked Mister Police to turn me loose,
But he said, I gon turn you every way but loose.
Lord, Lord, every way but loose.

OR: *I said, I got no money, but a good excuse,*
Lord, Lord, a good excuse.

I'm gonna drink my likker every place I go,
I'm gonna drink my likker every place I go,
Cause it makes me feel good from my head to my toe,
Lord, Lord, from my head to my toe.

I'm so bad I don't never want to be good,
I'm so bad I don't never want to be good,
I wouldn't go to heaven, even if I could,
Lord, Lord, if I could.

They say I'm a poor lost boy, Lord,
They say I'm a poor lost boy, Lord,
Lost for evermore,
Lord, Lord, lost for evermore.

But I'm goin to live anyhow, Lord,
But I'm goin to live anyhow, Lord,
Until I die,
Lord, Lord, till I die.

I told my Baby not to worry a-tall,
I told my Baby not to worry a-tall,
Cause I'm gonna go to heaven or not at all,
Lord, Lord, or not at all.

Oh, looka yonder: hot boilin sun turning over,
Oh, looka yonder: hot boilin sun turning over,
And it won't go down,
Lord, Lord, won't go down.

I asked the Capm, What's the time of day?
I asked the Capm, What's the time of day?
But he shook his head and sadly walked away,
Lord, Lord, sadly walked away.

This old hammer, Lord,
This old hammer, Lord,
Gets heavier and heavier,
Lord, Lord, heavier and heavier.

But I'm gonna lay it, Lord,
But I'm gonna lay it, Lord,
To save my hide and feet,
Lord, Lord, to save my hide and feet.

I don't want no cornbread nor no molasses,
I don't want no cornbread nor no molasses,
For supper-time,
Lord, Lord, supper-time.

Ev'ry mail-day I gets a letter,
Ev'ry mail-day I gets a letter,
Sinnin son, come home,
Lord, Lord, son come home.

But this old chain gang, Lord,
But this old chain gang, Lord,
Aint gonna let me go,
Lord, Lord, aint gonna let me go.

I'm gonna write one more letter to the Govnor,
I'm gonna write one more letter to the Govnor,
About my time,

Lord, Lord, 'bout my time.

Old Capm Bill from Campbell Hill,
Old Capm Bill from Campbell Hill,
Always mean to a nigger, and always will,
Lord, Lord, always will.

OR: *That's one man I'd like to kill.*

My Capm's a mighty big man,
My Capm's a mighty big man,
He the biggest man ever I see,
But I don't bar him,
Lord, Lord, don't bar him.

My Capm's got a big gun that shoots mighty long,
My Capm's got a big gun that shoots mighty long,
But Capm, I'm gonna run,
Lord, Lord, run by sun-down.

Did you hear bout the chain gang breakin up in Georgia?
Did you hear bout the chain gang breakin up in Georgia?
I'm goin back home,
Lord, Lord, goin back home.

GREAT BIG BARS

Capm took me to the phone and rung that bell,
The wagon come and I begun to catch hell;
I didn't have nobody to stand my bail,
So now I'm in this broken-down jail.

The Day is hot and my stripes do stick,
Please, Capm, don't use that trick,
Of makin us niggers get in the ditch.

Water me from the limerock,
So I won't need the Doc;
Branch water I cannot drink,
Cause it makes my body stink.

Capm gotta shotgun, and he tryin to play bad,
But I'm goon run if he make me mad.

Capm got a owl-head, just like mine,
If he beats me to the trigger, I won't mind dyin.

If I'd a knowed the Capm was bad,
I wouldn't a sold that Special I had.

Bed is hard,
Work is too;
Beans all week,
Sunday—stew.

Great big bars,
Cast iron locks;
If I tries to leave,
I'll get the box.

Tell me how long I gotta wait—
Or is I gotta do a little hesitate?

SOUTH ON THE RANGE

When you wore your dewlap,
Your long swinging dewlap,
And I wore my big bass ring;
When you caressed me,
'Twas heaven that blessed me,
Breath and eyes and everything.

Few folks outside the Palmetto Country know that it is cow country. Not only cattle, but horses and swine were introduced by the first Spanish explorers, and ranches were flourishing on the Florida peninsula at least 250 years before the Wild West became cattle domain. Today there are 1,500,000 beef and dairy cattle in the state—more than there are in Wyoming.

All parts of the region raise some cattle, but the verdant Kissimmee Valley north of Lake Okeechobee is the center of the industry. In Kissimmee, the cow capital, it is said that no one is recognized as a bona-fide citizen who doesn't wear a broad-brimmed hat; and the high-school football team is called the Kissimmee Kowboys. Arcadia, farther south, is another important cow town; until 1886 it went by the un-Arcadian name of Tater Hill Bluff.

The first herds to be brought into the region were communally owned and multiplied under a five-year ban against butchering. Though the

Spanish in Florida showed little interest in ranching; the British in Georgia were exporting beef and pork as early as 1775. But it was the Indians who proved to be the most capable herdsmen in the Palmetto Country. With foundation stock obtained by costly barter, they soon developed large herds. Especially fine stock was owned by the Miccosukees in the Alachua area, and their chief was called Cuscowilla, the Cow-keeper.

The refugee Negro slaves and Maroons also proved adept at cattle raising, and the memory of their prosperity still irks some white folk. George Dacy, in his *Four Centuries of Florida Ranching,* says, "The Negro Fort became a haven for rustlers and robbers and a center of terrorism. It was the only place on the American mainland where Negroes ever established a free and independent domain. White the fort endured, it was a center of iniquity." However, he added, "But those who thought that cattle stealing

48.........PENNED CATTLE.
   Men with penned cattle, Kissimmee, Florida 1946. The Spanish brought domesticated cattle to Florida, Native Americans developed herds, and Cracker pioneers took over the cattle industry. State Library and Archives of Florida.

would end with the destruction of the Negro Fort were as wrong as a right shoe on a left foot."

With the annexation of Florida to the United States there was a rapid influx of American cattlemen. Together with the slavers, they were responsible for many of the gross betrayals and injustices which brought on the Seminole Wars. They even organized their own Independent Mounted Volunteers to fight the Indians—especially those who owned cattle and occupied range land. When the Seminoles finally agreed to emigrate, it was with the understanding that their herds would be restored to them in the West.

Georgia, Alabama, and the Carolinas were complaining of overstocking by 1850, and during the following decade many cattlemen in those states drove their herds down into Florida. The remaining Seminole chieftains had voted to give up cattle raising to keep peace, so the newcomers took over their ranges and became the cattle kings of the peninsula.

Even before 1850 these cattlemen were supplying the Cuban market, shipping their herds from Tampa and Punta Rassa. Because of its wild venison-like flavor, the Cubans preferred the region's beef to all other. With the outbreak of the Civil War the Federal blockade put an end to the Cuban trade, and the Palmetto Country became a principal source of supply for the Confederate armies.

One of the early cattle kings was Jake Summerlin, who got his start in the business by trading twenty Negro slaves, worth $1,500 each, for 6,000 steers. He was appointed Confederate commissary-sergeant at Tampa, and during the first three years of the war sold 25,000 cattle to the Confederacy for depreciated Confederate currency.

Realizing the futility of this, Summerlin, upon the completion of his contract in 1863, formed a partnership with Captain Donald McKay, who owned a sidewheeler, the *Scottish Chief*. Summerlin loaded the *Scottish Chief* with 600 cattle, and McKay, piloting his ship through the shoal "graveyard waters" of the Florida Keys, slipped through the Federal blockade and landed the cattle in Cuba. For them he received top prices in gold—worth much more than Confederate script. McKay converted the gold into a cargo of wheat flour, bacon, sugar, salt, and tobacco. Meanwhile Summerlin sent word all over South Florida that a boatload of contraband commodities would soon be offered for sale at the mouth of the

Caloosahatchee River.

When the *Scottish Chief* arrived it was met by a large gathering of settlers, some of whom had been traveling a week by oxcart to get there. Summerlin—who knew everyone by their first names—conducted the sale. Wheat flour sold for the equivalent of $125 per barrel, and sugar brought forty dollars per sack. The buyers simply promised to deliver a specified number of cattle at Boca Grande in time for the next trip. Summerlin & McKay carried on this lucrative trade for the duration and not once did a Federal ship even sight the *Scottish Chief*.

The Reconstruction years from 1865 to 1870 were hard on the cattlemen. But then Cuba began ordering cattle again, and 165,000 head were shipped in the following decade. In addition to beef cattle, quite a number of wild Florida bulls were sold to Spain and Latin America for bull-fighting. Stock sold in Cuba was usually paid for in gold Spanish doubloons worth about $15.75 each. These coins were so heavy it was almost safe to leave them stacked on a shelf. For a long time there was no bank in South Florida, and the ranchers kept as much as $10,000 in gold in "gourd safeboxes" in their homes.

Frederic Remington, the noted writer and painter of Western scenes, visited the ranges of the Palmetto Country in 1895 and reported: "The poor little cattle, no bigger than donkeys wander half starved and horribly emaciated in search of the tough wire grass." These scrub cattle, which owe their poor qualities to undernourishment, premature breeding, and inbreeding, were recognized as a distinct type even before 1825. Often weighing much less than 500 pounds, these ramble-boned creatures manage to put on a little flesh during spring and summer, but by the end of winter they become bovine prototypes of the wild razorback hogs, and are so scrawny "you can hang your hat on their hips."

Several centuries of natural selection have not gone for naught, however. The breed is blessed with the stamina to cover range so sparse that heavier blooded stock literally walk themselves to death trying to find enough to eat. In addition, these natives have a great deal of woods-sense; they can travel through thickets of saw palmetto without lacerating their legs, they know how to sidestep rattlesnakes, keep out of gopher holes, avoid bogging down, wade neck deep after water hyacinths, and perform many other practical feats.

In describing the cracker cowboys, Remington wrote: "Two emaciated ponies pattered down the street, bearing wild-looking individuals whose hanging hair, drooping hats, and generally bedraggled appearance would remind you at once of the Spanish moss which hangs so quietly and help-lessly to the limbs of the oaks." So far as appearances go, this description still holds good for cracker cowboys—but they have never been quiet or helpless. They dress much more simply than their Western counterparts, and often their only distinguishing mark is a broad-brimmed, half-bushel pumpkin hat.

P. E. Lehman, a writer of cowboy stories, recently declared in *Travel* magazine, "In cowpunching and horsemanship the Florida cowboys are the peers of the men who ride the range from Wyoming to Texas." Cracker cowboys like King Kong Smith, Hub Boney, Top Barlow, and Dusty Dolan

49 ....REMINGTON DRAWING OF FLORIDA COWBOYS.
Frederic Remington drawing of Florida cowboys included in an article entitled "Cracker Cowboys of Florida" published in Harpers's New Monthly magazine, volume 91, issue 543, August 1895. State Library and Archives of Florida.

50 .... KING KONG SMITH.
King Kong Smith was one of Florida's best known cowboys and a familiar figure at rodeos around the state. State Library and Archives of Florida.

have sometimes defeated national champions from the West in rodeo competition. Rodeos are held annually at Arcadia and Kissimmee, attracting some 10,000 spectators. The programs follow the traditional round of roping, bronco-busting, and steer-riding, with whip-cracking, wild-cow milking, and cow-girl relay racing thrown in. Cracker cowboys generally subscribe to the maxim that "There aint no horse that can't be rode; there aint no rider that can't be throwed."

Between branding and penning seasons the cowboy's daily routine of twelve to fourteen hours of driving, herding, and mending fence is diversified by splitting rails, mending gear, laundering saddle blankets, skinning deceased inmates of the "hospital corral," and gathering palmetto fans to thatch bunkhouses and stables. Besides incidental joking, the cowboy's recreation is provided by weddings, funerals, and an occasional cow-camp frolic.

Like the *vaquero* of South America, the Palmetto Country cowboy uses a rawhide whip in herding. From twelve to eighteen feet long and costing from five dollars to twenty dollars, these plaited whips are mounted on hardwood handles from ten to eighteen inches in length. Their loud musket-like cracks drive the cattle in the desired direction, and only rarely do the whips actually touch the cattle. Augmenting the sound of the whips are the shrill cow-whoops emitted by the herders. Herd dogs and catch dogs, "generally a cross with about thirty percent bulldog and the rest common cur," have been widely used, but catch dogs have fallen into disfavor since it was learned that the wounds made by their teeth were a source of screw-worm infection.

At roundup time the cowboys used to co-operate with each other, herding their owners' cattle together into cow-pens. Most of the cattle bore their owners' brands, and the cowboys were so skillful at selecting the proper calves by their similarity to their dams that there was seldom an argument on that score.

In the old days tremendous herds of cattle, often extending several miles, were driven to the market or shipping place. These picturesque drives resembled those of the Western plains, except for the terrain covered. In the Palmetto Country, cowmen must constantly cope with dense woods, boggy marshes, and deep rivers. The drives were accompanied by an oxcart which carried the equipage. The teamster, who also served as cook, drove his beasts with a special ox-whip—a twelve foot lash on an eight-foot staff. Walking to the left of the cart, he swung the whip back over his shoulder and whipped it forward to crack near the ears of the oxen, scaring them into a temporary trot.

Oxen were used, rather than mules, because they could better withstand the attacks of horseflies, which were so numerous that their swarms could be heard before they were seen. Upon being attacked by flies the cattle would bunch themselves and whip their tails in unison, and the same procedure was followed in fighting mosquitoes at night.

Standard fare on the drives was fresh meat, hot biscuits, grits, and coffee. A steer was usually killed on the second day out, and after that it was up to the cook to bag deer, turkey, or other wild game. During dry season the riders drank from alligator holes. These supported clumps of green maiden cane, and when the cowboys sighted this cane they could usually find water by digging from eighteen to thirty inches. Camp was pitched in

51 .... LYKES BROTHERS.
The Lykes brothers helped transform Florida while building their dynasty. They are, standing from left, James, John, Frederick and Lipscomb, and sitting, Dr. Howell T., Thompson and Joseph. State Library and Archives of Florida.

the open, and in rainy weather the men slept with their heads and shoulders under the cart, and covered their bodies with palmetto fans.

Cattle Kings

The pioneer ranchers founded a cow-country dynasty that has fallen into

52........FLORIDA REPRESENTATIVE IRLO BRONSON.
Portrait of Florida Representative Irlo Bronson from Kissimmee, Osceola County, 1947. State Library and Archives of Florida.

the hands of their sons. The cattlemen have made their occupation traditional by creating a brand for their sons at birth, and parents, friends, and relatives customarily present the youngsters with calves as birthday and Christmas gifts. And so by the time the boys are old enough to ride they have herds of their own to manage.

Today the seven Lykes brothers are reputedly the largest cattle owners in the region, with 100,000 head in Florida, 15,000 in Cuba, and additional herds in Texas. Some 50,000 Florida cattle owners have herds of 100 or less, while another 10,000 cattlemen have herds with from 101 to 25,000 head or more. The total industry investment of $155,000,000 pays a profit of from ten to fifteen per cent. Beef raising on a sizeable scale has definitely become a rich man's enterprise; according to the agricultural agent for Osceola County, no less than $50,000 for cattle and land is sufficient for a good start.

Irlo Bronson, descendant of three generations of ranchers, owner of 10,000 cattle, and treasurer of the Florida Cattlemen's Association, has this to say regarding the opportunity for a cow hand to work his way to the top: "Some good cow hands work up to be foremen, but only a small minority make the long leap from puncher to rancher. The lure of range life, however, holds them in the cow country. They ride as long as they can sit saddles, then turn to cooking, driving trucks, or working as handy men around the ranches or stockyards."

Many fabulous stories are told about the exploits of the oldtimers. For example, there was Zibe King, the beef baron of South Florida who stood six feet six in his stockings, weighed 225 pounds, and could out-eat all competitors. Zibe didn't "rile" easily, but once when a wild steer attacked him he swung a haymaker from the floor, striking the 600-pound animal near the heart and killing it instantly. On the other hand, there was the time when Manatee County couldn't pay its schoolteachers, and Zibe handed out enough gold to pay their salaries for six months.

Zibe was never known to be beaten at stud poker. When the card sharps of Savannah got wind of the Florida cattle king named King who had plenty of money and a hankering for cards, they packed their kits and started south. Zibe's former storekeeper tells of the procession of dapper gamblers who inquired for Zibe; he would direct them to the ranch house, and after some hours they would return, broke and dejected. The storekeeper had standing orders from Zibe to advance the gamblers enough money to take them back where they came from.

Zibe liked to tell this story about one of his cow hunters named Bone Mizell. Bone was a heavy drinker, and one night when he was utterly inebriated some of the boys left him lying in a cemetery, and one of them concealed himself near by to observe Bone's awakening. After many hours Bone finally sat up, looked around and exclaimed, "I'll be danged if it aint Judgment Day, and me the first one up!"

53.........Legendary Cracker Cowboy Bone Mizell.
Portrait of Cracker Cowboy Bone Mizell painted in1895 by artist Frederic Remington in De Soto County. Special Collection, Univeristy of South Florida Library.

One of Zibe's sons, Bet King, is a folk character in his own right. For one thing, it is said that his teeth are filled with diamonds instead of gold. It is also said that when Bet attended Stetson University at DeLand, Florida, he took a horse from the stable and rode it so hard the animal dropped dead under him. Still another story records Bet's way with Negroes. While on a cattle drive, ravenous Bet is said to have yelled to the colored cook, "Boy, if you don't hurry up and scramble them eggs, you gonna have to finish em in hell!"

Another storied pioneer cowman is Jessie Hope, who in 1940 was still riding the range at the age of eighty. Hope began herding cattle in 1876 when he was fifteen years old. In 1878 he was driving cattle from Valdosta (Georgia) to Tampa for shipment to Havana. In those days, he says, the cattle were "wilder than wildcats," and would stampede at the crack of a stick. Sometimes a "rambunctious" herd would keep him from unsaddling for five days and nights. Cow punchers with their own horses were then paid $1.50 or less per day, and had to provide their own rations and horse feed.

Once when Hope was fording a herd across the Suwannee River he swam after a steer that was trying to escape. A big 'gator came lunging after him, so he scrambled up on the steer's back. The 'gator whammed the steer with his tail, the steer sank like a rock, and Hope is said to have broken all records swimming ashore.

On another occasion Hope tackled a bear cub barehanded; the cub turned out to be older than it had first appeared to be, and "chawed" off one of Hope's fingers before he subdued it. "Cubby" grew up to be the unofficial mascot of Brooksville. One of his tricks was to drink a bottle of beer, pretend to be intoxicated, and stage a mock attack on the person nearest at hand. One time the boys in the saloon secretly gorged Cubby on a bucket of beer, and then asked Hope to stage the bottle-of-beer trick. Hope obliged, and the genuinely intoxicated Cubby attacked him so ferociously that he had to be rescued. Cubby had another cute trick of terrifying strangers by charging headlong at them—and then extending his paw for a handshake.

One day Hope returned from cow hunting to find that Cubby had spilt a fifty-pound pail of lard on the kitchen floor and rolled in it, then ripped open a sack of sugar and rolled in that, then climbed the stairs and into the guest room bed. Hope sat down and wrote this note to a neighbor who wanted the bear, "Come and get Cubby; he's yours."

The hardiness of the pioneer ranchers is portrayed in a story about Bob Whidden. He had ridden from his home in Arcadia to Crabgrass at the mouth of the St. Johns River, where he covered another fifty miles rounding up a herd he had purchased. Upon reaching camp at dusk he received word that his wife was seriously ill. Saddling a fresh horse, he set out for home in a heavy rain. He tried a short cut, got lost, and at dawn came out at Fort Bassinger after traveling seventy miles. Stopping for a cup of coffee, he happened to set in a bed of fleas, which served to keep him awake during the rest of his journey. By loping his horse two-thirds of the way he made the total of 220 miles in thirty hours. Upon arriving he found his wife rocking contentedly on the front porch—she had been ill, but had speedily recovered. After a night's rest, Whidden rode back to Crabgrass to drive home his herd.

The early ranchers were not only hardy, but were often eccentric. One Irving Lockler hid his gold in hollow logs rather than entrust it to banks. After he had lost some $10,000 in this way, he sent one of his sons to a school in North Florida for the primary purpose of letting the boy hold the money and send it back as needed.

Polk County ranchers tell a bizarre story about Tappan Mann, who once needed $1,300 to swing a cattle deal. Mann obtained the money by mortgaging his home, herd, and ranch to a neighboring rancher. This rancher coveted Mann's property, and so offered to pay a cowboy to kill him. The cowboy "reckoned as how" if the property was worth a $1,300 mortgage, it was worth the same amount to kill Mann. So he demanded and got $1,300 in advance to do the job. But instead of killing Mann he gave him the money, and Mann used it to liquidate the mortgage.

Another strange tale is told about William B. Hooker, a cattle king who built the first large residence in Tampa. His wife died soon after its completion, and he married a Mrs. Cathcart from Ocala, who already had children of her own. Her children were not at all congenial with his children, so he had two sets of stairs built outside the house. The Cathcart children used the east stair and the Hooker children the west, while he and his wife used the inner stairway.

The Kissimmee cow country has also produced Hughlette Wheeler, the noted sculptor of thoroughbred horses and cow ponies. A native of Fort Christmas and the son of a cattle-raising family, Wheeler is best known for his statue of Will Rogers on horseback.

Though there are no dude ranches in the Palmetto Country, some of the modern cattle kings have ranch houses no less palatial than those of the Hollywood cowboys.

Hungry Land

Cracker cattlemen have taken for granted a limited amount of cattle stealing by people who need meat to eat, but anyone who rustles for profit does so at the risk of his life. Though the legal penalty is five years' imprisonment, it is one of the folkways of cattlemen to take the law into their own hands and exact the death penalty.

Backwoodsmen once made a practice of stealing unbranded calves, hiding them in remote swamps for about six months, and then bringing them out for sale—sometimes to their rightful owners. This sort of petty rustling was especially prevalent around the 'Glades, where "boats don't leave no trails." Halpatiokee Swamp (*Indian*: alligator water) near Fort Pierce was long a rustlers' hideout, and the adjacent territory is still know as "The Hungry Land."

Most likely candidates for rustling are unbranded calves and cattle, called "mavericks" in the West, but, for 150 years more or less, known as "hairydicks" in the Palmetto Country.

Rustling was especially widespread after the Civil War. Cattle buyers from neighboring states even complained that there was no profit in buying Florida cattle, because the original owners would send out their cowhands to steal back some of the cattle before they could be driven a safe distance away.

Big-time rustlers sometimes undertook the difficult job of changing brands, but usually they hurried their stolen herds to Tampa or some other town where "hot beef" could be disposed of at low prices. An epidemic of rustling broke out in the Arcadia section in 1890, when a quartet of rustlers got as far as Titusville with 200 stolen cattle. A posse of swift-riding cattlemen overtook them, shot two, and lynched two. Lynchings conducted by cattlemen were often characterized by a certain grim solemnity;

the rustler was stood in an oxcart with a noose around his neck, a cowman cricked his whip, and the oxen moved ponderously forward, leaving the victim suspended from a moss-bearded live oak.

Juries frequently endorsed such killings. On one occasion in Hernando County (Florida) a white man's body, with a bullet hole through the head, was found crumpled over the body of a stolen hog. A coroner's jury rendered the verdict that "the hog met death at the hands of parties unknown, and the man died from a wound which he received by falling on the hog's tusks."

One South Florida rancher estimates that he and his friends lost nearly 3,000 cattle between 1891 and 1896. In the latter year a band of rustlers ran off 300 steers in De Soto County. By tying blankets around their horses' hoofs, a posse of ranchers took a short cut across the Canoe Creek bog and came up with the rustlers in Polk County. Those of the rustlers who were not killed in the ensuing gun battle were sentenced five years for cattle-stealing and five years for changing brands. This discouraged large-scale rustling for a time.

But with the advent of Prohibition a number of cow-hands became bootleggers, and when that occupation became overcrowded, or when they needed ready cash to finance their operations, they often used their trucks to rustle cattle. When Prohibition came to an end, some of these men began to devote themselves entirely to rustling. Cattlemen offered a reward of $250 for evidence to convict rustlers; when this failed they oiled up their shooting irons and hid among their herds. An undetermined number of rustlers were killed and left in palmetto thickets for the buzzards.

In spite of such drastic treatment, rustling has not entirely disappeared. As late as 1940 several men were caught and sentenced for mechanized rustling.

Jackpot Herds

In the Palmetto Country a herd of mixed cattle is called a jackpot—and, taken as a whole, that is what the herds of the region are. Also in cracker cow-jargon, a bow-wow is a runty steer; a dogey or yellow-hammer is a small steer suitable only for canning; and a counterfeit is an animal whose markings suggest good stock, but whose figure does not.

The campaign to introduce better cattle blood to the region has been long and hectic. The 7,500 pure-bred bulls now in Florida represent an increase of 2,727 per cent since the tick-eradication program of 1936; prior to that time few pure-bred animals could survive on the peninsula longer than a year. The scrub cattle, representing a mixture of Andalusian Spanish stock and British colonial breeds, are rapidly being replaced by a wide variety of hybrid animals happily combining the beefy qualities of their sires with the endurance and woods-sense of their dams. Today at least thirty per cent of the region's cattle show evidences of improved breeding.

Not a few of these improved cattle resemble the hump-shouldered sacred cows of India—and with good reason, as they have 50 per cent more or less of Brahman (Zebu) blood. The first Brahman cattle were introduced to the region in 1849. Coming from a tropical climate, they are well adapted to

54 .... KING OF THE BRAHMANS.
   King of the Brahmans, "Emperor Jones VIII" selected as grand champion bull of the 3rd annual show of registered Brahman cattle in Ocala. State Library and Archives of Florida.

the Palmetto Country; heat-resistant and air-conditioned, they sweat as much as horses.

When bred to native stock the offspring are large and mature rapidly, are wide rangers and good mothers. Some cattlemen complain that if these hybrids are again crossed with Brahmans the resulting cattle are shy about breeding. The preferred procedure is to cross the Brahman-native hybrids with some heavy-beef breed.

The Most popular beef breeds in the Palmetto Country are the Angus, Hereford, Shorthorn, Red Poll, and Devon. One rancher has named his Angus bulls after such Seminole chieftains as Osceola, Micanopy, King Payne, Billy Bowlegs, and Seecoffee. Native beef is rapidly improving in quality, and less and less do the markets and restaurants of the region advertise "prime Western meats." During tourist season the "Gold Coast" of Miami and Palm Beach orders most of the prime native carcasses, while St. Petersburg, Tampa, and Sarasota can afford only the short loin prime cuts. A surprising amount of low-grade beef is consumed each winter by

55 .... YOUNG KAY DAVIS WITH CHAMPION STEER "JACK".
Kay Davis with her grand champion aberdeen-angus steer in Quincy, Florida, 1946. "Jack" weighed 885 pounds and sold for $1.15 per pound. State Library and Archives of Florida.

the thousand or more racing greyhounds which come to Florida.

During the drought of 1935, thousands of Western longhorns were bought by the U.S. Government and shipped to the Florida range to recuperate before being canned for relief distribution. Untold hundreds of them, however, mysteriously vanished before canning time. Folks in the Palmetto Country don't like their beef canned, anyway.

Tick Fever

One of the great drawbacks to the region's cattle industry has been the Texas fever tick. Georgia and Alabama carried out successful tick-eradication programs, and protected themselves by a strict quarantine against Florida cattle. Georgia even erected a "tick fence" along her Florida border—two four-strand barbed-wire fences fifteen feet apart, and armed Georgia cattlemen patrolled the fence in twenty-mile beats.

For a time Florida tried a local-option system of eradication, but this proved useless and the 1923 Legislature enacted a compulsory cattle-dipping law. For reasons hard to understand, many of the state's leading cat-

56 .... CATTLE DIPPED FOR TICK FEVER.
First cattle shipped from Kissimmee after compulsory dipping, 1923. State Library and Archives of Florida.

tlemen strongly opposed the law. In 1926 their opposition took the form of dynamiting fifteen dipping vats and taking potshots at and wounding several representatives of the State Livestock Sanitary Board. When the state persisted, obstinate cattlemen sold 70,000 cattle at giveaway prices to avoid ducking them in the arsenic baths.

Finally, all cattle in the State were dipped once every fourteen days for a period of fourteen months, and the quarantine was lifted in 1928. But in 1935 fever broke out in South Georgia again, and was traced to cattle brought in from Florida. The quarantine was hastily reapplied. Investigation revealed that several counties harbored a species of tropical tick which, unlike the Texas tick, also thrives on deer. This meant that it could not be eradicated without also eradicating the deer in the infected areas. This discovery led to the quarantine being extended to cover racehorses and dogs, whose owners went quietly mad as the Northern racing season approached.

When the Legislature passed laws enabling the infected counties to kill all deer within their boundaries, a Deer Protective Association obtained an injunction from the State Supreme Court to halt the slaughter. Now thoroughly sold on the merits of tick eradication, the cattlemen also appealed to the Supreme Court, and the injunction was dissolved. The slaughter proceeded and the quarantine was lifted. By the end of 1939 Florida had spent three million dollars on tick eradication, a good part of which was paid to cattlemen at the rate of three cents per head for permission to dip their cattle.

To Burn or Not to Burn

Early visitors to the Palmetto Country were astonished by the omnipresent brush fires of winter and early spring. Their acrid smoke filled the air, turning the sunsets red and mixing with the blankets of fog which spread over the lowlands. At night their glow could be seen in every direction. In 1879 the Florida Legislature passed a law providing that fires should be set only between February 15 and March 31, and that two days' notice be given to all persons living within one mile of the site; but the law has never been enforced, and the fires are still burning—under the very noses of the fire towers which dot the region.

57.........DEER HUNTING PARTY.
    Deer hunting party, near Sebring. Note Seminole guide. State Library and Archives of Florida.

The practice of burning the range to provide better pasturage is an ancient one. The American Indians traditionally set fire to the Western plains for the benefit of the bison and antelope. The custom has always been popular with the cattlemen of the Palmetto Country, who believe that burning is necessary to remove the heavy over-brush so the grass can find living space. Conservationists have long opposed this belief with the contention that burning destroys the valuable grasses, not to mention trees, soil fertility, wildlife, and insect food for fishes. The argument has waxed hottest, however, between owners of timber land and cattlemen who insist on firing the open range, including said timber land. Not infrequently feuds and bloodshed have resulted. As an early traveler in the region observed, "The Indians took much better care of this country than the white man does—they never allowed fires to run wild."

Cattlemen and others interested in promoting the Palmetto Country have long maintained that it offers the ideal combination of growing pines and grazing cattle under them. Recent experiments have shown, however, that although fires often stunt the growth of trees as much as ten years, they are decidedly beneficial in cattle raising. The U. S. Bureau of Animal Husbandry has reported that cattle grazed on burnt-over pasture have gained 44.4 per cent more weight than cattle on unburnt pasture. Thus the old question has been settled, but not the problem of getting the cattlemen to confine their fires to their own land. One effect of the anti-fire campaign has been that, instead of firing their pastures, some wealthy ranchers are giving them motorized haircuts at 30 miles per hour.

Rolling Stock

> *Sittin on a cow-horse*
> *The whole day long,*
> *Thinkin of those good times*
> *All past and gone.*

Time has not failed to bring progress to the Palmetto Country's cattle industry, and today it rolls on wheels. Big-time ranchers with farflung ranges use trucks to carry their horses from one range to another, and the cowboys follow with the equipment in small pickup trucks. Even small-time ranchers make use of handy two-wheel horse trailers.

Mechanization has also done away with the long overland cattle drives which caused such an enormous loss in weight and sales value. The cattle are now packed in trucks and driven to co-operative markets; this is a great advantage to the ranchers, who were formerly at the mercy of cattle buyers who visited their ranches and made them offers. Co-operative packing plants are also being established in various parts of the region.

The Spirit of Joe Stalin

The institution of private property, with its symbol and guardian, the fence, has had a bloody career in the Deepest South. Florida's first fence-cutting law, enacted in 1868, was aimed at cattlemen who were wont to destroy any fences which interfered with the free ranging of their stock. The conflict between community interests and livestock owners' interests also found expression in editorials like the following which appeared in the

58 .... SEMINOLE COWBOY CHARLEY MICCO.
Seminole Indian cowboy Charley Micco and grandson Fred Smith on horseback at a cattle ranch, Brighton Reservation, Florida, 1950. State Library and Archives of Florida.

Quincy Herald in 1890:

"Look after your cows at night or the marshal may have them in the pound in the morning, and it will cost you a dollar apiece to get them out. Last Monday the marshal sold a hog that had been impounded to Dr. Monroe. This is the first sale under the law and more will follow. A few hogs still defy the law and roam at large on some of our streets."

In 1903 the fence-cutting law was strengthened to provide a maximum penalty of ten years' imprisonment and a fine of $10.000. This time, however, the law was championed by wealthy cattlemen who had bought or leased land (usually at five cents per acre per year) and fenced it. This marked the beginning of a trend toward fenced pastures, and a corresponding change in the attitude of wealthy ranchers toward fences. Whereas they once invariably championed the open range, those who now have fenced land uphold the privileges of private *fenced* property, and at the same time continue to insist on open-range grazing privileges on unfenced land.

A fence war broke out in Polk County (Florida) in 1925, when a phosphate company fenced 10,000 acres that had been open range. Cattlemen cut the wires at night; the phosphate company replaced them. When it was cut again the company appealed to the sheriff, who warned the cattlemen that he was going to patrol the fence. One night the sheriff and his deputies came upon three men cutting the fence; the sheriff ordered them to halt, but instead they began shooting. All three fence-cutters were killed by the officers. The victims were "prominent" cattlemen, and their deaths discouraged fence-cutting for a time.

It was in 1934 that the Florida Cattlemen's Association was organized. According to Dacy, whose *Four Centuries of Florida Ranching* has been quoted, "Just as cattle bunch together to fight off horseflies, mosquitoes, and other insect pests, their owners are practically compelled to unite in a protective group." Be that as it may, the Association now boasts of being "one of the best-financed organizations in the State," and maintains a powerful legislative lobby to promote its interests.

By 1939 the increase of blooded cattle had caused an increase in fenced pastures to such an extent that when another fence war broke out in Manatee County the line-up of 1925 was reversed; this time the cattlemen took their stand inside the fence.

Dacy, unofficially stating the position of the Association, wrote; "This is a revolt of an organization which calls itself the Civil Liberties League against the legal rights of ranchers to fence previously unfenced ranges which they have purchased. The membership of this 'communistic' society consists of frog hunters, moss pickers, commercial hunters, and squatters, as well as rovers and derelicts. A group of CLLs presumable cut 25 miles of the new fence one favorable evening in 1939. The wire was completely ruined by cutting it between each post. It cost $90 per mile, or about $2,250 altogether. New wire was strung, and 14 miles of it was cut immediately. Armed riders are now patrolling the fence, and tragedies may result unless drastic suppressive measures throttle the trespasses of the CLL.

"A Committee from that body called upon one of Florida's former governors who is engaged in the cattle business and demanded that he leave the gates to his range unlocked. You can guess the forceful refusals that were made to these demands. There is no room for sit-down strikers or red-shirted objectors in Florida, even though the State is the second largest next to Georgia east of the Mississippi."

A similar and more official statement appeared in the Association's *Florida Cattleman* in 1940: "In October the editor held that a fence was prima facie evidence of private ownership and any who deliberately trespassed did so in violation of the owner's rights. If we interpret the *Polk County Democrat's* meaning correctly that they advocate violation of private property rights by those who own no property simply because they are too poor to do so, then it smells like Communism to us. We wonder what is happening to the people down in Polk County. It seems that they have taken it upon themselves to do away with private property rights. This is a generous spirit, but it sounds too much like Joe Stalin."

The charge was thrown back at the *Cattlemen* by the Fort Myers *News-Press*: "In the generous spirit of Joe Stalin, the cattlemen have turned their stock loose to graze on the public thoroughfares and State lands, to say nothing of village greens, private lawns, garden plots, and citrus groves."

Sacred Highway Cows

In most parts of the Palmetto Country, motorists are frequently confronted with signs warning: *Open Range, Beware of Cattle!* Newcomers are fortunate, particularly after nightfall, if they come upon the warning before they hit a cow. Collisions between cars and cows have nasty consequences, usually wrecking the car and injuring or killing its occupants—not to mention slaughtering the cow. A surprising number of cows bag two cars at once. Besides menacing human lives, the open range imposes upon the farmer the burdensome expense of erecting a fence to keep other people's livestock out of his crops.

During the day, cows congregate along the highways because the grass on the shoulders of the roads in the best available, and during the night they like to bed down on the pavement because of the heat it retains. Young calves are most dangerous because their actions are entirely unpredictable; alarmed by oncoming automobiles, they often dash in front of them. They also require special attention when engaged in play, or when their mothers are on the opposite side of the road. Mature cattle are somewhat more dependable; in them the laws of inertia and momentum operate with few rational interruptions. That is to say, a cow at rest has a tendency to remain at rest, and vice versa. Many folk say a motorist can prevent a cow from crossing the road by pointing a finger at it.

Bills to remove cattle from the highways have been introduced in every session of the Florida Legislature since 1931, but have always met defeat after being opposed by the Cattlemen's Association. The most recent of these measures was introduced in 1939 by Fuller Warren, popular leader of the anti-highway-cow campaign. Though Warren proved to be the life of the Legislature with his cow harangues, even his renowned wit and eloquence failed to carry the bill. Most people in the state have heard Warren speak on the subject of bovines on the boulevards. He also takes advantage of every cow-caused casualty to write letters to newspaper editors, and these pithy epistles are always printed and read with alacrity. Here are some typical examples of "Fuller's Fulminations" on "Florida's sacred highway cows," as he calls them:

"I am grateful for your fine and forthright editorial taking to task the

Junior Chamber of Commerce for making up and bedding down with the Cattlemen's Association on the question of removing cows from the public highways, after the Junior Chamber had waged such a courageous fight for so long to get these walking death traps off the roads.

"It was blandly announced that the problem was 'solving itself,' but it will never be completely solved until the Legislature and the Governor decide that the right of the citizens of Florida, and the millions of visitors to our State, not to be killed by highway cattle, is superior to the right of cattlemen to make private profit by grazing their private livestock on the public-owned, public-paid, public-traveled, public highways.

"Two young members of the Army Air Corps were killed by a highway cow last week near DeFuniak Springs. For decades, highway cows have

59 .... GOVERNOR FULLER WARREN.
Governor Fuller Warren in his office, Tallahassee, Florida, 1950. Fuller gained prominence as the legislator leading the anti-highway-cow campaign in the 1930's and '40s. State Library and Archives of Florida.

been slaughtering the civilians of Florida at the rate of about one a week, but as far as I know, this is the first time that soldiers have been killed by them. It can now be truthfully said that highway cows are sabotaging our national defense. The cattleman who insists on grazing his stock on the public highways and thereby killing American soldiers is helping Hitler just as surely as some subversive scoundrel who is actually engaged in espionage. A special session of the Legislature should be called for removing livestock from public highways, as has already been done in 39 states."

Some counties have enacted fence laws of their own. Meanwhile Warren carries on with his statewide campaign. In 1940 he ran for governor, standing most of the time on his platform plank against highway cows; in spite of his youth (he is thirty-five), he finished third in the field of eleven candidates.

The railroads traversing the region have suffered long from the extortion of exorbitant sums demanded by indignant cowmen for their "pure-bred Jerseys" killed on the tracks. In the early days these long-haired boys had a habit of suddenly dropping into the nearest railway station, and, with rifles suggestively in hand, demanding immediate compensation from the station master. If refused, they sometimes subjected the station house to a peppering of buckshot on the first dark night, and even trains were fired upon. This sort of thing soon led to the appearance of the "cow attorney," or claim adjuster. In 1899 the cattle interests succeeded in having the Florida Legislature enact laws making railroads liable for cattle killed on the tracks, and requiring the payment of double indemnity on claims not settled within sixty days. These laws remained in effect until declared unconstitutional in 1941. One of the reasons given for voiding the laws was that they did not require cattle owners to prove that the trains were operated negligently.

The Little Pigs Danced

A visitor to the Palmetto Country in 1879 wrote, "The prairies furnish sustenance for lowing herds which are captured by a song the cowboys sing resembling nothing else in the world. Where it originated none can tell, but the cattle gather from afar whenever it is sung." The magical song to which he referred is not known, but cracker cowboys often sing songs of the Western range, as well as some of local origin. Though the native lyrics lack the narrative quality of the Western ballads, they have a flavor peculiarly their own. The following are typical.

MY CINDY

I cannot marry my Cindy;
I'll tell you the reason who:
She's got so many relations,
They'd make the biscuits fly.

I cannot marry my Cindy;
I'll tell you the reason why:
Her neck's so long and skinny,
She will never die.

Chorus;
Apple like a cherry,
Cherry like a rose;
Oh, how I love my Cindy,
No God Amighty knows.

TURKEY HAMMOCK

Way down yonder
On Red Bug Branch,
The same old sun fiddled
And the little pigs danced.

Alligator hollered,
The panther squalled,
To see that nigger
Knock a hole in the wall.

Raised in the backwoods,
Suckled by a bear,
Got nine rows of jaw-teeth,
Got a right to rear.

BIG JIM IN THE BARROOM

My mama told me
Long time ago

Quit all my rowdy ways,
And drink no more.

Played cards in England,
Throwed dice in Spain;
Goin back to England
To play cards again.

Don't dance her down, boys,
Don't dance her down;
Don't dance her down, boys;
Her old man's in town.

Chorus:
Big Jim in the barroom,
Little Jim in jail;
Big Jim in the barroom,
Drinkin good ale.

Which reminds us that curb-service bars, where cowmen were served whiskey without having to dismount, originated in the Palmetto Country years before they became popular in the West, But now it's time to say:

Put the bottle on the horse,
And the saddle on the shelf;
If you want any more singin,
You can sing to yourself.

Hog Wild

Ole sow in the corner putting down bread,
Pigs outdoors a-combin their heads;
I drove that ole sow into the house,
And there had backbone, chitlins and souse.

There is an old story about a cracker who lived in a shack in the pine barrens of South Georgia. He had a little land cleared for farming, and considered himself especially fortunate because a herd of tasty wild razorbacks ran "hog wild" through the woods and sustained themselves on the nut-like pine mast. One day a Northerner happened to visit him, and suggested that he get rid of the razorbacks and start raising Poland China hogs.

"Why should I git shet of them hawgs?" asked the cracker suspiciously. "Aint costin me nary a cent to raise em."

"But think of the time!" exclaimed te Northerner. "You can fatten Poland Chinas in six months, while it takes two years for those razorbacks to get any meat on them."

The cracker expectorated with eloquent disdain. "Shucks," he said, "time don't mean a dad-blamed thing to them hawgs."

Ever since pioneer days, razorbacks have been a principal source of fresh meat for the white and Negro natives of the Palmetto Country. The first cold snap of winter ushers in "hog-killin time," and for a while there is an overabundance of fresh pork in the diets of rural natives, who are said to eat all of the pig but its squeal. The razorbacks are especially prized for

60.........RAZORBACK HOGS.
"Most dangerous animal in the Florida wilds"—razorback hogs. 'Tis said that "they will eat you alive if you mess with them!" From the Stetson Kennedy Collection.

making country-cured ham, bacon, and sausage; and all that is not consumed by the family finds a ready market in the towns and cities. An enterprising Georgia farm woman recently wrote to a friend:

"Am shore my hams would make you rudy so you wouldn't have to fret about lookin so puny. I been scared you got hookworm, as my brother looked a heap like you. We got him shet of them by eatin him right. Everybody herebouts calls me Aunt Sally, and a letter thataway will reach me."

There are two kinds of wild hogs in the United States—the native peccary of Texas, and the razorback of the Palmetto Country which, after generations of inbreeding and running wild, has reverted from what was originally domestic stock. Like the scrub cow, the razorback has been designed by nature for wide ranging in a region where food is scarce. Its proficiency as a forager has given rise to such expressions as "the root-hog-or-die-days,' meaning the Reconstruction period. The razorback's skull is low and elongated, the snout prolonged and tapering. The neck is scrawny, the back humps at the center and slopes toward the flanks. Altogether the animal has a streamlined appearance that is in keeping with its fleetness, which is almost equal to that of a horse.

Being omnivorous, the razorback seldom lacks food even during the worst seasons. An ancient cracker maxim has it that wherever razorbacks are numerous, quail and snakes are scarce. The hogs eat bird eggs, and snakes of all kinds. It is popularly believed that razorbacks are immune to the venom of rattlesnakes and moccasins. They also prey on mice, rabbits, skunks, young foxes, and other small animals. In addition to their predatory characteristics, as scavengers the razorbacks disdain no carcass, however putrid. On the vegetarian side they are fond of corn, peanuts, acorns, roots, palmetto buds, and pine mast. And as cattle king Hendry has written, "The razorback, or long-nosed wind-splitter, or Devil's right bower, as you choose to call him, rustles the marshes for wampee, a root similar to the arrow. It burns his mouth so badly it makes him squeal, yet he continue to eat and thrive on it." Folks also say that when all else fails the razorbacks eat pine knots; they also say that alligators gorge themselves on pine knots during the summer and thus keep fat all winter.

When in numbers, razorbacks are in every respect the most dangerous animals yet to be found in the Palmetto Country. Many men have had to save themselves by scampering up a tree, and even an armed or mounted man is not entirely safe. Hunters and campers must hang high in a tree everything which the swine might consider edible. Ordinary dogs are no protection, and only invite trouble, as they are the swine's pet hatred.

Cracker 'gator hunters maintain that "the best 'gator bait is a nigger or a hog." And some hunters actually lure 'gators to the surface by emitting pig-like grunts. The 'gator is indeed fond of pork, especially after he has ripened it in a mud bank. Other traditional enemies of the wild porkers are bears, pumas, and wolves. Upon occasion razorbacks have turned the tables on these formidable attackers and devoured them tooth and nail. Bears, incidentally, are still fairly numerous, some pumas are to be found in the big swamps, but wolves—except for the depression variety—are no longer present, though they were plentiful as late as 1850.

When hog-killing time rolls around the serious and often thrilling business of bringing home the bacon begins. This is usually done with the aid of a pack of catch dogs, and the men follow closely, often on horseback. The dogs capture the hogs by seizing them by an ear, throwing them, and hanging on until a man arrives with a rifle.

The most propitious time for hog-killing is said to be on a Saturday morning when the moon is in its ascendancy; hogs butchered on such a day are not supposed to dry out or be attacked by blowflies. It is also believed that boars should be castrated while the boar-sign dominates the zodiac.

Razorbacks on the open range are a far greater menace to crops than are cattle, and it is much more expensive to erect a "hog-tight" fence. Though the species is still numerous, the Florida Legislature—to put an end to the standard excuse of hog thieves—declared wild razorbacks to be nonexistent in 1937.

FISHERFOLK

Fishy, fishy bite,
Your mother said you could
Your father said you might
Fishy, fishy bite.

"The unfailing supply of marine products has kept, and at present is keeping, many settlers from a condition approaching starvation," wrote the U. S. Fish Commissioner at Pensacola in 1885. "For about one-hundred years the fishing of Florida was done mainly for home consumption. With the growth of towns, local fishing industries developed, and along the southeastern coast considerable trade in salted mullets and fresh groupers developed with Cuba. The most important fishing industries of Florida are but ten or fifteen years old; in 1880 there were 2,194 fishermen in the State. North of Tampa Bay, on either side of the peninsula, the mullet catch is sold to the nearest markets of Florida, Georgia, and Alabama. The stations are visited by many customers from the country who travel with ox-carts and carry their purchases home with them."

An interesting sidelight on fishing in those days has been recalled by John Reese, who worked on the Mulberry Grove Plantation near Jacksonville. "We used to catch hundreds of catfish in the mullet nets, and just leave them piled up on the banks. They were good alligator feed—the 'gators climbed out and had a feast of them. We wouldn't eat catfish in those days. The belief was founded on some teaching of the Old Testament. I have heard it said, 'Don't eat any fish without a scale.' But nowadays, since the preachers preach from the New Testament, you can eat catfish, eels, frogs, and even rattlesnakes."

The Palmetto Country's sub-tropical climate has made for particularly abundant aquatic life. The sea waters encircling the region contain more than 600 kinds of fishes—including twice as many edible varieties as can be found in any other part of the country. The business of catching fish constitutes one of the region's largest industries; in 1941 Florida alone had 75,000 fishermen and their catch for the year was 137,000,000 pounds.

Fishing ways vary from the native whites and blacks who take a cane pole and can of worms to fish for perch in the nearest creek, to corporations which operate everything from fishermen's quarters, commissaries, fleets of sea-going boats, docks, icing plants, trucking lines, oil and fertilizer plants, and retail markets. Associated industries deal with shrimp, oysters, sponges, turtles, crabs, crawfish ("Florida lobster"), octopi, conchs, and other marine products.

Commercial fishing engages men of many races, including crackers, Negroes, Scandinavians, and Latins. But in the Palmetto Country as else-

61 .... BOYS FISHING.
"Fishy, fishy bite, Your father said you could, Your mother said you might; Fishy, fishy bite!"
Palm, Beach. Michael Thomason photograph. State Library and Archives of Florida

where, the folkways of fishing communities tend to be alike, regardless of their racial make-up or geographic situation.

A peculiar lot are the Negroes who man the pogy (menhaden) fishing boats—some are Geechees from South Carolina, while others are from the West Indies. At the heavy work of hauling in the nets they sing characteristic songs known as sea chanteys. Usually a soloist renders the narrative lines, while the refrain is sung by the entire gang. One of their most popular chanteys tells about:

THEM JOHNSON GALS

Them Johnson gals is mighty fine gals.
  Walk around, Honey, walk around.
They's neat in the waist and has mighty fine legs.
  Walk around, Honey, walk around.
Great big legs and teenincy feet.
  Walk around, Honey, walk around.

62.........MAN CASTING NET.
   Casting nets as a method of fishing dates back to prehistoric people in Florida and is still popular today. From the Stetson Kennedy collection.

The got sumpum called Jamaica Jam.
Walk around, Honey, walk around.
Hot as cayenne pepper, but good, goddam!

Some sea chanteys are adaptations of road-gang songs, to which have been added a salty flavor.

Crackers are especially partial to fish as a food and may frequently be heard to say, "I done et so free of fish my stomach rises and falls with the tide." The old-fashioned fish-fry—where folks get together for a day's fishing and then gather on the shore to fry their catch—is one of the Palmetto Country's most typical folkways. Until prohibited by law—and even yet on dark nights—the crackers have had their own ways of obtaining abundant supplies of fresh-water fish—by dynamiting, seining, and toxic stupefaction with sawdust or berries. Their ancestors learned the berry trick from the Indians.

Sport fishing, both by regional folk and tourists, is a multimillion dollar pastime in the Palmetto Country. The business men of the region are particularly keen about this form of recreation, and perhaps a majority of them spend their vacations and/or week-ends in this manner. In fresh water, the custom is to employ a local Negro to serve as guide and to row the boat. Artificial plug lures are cast by rod and reel to catch the large-mouthed black bass, which is said to be "inch for inch and pound for pound, the gamest fish that swims." Of course, sportsmen in other regions make this same claim for other fish. The major attractions in salt-water sport fishing are the mighty tarpon—the Silver King of the angling world, sailfish, swordfish, tuna, sharks, and numerous others. Annual fishing contests are conducted by many communities, and the attendant newspaper and radio publicity receives almost as much attention as Florida's perennial bathing beauty.

Needless to say, there is a vast difference in fishing for sport and fishing for a living. Listen to what the wife of a typical commercial fisherman has to say:

"Tom works for a fish-house at Fort Pierce. In the winter he fishes along the coast, and in the summer in Lake Okeechobee. The lake fishin is best in hot weather durin the full moon; the trouts [black bass] bite extra good whenever the redbirds sing.

"The fish-house has branches at Miami, Fort Lauderdale, and Okeechobee, and takes all the fish Tom can catch. They furnish him with a boat, but he has to buy his own gasoline and nets. Sometimes it takes fifty gallons of gas for one trip. And if there is a big haul the nets are always broken. He tries to keep several nets so we can be mending the broken ones while he's usin the others. They don't last long cause the salt water rots em out; and they costs so much to buy.

"Lately Tom hasn't gotten but three cents a pound for his fish. I don't know why the wholesalers pay so little, because the very same fish sell for twenty-five cents a pound in the markets. Sometimes when there is large catches, or the weather is bad, Tom is laid off for a week or two. It is a mighty uncertain life and I wonder why people will stick to it. That is something I just can't explain. Once you get in it you just can't give it up, kind of like farmin. I know some farmers that are as poor as we are, but they keep right on farmin. When they make good crops they can't get a decent price for them; but usually they don't make much of a crop on account of the weather and bugs.

"I expect it was fishin started me on my sickness, just like it has Tom. Workin in all weathers and in the winter and at night-time like he has to do has caused him to have arthritis and rheumatism. Fishin is sure hard work, but what's a body to do that don't know nothing else? I don't want my boys to follow their daddy's trade, even if it has been in both our families for generations."

To this common complaint of hard work and low pay must be added the actual danger involved in fishing. One storm-wrought catastrophe has been recorded in a folksong, "The Lost Boys of East Bay," the original version of which was written by Harry Evans. The wind blew in October of 1894, and the fatalities occurred at St. Andrews Bay, Florida where the song is still current. It concludes:

Saddest of all is the tale I now tell,
How the storm swept Sand Island like the furies of Hell,
How each raging sea claimed its victims that day,
Those sixteen brave lads from the shores of East Bay.

Oh, that mother who's left without husband or son,
To cheer her at evening when the day's work is done!

Those kind-hearted men will go out never more,
In struggle to drive the grim wolf from the door.

Conch Talk

Conchy Joes, all they know
Is after supper to the crawls they go,
Talkin bout fish and turtle too,
Mark my word, you'll find it true.

Went a-fishin, fished all night;
Grapple got hooked, fish wouldn't bite;
Hard times, nothing to do—
Lost my grapple and mainsail too.

In South Florida there are some 5,000 Anglo-Saxons of Bahaman descent who have come to be called Conchs, probably because the conch shellfish is an important item in their diet.

Several thousand live at Key West, 1,000 along the Florida Keys, and another 1,000 at the fishing village of Riviera above West Palm Beach. Most Conchs follow their traditional occupations of fishing, sponging, turtling, or boat building, but in Key West they also hold a host of other jobs—from that of mayor on down. Any Key Wester likes being called a Conch—provided the context is not derogatory.

In some ways the story of the Conchs is typical of the region's fisherfolk, yet it also has many exceptional aspects. Their saga began in 1646 when Captain William Sayle, oft-time Governor of the Bermudas, professed to have obtained from the British Parliament a grant of one of the Bahama islands (no record of the grant has ever been found). At any rate, a company of Eleutheran Adventurers was founded in London that year with the purpose of establishing a colony in the New World "where every man might enjoy his own opinion or religion without control or question."

Captain Sayle led the Adventurers to the Bahama island which had been named Segatoo by Columbus. They changed its name to Eleuthera, but it later become known as Abaco. Thus was founded, forty-two years before Jamestown, one of the first Anglo-Saxon settlements in America. Probably

63.........KEY WEST FISHING DOCK.
Key West fishing dock. Arthur Rothstein photograph. State Library and Archives of Florida.

no colony was ever established with broader (more anarchic) concepts of freedom.

Most of the Adventurers were cockney fisherfolk, and their fishing and turtling expeditions carried them to many islands of the West Indies and along the Florida coast and Keys. At first they sold their catches at Havana, and later at Key West. Settlers in New England once became fearful of the Adventurers' welfare, and sent them a cargo of food. In return the Adventurers loaded the ship with braziletto wood, which was sold by the New Englanders and the money donated to an institution which later became Harvard University.

As time passed there came to be many Negros on Abaco, many of them runaway slaves from West Indian plantations. Later, when England abolished slavery, British ships dumped the human cargoes of captured slave ships onto Abaco and other Bahaman isles. Considerable miscegenation between the whites and blacks took place.

One of the oldest stories about how the Conchs got their name says that it was given to them when they stoutly told the British authorities that they would "eat conchs" before paying the taxes which the Crown had levied against them. As the movement for independence of the British West Indies gained momentum, many revolutionaries and religious zealots sought refuge in Abaco, contributing further to the laissez-faire propensities of the colonists.

During the American Revolution, Abaco and other Bahaman isles received a large influx of Tories from the rebelling colonies. In 1783 the British commissary-general at New York reported that "near a thousand souls" were ready to embark for Abaco, and other refugees left at the same time for Cat Island. Later in the year, eight companies of British militia were evacuated from New York and transported to the Bahamas. And no less than 1,500 British Loyalists left St. Augustine for Abaco and New Providence islands.

A popular factual legend recalls how the Bahamas were recovered from the Spanish in 1783. Major Andrew de Veaux, a provincial officer from South Carolina, sailed on his own initiative from St. Augustine with two brigs, each mounted with twelve guns and manned by "fifty reckless and desperate adventurers and a few Negroes." Arriving off Nassau at night, they slipped quietly ashore and overpowered the Spanish garrison in the fort. After daybreak they pretended to introduce a large force of men into the fort. This was done by rowing ashore with all fifty of their men, and then setting up straw dummies in the fort. The men then hid in the bottom of the landing boats, which were rowed back to the ships; out of sight on the seaward side of the vessels, the men sat upright again and rowed back to shore. This process was repeated many times, much to the apprehension of the watchful Spanish forces in the distance.

When De Veaux ordered the Spanish governor to surrender, the Governor first refused, but changed his mind when De Veaux sent a cannonball over the Governor's mansion. The Spaniards were 500 strong, had seventy cannon and six galleys. The adventurers, having captured Nassau without official British sanction, hoisted a flag with a conch shell rampant on a field of canvas. Ironically, nine days before this incident Spain signed a treaty ceding the Bahamas back to England.

64.........."TURNING TURTLES".
"Turning turtles" on the Florida Keys. Once turned, the turtles cannot right themselves, and so remain on their backs until a truck comes to pick them up. State Library and Archives of Florida.

During one such unsettled period when the ownership status of the Bahamas was in doubt, an American ship stopped at one of the smaller islands. Not knowing what flag to raise, the islanders returned the American salute by hoisting a conch shell on a pone— "and ever since then they have been called Conchs."

Another bit of "Conch talk" tells a tale of the Civil War, during which Key West enjoyed the distinction of being the only Southern city to remain in Federal hands for the duration. Many Key West Conchs served as blockade runners for the Confederacy; but with most of the Federal fleet stationed at the Island City, they had a difficult time. Altogether, 149 blockade runners were captured and brought into the harbor, and the consequent bottling up of the Gulf was undoubtedly a large factor in the ultimate defeat of the Confederate States. The story tells of a Conch blockade runner who was hailed by a Federal ship. The Conch displayed no flag, so the Federal officer demanded to know his nationality.

"Conch," replied the Conch.

Being new to the area, the Federal officer thought the Conchs must be some breed of West Indian. Anxious to avoid difficulties with any independent nation, he allowed the blockade runner to proceed.

Probably that was the closest the Conchs have ever come to achieving national identity. Yet Bahaman postage stamps continue to bear the imprint of a conch shell.

"Wreck Ashore!"

Ever since the Conchs first arrived in the Bahamas they have been identified with the salvaging of wrecked ships. As more and more ships ran afoul of the jagged reefs along the Florida Straits, the Conchs migrated to the Florida Keys, establishing their headquarters at Key West, Tavernier, Marathon, and Plantation Key.

Besides wrecking, they fished, cut mahogany, and cultivated pineapples and their favorite fruits "sours and dillies" (limes and sapodillas). The fragrant half-wild Mexican limes they grew were in such great demand as a scurvy preventive on sailing vessels that the ships were known as "lime juicers." The limes were also pickled in brine and shipped to Boston, where they were sold to children. By 1942 the Keys were supplying ninety per cent of the limes grown in the United States.

The Conch settlements on the Keys were completely isolated except by boat transportation until the completion of the Oversea Railroad in 1912, and until that time some of the natives had never seen ice. The Conchs developed a means of communicating from key to key by blowing plaintive blasts on conch-shell bugles, and it was in this way that they let it be known that a ship had gone on a reef.

The cry "Wreck ashore!" was a familiar sound in old Key West, where a close watch of the sea was kept from the miradors on the housetops. Echoed from quarter to quarter, the cry seemed to electrify the population, and the streets rapidly filled with Conchs running to their boats. There was keen competition among the owners of wrecking vessels because—according to the laws of salvage—the first captain who could get a line aboard a stranded ship was appointed wrecking master and was awarded the largest share of the spoils. Often the race of the wrecking fleet was more exciting than any regatta, as the various craft vied with one another in the teeth of heavy gales.

The accusation has often been made that wreckers in various parts of the world are little more than pirates and that they deliberately lure ships onto reefs. There seems to be no evidence that this ever occurred among the Florida wreckers, who are entitled to credit for the lives they saved.

Wrecking had a profound influence on Key West, for the ships came from the four corners of the earth, their holds loaded with everything that the commerce of the world afforded. The city became a bazaar of salvaged goods, and the colorful auctions attracted merchants from Havana, Mobile, New Orleans, Charleston, and New York. In 1846 alone the wreckers recovered $1,600,000 worth of shipwrecked property. In those days Conch women were frequently attired in costly but water-stained silks, and their homes still contain salvaged articles.

Key West's most popular legend recalls how, in the heyday of the wreckers, the good Squire Egan was conducting services on a Sunday evening in the upstairs auditorium of the county courthouse. As he held forth in all earnestness, he suddenly saw, from his vantage point in the pulpit, a large vessel go hard aground on a reef.

As master of the wrecking vessel *Godspeed*, Squire Egan was very anxious to terminate his sermon and get to his ship. But knowing that a number of other wrecking masters were in his congregation, he gave no sign of his discovery, but instead waxed more eloquent. Exhorting his congregation with great vehemence, he left the pulpit and strode down the aisle. Upon reaching the doorway he quoted the Scripture as follows: "Know ye not that they which run in the race run all, but one receiveth the prize? So run that ye may obtain!" Then with a loud cry of "Wreck ashore!" he dashed for the waterfront, with the other wrecking masters hot on his heels. But to the *Godspeed* went the prize.

Wrecking reached its peak during the first several decades of the nineteenth century and continued to be a profitable enterprise until steam replaced canvas, and until the system of reef lights began blinking warnings to mariners in 1852. Yet today the reefs are as sharp and treacherous as ever, and one battered wrecking tug occasionally leaves her berth to rush to the aid of a stranded vessel.

The sinking of numerous United Nations' ships along the Florida coast by Axis submarines caused a revival of the wrecking business, and the wartime prices paid for scrap metal also inspired the Conchs to salvage old shipwrecks.

Sponger Money

For decades Key West was the center of the United States sponge fishing industry, but that position was captured by Tarpon Springs when the Greek spongers there began using modern diving equipment. Key West's Conchs adamantly cling to the hooking method of sponging, in the belief that the diving shoes worn by the Greeks destroy the fertility of the sponge beds. Greek divers who ventured into the Keys area had their boats burned by the militant Conchs and the Florida Legislature eventually prohibited diving for sponges in Key waters.

In 1940 and at intervals thereafter, a blight destroyed up to ninety per cent of the Key sponges. Though the U. S. Bureau of Fisheries succeeded in determining the microscopic organism which caused the blight, some Conch spongers preferred to believe that the blight was caused by a crystalline slime, by streams of "black water" washed by heavy rains from the Everglades, or by underground streams of fresh water released into the Gulf by volcanic action.

With characteristic individualism, the Conchs have refused to organize a co-operative market such as the one which gives the Greek spongers their great marketing advantage. When World War II brought a construction boom to Key West, the comparatively attractive wages led many old-timers to abandon sponging and accept laboring jobs for the first time in their lives.

But in the old days the small coffee shops along the Conch Town waterfront resounded with the singing of:

SPONGER MONEY

Sponger money never done, sponger money,
Look at my hand—my hand look new,
Cause I don't want no other money
But sponger money.

Look in my trunk and see what's there, sponger money,
One hundred dollars was my share, sponger money,
I'm gonna take away your woes, sponger money,
I'm gonna buy you fine new clothes, sponger money.

Then when we go out on the street, sponger money,
You'll be lookin nice and neat, sponger money,
Then all the boys will envy me, sponger money,
Then all the girls will fall for me, sponger money.

Money don't make me you know, sponger money,
Sponger money ever flow, sponger money,
Tell ev'rybody in town, sponger money,
Me and my gal gon dance em down, sponger money.

Sponger money never done, sponger money,
Cigarmakers on the bum, sponger money,
But I'll treat them just the same, sponger money,
Keep them boys from feelin shame, sponger money.

Look in the corner, see what's there, sponger money,
Champagne, whiskey, gin, and beer, sponger money,
Tell ev'rebody that you see, sponger money,
We're gonna have a shivaree, sponger money.

Negroes who were spongers in the Bahamas have added such Negroid verses as these to the song:

Round and round the barroom,
Foolin round the barroom,
Runnin round the barroom,
Them Nassau gals like tigers,
Tigers, tigers, tigers,
They tear you down like tigers,
Tigers for sponger money.

Grate your potato, grate your potato,
Put a piece of pumpkin in it,
To make it yellow, sponger money.
Baygrass was the weddin bed,
Seaweed was the bolster,
Sand-bank was the pillow,
Them Nassau gals like tigers,
Tigers for sponger money.

Though Negroes are tacitly barred from doing their own sponging in Key West, a number of them—natives of the Bahamas—are commercial fishermen. They continue to sing their Bahaman songs, which, like those of convicts, often reflect their longing to go home:

HOIST UP THE JOHN B SAIL

Hoist up the John B sail,
See how her mainsail set
Send for the Captain ashore.

Captain and Mate got drunk,
Open the people's trunk,
Stole all the people's junk.

The Captain raise cain up town,
Up come Policeman Brown,
Who took the Captain down.

The Judge he was sorta kind,
Scold him for drinkin wine;
"Let you off light this time."

The Captain told the Mate,
At nine o'clock to lock the gate;
Run, run before it's too late!

Chorus:
Let us go home, oh let us go home,
To see my Darlin, let us go home.

As boat builders the Bahamans—both black and white—are justly famous, particularly for that seaworthy creation, the Nassau dinghy.

BELLAMENA

Bellamena, Bellamena,
Bellamena in the harbor;
Gonna put Bellamena on the dock,
Gonna paint her bottom black, black.

Oh, the Mystery, oh, the Mystery,
That boat she tote the whiskey;
Gonna put the Mystery on the dock,
Gonna paint her bottom black, black.

Oh, the Maisie, oh, the Maisie,
That boat she sets me crazy;
Gonna put Maisie on the dock,
Gonna paint her bottom black, black.

Man's difficulty in obtaining a house and land has inspired this striking comparison with the crab;

> *Crab is a better man than man*
> *Cause he got his house and land;*
> *Crab don't need no helpin hand*
> *To get his house and land;*
> *Crab can play about the sand*
> *And build his house and land.*

Insects make their inevitable appearance in:

> *Mosquito had a spree,*
> *Sandfly went to sea;*
> *Poker [gallinipper] stand behind the door,*
> *And throw breakers on me.*

Conch Eats Conch and Grunts

On days "when the wind is walkin right" Key waters are "as crystal as gin"—to use expressions of the Conchs. On such days conchs can be sighted at great depths on the sea bottom. Conch spongers, peering through their glass-bottomed buckets, are able to bring up conchs with their sponge hooks from depths as great as sixty feet. But almost all Conchs are excellent swimmers and capture their conchs by diving for them.

Some prefer to eat their conch raw, as soon as it is caught. With a chisel or screw-driver they pierce the shell near the spiral tip and sever the muscle that binds the flesh to the shell. Grasping the protruding "heel" of the conch, they draw out the mass of flesh. Strips of the best parts are pared off and dipped over the side of the boat to season them with the salty sea water. Then the strips, perhaps still squirming a bit, are chewed and eaten with great gusto. It is popularly believed that raw conch is a powerful aphrodisiac.

Conch is also eaten raw as a salad, with a dressing of lime juice, olive oil, vinegar, salt, and pepper. Few Conch homes are ever without their bottle of "sour"—which is nothing but lime juice; it is even said that a Conch without sour will gladly swap a bottle of whiskey for a bottle of sour, and no questions asked.

Conch meat is also served in sandwiches and prepared as steaks, but the most popular conch dish is chowder made with tomatoes, onions, garlic, salt, and hot pepper. Conch in all these forms is served in most Key restaurants and is even more in demand that another Key delicacy, the turtleburger, made from ground green turtle meat.

Countless Florida souvenir shops along U. S. Highway 1 maintain heaps of conch shells which they sell or give away to customers. Other shops make the shells into attractive lamps and similar curios. This market for conch shells so depleted the supply of conchs that the Florida Department of Conservation has been forced to restrict the business. Strange to say, the Conchs who supplied the conch shells believe that they bring bad luck and will not allow the shells to remain in their houses.

"Besides conchs, grits and grunts is our favorite ears," the Conchs say. "We can't afford much else, but even if we could, I guess they would still be our favorites." The grunt, it should be explained, is a small bottom-feeding fish (*Haemulon plumieri*), which derives its local name from its habit of emitting loud grunts upon being pulled from the water. In other parts of the region this fish is known as a croaker. The grunt's popularity is by no means confined to the Conchs—it is one of the region's most important food fishes. In Key West, waterfront markets keep their grunts and other fishes alive in pens along the docks. Customers peer into the water, point out their preferences on the fin, and the fish are scooped up with a dip-net.

A story which bears out the Conch's preference for grunts is told about an old-time Conch wrecker who became so prosperous that he took his wife to New York City and established residence at the Waldorf-Astoria. His wife soon tired of the hotel's rich French cuisine and told her husband that if he did not wire Key West immediately for "a sack of grits and a barrel of grunts," she was going to return to the Keys "where she could get some decent eatin." The grits and grunts were sent for, and, in keeping with the tradition of American hotels to cater to the whims of their guests, were cheerfully prepared and served by the Waldorf.

"When the Blues Is Runnin"

The Riviera Conchs did not migrate from the Bahamas until about 1918. They first settled on Singer's Island in Lake Worth opposite Palm Beach, where they lived until driven off by a real-estate boom, and then took up residence in Riviera. Some of them are still British citizens, and retain a patriotic feeling for the Crown Land, as they call it. Most of them are natives of Abaco, and they often sing:

> I want to go to Abaco, do-ma, do-ma,
> Cause Abaco is a pretty place, do-ma, do-ma-ma;
> You see them gals with the wire waist, do-ma, do-ma,
> The wire waist and the figure face, do-ma, do-ma-ma.

Other of their folk stuff harks back to London, as in:

> Biddy, biddy, pass my old gold ring
> Till I go to London—back again
> To seek out Simon, who's got the pawn.
> When I eat my rotten egg, aint gon give you none!

Although their Conch Town is situated in a white neighborhood, the Conchs are compelled by their neighbors' prejudices to remain socially apart. About 1935 a group of white Riviera residents launched a campaign to have the Conchs subjected to the segregation laws affecting Negroes, but the movement failed. Some Riviera parents, however, withdrew their children from the school attended by the Conchs.

Conch women are highly skilled at handicrafts. Hats, purses, rugs, table mats, and baskets are woven from palm fronds, and colorful flowers are made of sea shells and fish scales. The Riviera women meet one afternoon each week at their Community Club, which they use as a workshop and recreation center. Finished articles are displayed for sale to tourists, and the handmade quilts are given to the neediest families in the community.

Some of the Riviera Conchs attend the Pentecostal Church of God, Carl L. White, pastor. An interviewer found Reverend White at his home, strumming a guitar and singing a hillbilly tune. He told how he had completed the fourth grade in school and left his home in the mountains of North Carolina to work with his father in sawmills through Georgia, Alabama, and Florida. He learned to preach at a Church of God Bible Conference at Winona, Florida.

"The Conchs prefer my church to their old Episcopal Faith because of the better benefits and moral values derived," Reverend White declared. "The Pentecostal Church of God will have nothing to do with the works of Satan. We strictly forbids dancing, frolicking, face paint, bobbed hair, too much jewelry, loud clothes, men and women bathing together on public beaches, imbibing alcoholic liquors, attending movies, shorts on women, all forms of gambling, belonging to any secret order or club, and so on. Anyone charged with breaking any of these laws is summoned before a church council and given a chance to defend themselves and their actions; also to repent and be saved.

"The Conchs is God-fearin honest people. Them that has, gives. When the blues [bluefish] is runnin they give handsome contributions to the church—from one to five dollars. There is one man who doesn't come to church, but he gives contributions in lieu of his sins. They are all like a bunch of children seeking guidance in a strong hand; they trust practically everybody. They have been betrayed and gypped right and left, which accounts for their impoverished condition."

TURPMTINE

Living as we do in this marvelous age of science, with high-speed cars, aeronautics, radio, television, talkies, electricity and its myriad uses, it seems a far cry to Civil War days. It doesn't seem possible that a basic industry that was flourishing in those days can yet be flourishing without *any* form of change.

"Here lives 'Uncle Doug' Ambrose, famous ex-slave, father of thirty-eight children and hale and hearty at the age of ninety-seven. Here live some 200 other happy descendants of former slaves; pickanninies are at play in the sand, an old hound dog watches indifferently, a carefree darkey plaintively strums a guitar with a melody to his lady-love, and typical mammies are washing clothes in primitive black iron boilers. Here is the last link between slave days and modernity."

All of which goes to show that in the Palmetto Country even a thing as repulsively medieval as a turpentine camp can be glorified into a tourist attraction by a promoter with talent and imagination. The advertising leaflet from which the foregoing text is taken is beautifully illustrated with photographs labeled; "On Their Way to Work or Play—Always Cheerful."

A much more authentic picture of the turpentiners' life is given by the Negro workers themselves in this "old-timey turpmtine song":

I'SE GWINE TO GEORGY

When I left old South Ca'lina,
I left in the winter-time.
"Where you gwine, nigger?"
"I'se gwine to Georgy, I'se gwine to Georgy,
To work in the turpmtine."

When I gits in Georgy,
They gimme a hack and stock
And put me in a crop; they say,
"If you wants to see that double line,
You shorely got to chop."

You see that Woodsman comin, ridin through the pine;
He turns round and 'gins to peep;
You hear him say to the black man,
"Old nigger, sink em in deep!"

65 .... PRISONERS WORKING A TURPENTINE FARM.
These prisoners are doing difficult work at a Florida Turpentine farm. State Library and Archives of Florida.

The nigger pull off his hat,
And throwed it on the ground;
You hear him say to the Woodsman,
"Do you want me to cut em down?"

They worked this nigger all year long;
It's time for him to go home.
You hear the Bossman say to the Bookkeeper,
"How do this nigger stand?"

The Bookkeeper goes in the office,
He sit down and 'gin to figger;
Then he say to the Bossman,
"That nigger's just even now!"

When I libbed in Georgy I heered a lion sing,
And I didn't have long to stay;
I got in debt, and I had to run away.

The Woodsman went to the Bossman,
And begin to fret; he said,
"I'll bet that nigger has left in debt!"
The Woodsrider caught me and brought me back;
He said, "If you don't work, I'll beat your back!"

That song is still sung by turpentine workers throughout the Palmetto Country, and has not lost its meaning in the least. Evidence of this was recently found by a Negro collecting folklore in a West Florida turpentine camp. The fact that she feared to fill her notes out in greater detail only adds to their import.

"A colored woman can't make more than $2.50 or $3 a week. I'll see many a hungry day before I'll work for that.... Relief here is just an under-cover way to buy votes. Once they gave away chicken feed and a rich farmer drove up and filled up his truck. No colored people are given relief work.

"No schools at all in some of the camps; no Negro high school in the county...Social Security not turned in.... Not long ago the Woodsrider got in an argument with a young colored girl who was going to have a baby. He slapped her down and kicked her in the stomach.... One time a Negro hand left the camp owing the company $129. The sheriff had all the roads guarded and nobody was allowed to leave.... The Klan paraded last night over in—.... There is a grave not far from here of a hand they beat to death."

A few weeks after those notes were taken I visited the same camp to make phonograph recordings of Negro folksongs for the Library of Congress. As a guest of the camp's owner-operator I gained an intimate insight into the *modus operandi*. He carries a revolver, sleeps with two double-barreled shotguns by his bed, and keeps another shotgun and an automatic rifle near the front door.

I was further enlightened by visits to the company commissary. Its windows are barred. The manager volunteered the following information: "With the commissary we makes a gross profit of sixty per cent and a net profit of twenty per cent. You know that's pretty good—it takes a good slice offen the salaries. We don't hardly have to pay no salaries. The private

66 .... 1920's WAUCHULA TURPENTINE STILL.
A 1920's turpentine still in Wauchula. State Library and Archives of Florida.

stores around here do good to make five to eight per cent profit. Of course we have to charge the niggers more, but they save in the long run. Just think how much it would cost them to drive thirty miles into town for vitals if they had cars!"

While making recordings we were interrupted when the sheriff telephoned the camp owner for a description of a "nigger who pulled out without payin his debts." While the camp owner was at the telephone, Robert Butler, Negro, age twenty-one, quickly told this story for recording. Recently when he became ill he made arrangements with his Negro landlady not to pay rent on his company-owned shack while he was unable to work. After three months he was able to go back to his job, but instead of wages at the end of the first week he received a bill for fifty dollars back rent. Rather than pay this bill, Robert decided he would prefer to "work it out with the county." Some time later he was in town trying to earn a living shining shoes. When he saw the policeman coming he knew his time had come.

"Robert, are you comin with me?" asked the policeman.

"Yes, sir, I'm comin," Robert answered. While he was being taken to the county prison camp to serve three months he sang:

67 .... TURPENTINE STILL, CIRCA 1930.
A turpentine still in Florida's Panhandle photographed by Dorothea Lange in 1930. Pace Library, University of West Florida.

Oh, my dear mother,
She prayed this prayer for me;
She said, "Lord, have mercy on my son,
Wheresoever he may be."

The Story of Naval Stores

Having seen something of what the modern naval stores industry is like—as well as what it is not like—we might as well take a look at its background. Involving the chipping of pine trees to obtain resinous gum, and the distillation of this gum to secure spirits of turpentine and rosin, the industry received the name "naval stores" about the sixteenth century, when pitch and tar were widely used in shipbuilding.

The first naval stores to be shipped from America to England were sent from Virginia in 1608. Following the settlement of New England in 1620 the industry developed rapidly there—so rapidly, in fact, that the forests were soon depleted. Such nearsighted exploitation drove the industry southward in search of richer yields; North Carolina became known as the Tar-heel State, and naval stores were even recognized as media of exchange.

Suffering its now traditional fate, the industry moved into Georgia in 1875; Georgia's pines lasted until 1905, and then it became necessary to move into Florida. Florida held the lead until 1923, when a new crop of pines carried it back to Georgia. For some time Alabama has also had about a ten per cent share in the nation's total production. Not until recently has agitation for more conservative methods of exploitation begun to take effect. In 1942 the wartime need for naval stores led the Government to ask for a fifty-per-cent production increase over 1941. To do this the industry adopted a method developed in Russia—the application of a sulphuric acid solution to the tree face. For some unknown reason, this increases the gum flow of slash pine by fifty per cent, but does not affect the longleaf pine.

At present the 15,000 employees of the Florida naval stores industry represent the second largest occupational group in the state. The great bulk of these workers are Negroes, who theoretically earn from $1.00 to $1.75 per day on a piece-work basis of trees chipped, cups dipped, barrels filled, etc. This means that rainy weather or poor markets may cut off the workers' incomes for days, weeks, and even months, while they accumulate debts at the company commissary.

Further information on these commissaries is provided by a turpentine man who says, "My Pa used to have a commissary where he sold every-thing from horse collars to ladies' millinery and from coffins to groceries. He made plenty money—seemed like everything he touched turned to money almost like magic. He had more money than he knew what to do with—used to carry a $1,000 bill and two $500 bills just to play with. Pa always said his success depended on bein able to call a lot of men by their first names."

Negroes have provided the labor for the naval stores industry since the beginning of slavery in America. Generation after generation they have followed its southward migration, and the majority of those engaged in it today are descended from a long line of turpentine workers.

More than any other occupational group, these Negroes are denied the rights for which the Civil War was supposedly fought. As one who knows told me, "A Negro who is foolish enough to go to work in a turpentine camp is simply signing away his birthright." They are held in abject pov-erty and peonage by a combination of forces quite beyond their power to oppose.

Supplementary mores making for the perpetuation of this slavery in modern clothing are the denial of education and the use of child labor. The few schools which serve some turpentine camps could hardly be more primitive, and their attendance drops off thirty per cent as soon as the weather becomes warm enough to make the sap run in the trees. Some of the younger generation get something of a grammar-school education which at least carries them beyond the stage of illiteracy. The result is a type in interesting contrast to the "old-timey" turpentine Negroes. The fol-lowing song, composed by a young worker and adopted by the younger set in the camp, is typical of the group.

> *Just a jitterbug,*
> *Just a crazy mug,*
> *He's young and wild*
> *And not the style,*
> *Just a jitterbug.*

Drink whiskey by the jug,
That foolish crazy mug,
He's young and wild
And not the style,
Just a jitterbug.

They threw him outa school
Cause all he learned was Tiger Rag;
He never learned the Golden Rule,
But boy, he could shag.

In some turpentine camps Negroes are so thoroughly intimidated, it is well-nigh impossible for a white person to talk to them. An interviewer calling on Rich Gray, the Negro woodsrider at Carter's Camp, owned by the South Florida Turpentine Corporation, was asked, "What's your business? We got rules and regulations here. I'm foreman of these quarters and I have to know the business of all who comes around. Just last week I had dealins with one of them Social Security snoopers, and now you want to know about my life. My Bossman tells me not to talk. You let me get you a

68.........STRIPPING BARK AND DIPPING SAP.
Workers strip the bark and collect the sap from pine trees to make turpentine. State Library and Archives of Florida.

carbon so you can give me a copy of whatever you write down. I have to report on everything."

Rich said he was thirty-nine years old, although that was not his "insurance age," and went on to explain that he and his wife claimed to be younger in order to get lower rates on their insurance policies. "I goes to church now and then," he said, "but the other people here goes reglar. That's all they got to do besides work—go to church and drink shine." When asked if he ever voted, Rich said emphatically, "No, man, I don't vote. I don't fool with it. A man has to watch hisself. If you stick your finger in the fire you sure to get burnt."

The Social Security Act brought the turpentine workers their first ray of hope since the Civil War; but like the war, its effects are no longer visible around turpentine camps. Turpentine operators bitterly opposed the Act, and Government investigators found the workers so terrorized that it was difficult to obtain witnesses in prosecuting violations. Some Government men who entered turpentine camps without warrants were jailed for trespassing. It all came to an end in 1940, when the Fifth Circuit Court of Appeals in New Orleans ruled that turpentine workers were engaged in agriculture, and therefore not covered by the Act.

Some other ways of the operators are reflected in *The Naval Stores Industry*, a recent study by the Bureau of Economic and Business Research at the University of Florida:

"The work is too severe and the pay too small for white workers. Too, there is a feeling among white workers that such disagreeable work is negroes' work, and that white men would demean themselves by doing it. The problem of managing the negro laborers is a difficult one. The practice of cash advances to them is vicious, as the losses from unpaid accounts is enormous.

"The negroes are a shiftless class and it is estimated that three-fourths of them are constantly in debt. Without any notice, they frequently leave one operator and go to work for another, usually leaving an unpaid account behind. Some operators will pay the moving expenses of a negro's family in order to obtain another workman.

"RECOMMENDATIONS FOR THE INDUSTRY

"1. When a negro leaves a still, or applies for a job at another still, have the operator give his name and description to a central agency. In this way a full check on the whereabouts of negro workers would be kept.

"2. Having a gentlemen's agreement between operators not to hire run-away workers of other operators without their consent.

"3. Setting up a dictator for the industry. This suggestion comes from persons connected with the industry. We admit that a wise, strictly honest, and impartial dictator might do a great deal for the industry and everyone connected with it."

Still another view of life in a turpentine camp is provided in the following story by a white foreman. As "a man who knows his niggers," he is typical of an influential group of Palmetto Country whites whose job is to get the most out of Negro labor.

The Man

"Yeah, man. I was born in the turpentine business. Spent near-bout forty years in it, and woulda been in it yet if the bottom hadn't dropped out of it. I've soaked up so much turpentine in my life that if you was to run me through a still I reckon you'd get about ten gallons outa me.

"My father was manager of a twenty-crop camp near Eastman, Georgia, where I was born in 1899. There was six of us children, and as soon as us boys was old enough we shore had to work. When I was about two years old my folks moved to a camp at Bay Lake, Florida. I started school when I was six, in a little one-room log schoolhouse. When I was about ten years old we moved to another camp at Martin, and I was promoted from water-boy to talley man, whose job is to keep talley of the number of trees boxed or streaked by each nigger. At each camp there will be from fifty to 200 niggers, accordin to the crops worked. A crop is about 10,000 trees.

"The white fokes live in fairly good houses at one side of the camp, and the niggers live in their quarters at the other side in two- or three-room cabins. We always aimed to have separate quarters for the single niggers to keep them from messin-up with the married men's wives. But this didn't always work, and there was many a fight on account of them mixin in the woods at night.

"Turpentine niggers are a class by themselves. They are different from town niggers, farm laborers, or any other kind. Mostly they are born and raised in the camps, and don't know much about anything else. They seldom go to town, and few of them ever saw the inside of a schoolhouse. In nearly every camp there is a jack-leg preacher who also works in the woods, and they have church services at one or another of their houses. Every camp has its jook, as they are now called, but the original name of this kind of a joint was 'tunk.' This is a house where the men and women gather on Saturday nights to dance, drink moonshine, gamble, and fight. Between dances and drinks, young couples stroll off into the woods to make love.

"The supreme authority in the camp is the foreman. To the niggers he is the law, judge, jury, and executioner. He even ranks ahead of God to them. In speakin to him they call him Capm, but among themselves they call him The Man. And believe me, he better be a man from the ground up! If he ever stands for any back-talk or shows a streak of yellow he's through, and might as well quit. For they lose all respect for him and won't mind him. Even though they keep up a pretense of respect to his face, they'll laugh at him behind his back and gang up to make his life miserable. They like to be ruled by an iron hand and no velvet glove.

"Seems like I always had a knack of handlin labor. Bein born and raised with turpentine niggers I learned their nature. They all liked me because I

69.........WAUCHULA TURPENTINE STILL.
This Burgert Brothers photograph shows a Florida turpentine worker in the 1920s. Florida Historical Society.

was fair and firm, and they'd do anything for me. If I quit a job and went to another, ever last nigger on the place would follow me if I told em to.

"Most camps are so deep in the woods that law officers don't bother with em much. Outside of murder, the officers usually leave it up to the camp foreman to make and enforce his own laws. In the old days there were very few legal marriages or divorces among the niggers. For the sake of good camp government and economy in housing, it was to the interest of the foreman to see that all unattached men and women got 'married' to each other. This was done by what the workers called a 'commissary weddin.'

"The foreman was a pretty good matchmaker, and when it was decided between him and a couple that they should 'marry-up with each other,' they simply went to the commissary and were assigned a house, and an account for rations and clothing was opened for the pair. Once in a great while, when a couple had some extra money and wanted to put on style, they would go to the county seat, get 'a pair o'licences,' and have a 'cote-house weddin,'

"In 1916 in Manatee County there were about fifty nigger couples livin together without benefit of 'cote-house' or clergy. One elderly pair had been happily joined in commissary wedlock for more than fifty years, and had a large family of children and grandchildren. Somehow a white preacher from the North heard of this 'unholy' state of affairs, and made such a loud complaint that the county officials finally issued orders that the nigger couples had to be legally married or stop livin together. The camp foreman had to pay for some fifty marriage licences and hold a mass weddin. All it meant to the niggers was a big holiday.

"In 1922 I had a job as manager of eight camps owned by a New York concern at Opal, Florida. I had charge of 400 niggers and nine white woodsriders. Then came the damndest rainy season I ever seen. It poured down bullfrogs for weeks, and water stood knee-deep all over the woods. We had to set in camp and do nothing. Besides the 400 niggers, there was thirty head of horses and mules eatin up rations; and the wet weather make the horses' and mules' backs so sore we couldn't have worked even if it had stopped rainin. I shore had a peck of trouble on my hands. To make everything worse, the big bosses in New York kept telegraphin me wantin to know why no production. Finally I got mad, told em to go to hell, and waded off the job."

OUR CIGARS PUT FLORIDA ON THE MAP

There are in the Palmetto Country some 40,000 Latins who have contributed more than their pro-rata share to the industrial and cultural life of the region, and their colonies constitute highly volatile centers of advanced and progressive thought in the comparatively backward Southern setting. Unlike the majority of Southern poor folk, these Latins have strenuously sought to better their condition by group action. Inherently sociable, traditionally co-operative, they uphold a heritage of militant unionism developed over a period of centuries in Europe, Cuba, and the United States. There co-operative approach to the problems of security-through labor unions, political organizations, and social-benefit societies-is of timely significance to the South and the nation.

Tampa's Latin colonies, Ybor City and West Tampa, where live some 12,000 Cubans, 8,500 Spaniards, and 8,500 Italians, comprise the Largest Latin community in the southeastern United States. Another 3,000 Cubans live in Key West, there are several thousand descendants of Minorcans and Spaniards in St. Augustine, and smaller Latin groups are scattered about the region, chiefly in Jacksonville, Miami, Mobile, and other port cities. In recent years there has been an increasing interest in these Latin culture groups, in the hope of enhancing relations with Latin-America.

With the exception of those in St. Augustine, Florida Latins represent comparatively recent immigrations. The Cubans, comprising the largest national group, began to pour in about 1868 with the intensification of the movement for Cuban independence, which also brought the partial transfer of the Cuban cigar industry to Florida, where it first developed in Key West and then in Tampa. The heaviest immigration of Spaniards occurred during the first decade of the twentieth century; after Cuba had achieved independence the Spaniards there thought their chances of employment would be better in Tampa. The majority were of Asturian origin; ninety per cent of them came by way of Cuba. The Italians, mostly Sicilians and Sardinians, came very largely from New Orleans after anti-Italian riots there in 1891. The immigration of all these Latin groups continued steadily until halted in 1921 and again in 1933 by the United States quota limitations.

For the most part the Spaniards left their native land in the hope of bettering their economic condition, although many were seeking to escape compulsory military service and the Inquisition.

The Cubans, in the diversity of their racial origins, are almost as cosmopolitan as Americans. The Spaniards who conquered and settled Cuba were themselves made up of a multitude of racial strains, including those of the Iberian, Moor, Roman, Basque, Celt, Visigoth, Mauretanian, and Jew. The *conquistadores* were fighting men from the northern provinces of Spain. Having driven out the Moors, these men were idle and actually hungry; consequently it was with alacrity that they set forth to conquer the New World. They brought with them the traditions of their class, inculcated by eight centuries of warfare; and it was they who established the aristocratic Castilian structure that persists in Cuba today.

Spain soon put a stop to emigration from her northern provinces, and the real colonization of Cuba began in 1794 when an organized campaign was launched to encourage the emigration of laborers from Spain's southern provinces.

The cigar industry was one of the first to be developed in Cuba. A majority of the cigarmakers worked in small household shops called *chinchares* (chinches), although in time large factories were established in Havana and other cities. From its inception the industry was marked by conflict between the Cuban workers on one hand and the Spanish manufacturers and Government officials on the other. Serious rebellion broke out as early as 1716 in protest against the compulsory shipment of tobacco to Spain under heavy tariffs.

The Spanish Government retaliated by imposing additional taxes. Protesting demonstrations became numerous, and in 1817 a large group of rebellious Cubans marched into Havana, forcing the Governor to flee to Spain. The strife continued with the Government promising to reduce the tariffs, yet failing to do so. When widespread rebellion again broke out in 1823, the Government enforced its edicts by mass assassinations.

The first cigar factory to be established in Key West was that of William H. Wall in 1831. Other *chinchares*, or "buckeyes," as the Americans called them, were established in rapid succession, but until 1868, when the Ten Years' Warefare broke out in Cuba, the Key West industry was still in its infancy. At that time Vincente Martínez Ibor, a Spaniard who owned the famous El Príncipe de Gales factory in Havana, became interested in moving his factory to Key West in the hope of escaping the difficulties he was having with the Spanish authorities over his alleged sympathy with the Cuban independence movement. With encouragement and material assis-

70........KEY WEST CIGAR WORKERS PACKING CIGARS.
The cigar industry in Key West began as early as the mid–1800s. State Library and Archives of Florida.

tance of Key West merchants, Ibor moved his factory to that city in 1869, and thus became the real founder of the cigar industry in Florida.

Ibor's factory proved highly successful and was soon followed by La Rosa Española and other factories from Cuba. Thousands of cigarmakers came from Havana, Bejucal, San Antonia de los Baños, Güines, Santiago de las Vegas, and other small towns near Havana. At first the cigarmakers came alone, and returned to Cuba after saving some money. But usually they returned to Key West, bringing their families with them; they liked America better than Cuba because they earned better wages, enjoyed more personal freedom, and were not bothered by such rigid class distinctions. A sizable Cuban colony soon developed, and the Cubans were no longer able to refer to Key West as La Isla Solariega (The Isolated Island).

Among the motives which caused the manufactures to move to Key West was a desire to get away from the import duty charged on Cuban-made cigars, and the growing pressure of La Liga, the Cuban labor union. But in the latter regard they were sadly disappointed, as the cigarworkers brought unionism with them. The unions, which were flourishing in Key West ever prior to 1879, were the first in Florida. The wives of the cigarmakers were frequently employed as strippers, whose job it was to remove the center stem from the tobacco leaves; and these women were organized in a strippers' union, one of the most active of the Cuban revolutionary groups in key West. Strikes for better wages, better working conditions, and in protest against discrimination against Cubans in favor of Spaniards, were frequent.

The attitude of the city's Anglo-American leaders toward unionism found expression in the organization of the Key West Rifles, "a volunteer military company" formed in 1877 with eighty members. This group answered two "riot calls," the most serious of which occurred when a group of cigarmakers gathered at the factory of Francisco Madero, who had shot and killed a union organizer. "To satisfy the demonstrators" Madero was jailed; but later the same day the authorities decided to free him. The Key West Rifles were summoned by ringing the fire bell, and they escorted Madero to his factory where they maintained guard for twenty-four hours until "wiser heads" calmed the demonstrating cigarmakers.

In 1868 fire destroyed almost half of Key West, including the factories of Ibor and Sánchez & Haya. Ibor had already considered moving to some other locality to escape the pressure of the unions. He and Haya investigated the advantages of Tampa, to which the South Florida Railroad had just been completed, and whose port was being improved. In consideration of a $4,000 tract of land offered free, both manufactures decided to establish themselves there. A race was begun to see which factory would be first to begin operations and to receive Tampa License No. 1. By importing his tobacco already stripped from New York, Haya was able to begin operations about a week before Ibor.

For several years the passage of cigarmakers and their families from Key West to Tampa was paid by the manufacturers. When the cigarmakers arrived, Tampa was a wilderness settlement comprising some four blocks of houses. The manufacturers had built numerous small cottages, which they offered for purchase at $750 to $900, with monthly payments of five dollars, and no interest. The first-comers found these domiciles furnished with nothing more than kitchen utensils and candles. As the colony gradually grew on the swampy ground surrounding the factories it came to be known as Ybor City. There were two large lagoons that overflowed after heavy rains to form a lake. Snakes were numerous, and at night the frogs made a terrific noise. Alligators crawled out on Seventh Avenue-the main street- and it was necessary to carry a lantern at night to avoid them.

Hardly a person failed to suffer from the ravages of malaria and other diseases, which spread because of the polluted drinking water, mosquitoes, and poor sanitary facilities. Plagues of gnats caused temporary blindness, and forced many people to wear goggles. Drinking water had to be strained to remove insects and other foreign matter. The first winter many of the cigarmakers became disgusted and wanted to leave, but Ibor held them with the promise of a huge Christmas picnic. The affair took place on Ibor's farm, and he personally drove his buggy and brought each family. It was a festive occasion, and many roasted hogs were consumed. The farmyard was lighted by countless candles place on tree stumps, and a large Negro was kept busy relighting and replacing them.

Conditions gradually improved, and the settlers remained. One of the principal attractions was the cheapness of food. Farmers came to the houses selling eggs for ten cents a dozen and pork for five cents a pound. Half a bushel of sweet potatoes could be bought for ten cents, and by taking a pitcher to a dairy you could have it filled, the milking done before your eyes, for five cents.

Transportation between Ybor City and Tampa was sporadically effected by small steam engines that ran along narrow-gauge track on a schedule of once-in-a-while. It is said that the odds of arriving at one's destination aboard one of these locomotives were about fifty-fifty. The engines were popularly named after Fannie, wife of Ignacia Haya the manufacturer, and the daughters of Ibor; Tereita, Mirta and Jennie.

There were relatively few women at first, and the prostitutes, even the Negro ones, did a thriving business.

As the cigar workers increased (and opportunities for employment decreased) they became unionized. But when the unions sought to maintain or improve the lot of their members they were met with the same violent opposition which the manufacturers had employed in Cuba and Key

71 .... WORKERS SELECTING CIGAR WRAPPERS.
   Cigar wrappers at the Sanchez & Haya Plant in Ybor City. The highly skilled wrapper selectors separated the leaves and selected the wrappers for different cigars.   State Library and Archives of Florida.

West. Applicants for jobs were often turned down or accepted depending upon whether or not they were available as roomers or boarders, as many of the manufacturers and managers owned restaurants and rooming houses. Windows for paying rent were set up next to the pay windows in some factories. Manufacturers and company officials sometimes forced their attentions on women employees by the threat of discharge; and this practice has not entirely disappeared.

What the coming of the cigar industry meant to Tampa is indicated by the fact that its population in 1880 was but 720; the cigar industry was established in 1886 and by 1890 the population had leaped to 5,532.

Meanwhile the industry continued to grow in Key West, and by 1888 there were over 200 factories there employing 6,000 persons at an annual payroll of $3,000,000. Weekly wages varied from eight dollars to fifty-five dollars, and the average yearly earning was $800. The Key West industry reached its peak in 1890, when 12,000 cigar workers produced 100,000,000 cigars. The Island City was the cigar manufacturing center of the United States, and the industry constituted the axis upon which the economic life of the community revolved.

"An Odious Spectacle"

In 1889 a general strike was called throughout the Key West industry, demanding that the rate of pay be increased by one dollar, and that a bargaining Comité Nivelador, composed of six union representatives and six manufacturers representatives, be established. During this strike the Tampa cigar workers contributed a dollar each from their weekly salaries to aid the families of the striking Key Westers. Some of the strikers left Key West and went to Havana or Tampa. The strike was won early in 1890, and most of the Cuban and Spanish cigarmakers who had left during the strike returned. The Spaniards, however, found feeling against them so high that they went back to Tampa. Yet the Key West manufacturers continued to encourage the migration of Spanish cigarmakers from Cuba, and gave them preferential employment. In 1894, when the manufacturers refused to stop importing Spanish labor, the unions again called a general strike.

Seidenberg, operator of La Rosa Española factory, appealed to the Key West Board of Trade. According to Jefferson B. Browne in *Key West–The Old and the New*:

"This body assured him that he would receive not only the protection of the law, but the support of the citizens of Key West, who felt that the right of the people of any nationality to come to the United States to obtain work should not be infringed. The Board then appointed a committee, composed of A. J. Kemp, the county judge; L. W. Bethel, circuit court judge; W. R. Kerr, a financier; George W. Allen; Wm. H. Williams; John F. Horr; and the Rev. Charles W. Fraser, a militant Christian, to go to Havana and assure the *Capitán-General* that if any Spanish subjects desired to come to Key West to work they would receive the full protection of the law."

Meanwhile the Cuban cigarmakers in Key West threatened the lives of any Spaniards who might come with the purpose of breaking the strike. When the committee returned from Cuba accompanied by a group of Spanish workers, the atmosphere was tense. A large "delegation of citizens" headed by Mayor Robert J. Perry met the boat and escorted the Spaniards to a place of safety. According to the eminent Cuban historian Gerardo Castellano in his *Motivos de Cayo Hueseo* (a history of Key West):

"The conflict reached such a temperature that Key West was in an uproar. What an odious spectacle of a city-created by its adopted sons-leaving its land and laws to go out and bring in the enemies of its sons! A city that, in the hands of the Yankees had been nothing but sand and huts, but now boasted of factories like academies with their lectures, societies of art and recreation, and lyceums where hands that folded the tobacco leaf during the day rested on books of learning at night.

"This crisis, this acute tension between the Anglo-American sector and the Spanish-speaking ethnic group should demonstrate to us Cubans the difficulty of reaching a clear-cut social and political understanding with the ponderous North American conglomeration. More than one-third of a laborious and honorable century of evident progress was not sufficient to amalgamate the aspirations of the two races."

Feeling on this subject has affected all susequent relations between the two groups, particularly in labor matters. Castellano, for example, was writing in 1935.

At the time of the occurrence, the Junta Revolucionario Cubano, which by this time had gained considerable influence in the United States, charged that the collector of customes, the district attorney, and immigrant inspector of Key West had aided and abetted a violation of the labor contract laws of the United States. A committee sent by the Key West Board of Trade to Tampa with the same purpose was similarly charged. In spite of the protests of Mayor Perry, George W. Allen, and Jefferson B. Browne-who went to Washington and conferred with the Secretary of State, Attorney general, and Secretary of the Treasury-the Treasury department ruled that the committee had committed a violation as charged, and ordered that the Spaniards be deported.

The committee frustrated the order by bringing the complaint before Circuit Judge Alex Boarman in Key West, who ruled that "no contract, written or verbal, expressed or implied, had been made by the committee of anyone for them." Nevertheless, the local immigrant inspectors were ordered by their Washington office to arrest and deport the Spaniards. Judge Boarman granted writs of habeas corpus, and the Spaniards were released under bond, pending an appeal before the Supreme Court (which was never made).

Browne reports, "A spirit of unrest took possession of the Cuban population, who considered the action of the citizens unfriendly to them. This feeling, however, would have soon worn off, had not a committee come from Tampa to take advantage of the delicate situation. They offered attractive inducements to the Cuban manufacturers, and succeeded in getting four large factories to move."

Castellano, however, attributes this removal to the patriotism of the Cuban manufacturers, who wished to abandon Key West after its anti-Cuban actions. "Considering that the manufacturers were business men, who prefer, above all, that which can be reduced to money, their action was a wonderful proof of unity with the Cuban workers. On this occasion the Creole temper predominated over bourgeois egotism. It proves that the Cuban immigrants were pre-eminently patriots. And because of the censorable and perfidious action of a few Conchs, the industry which would have remained permanently concentrated on the rock vanished forever from the place.

The Cradle of Cuban Independence

Cuba's terrible year, 1871, saw mass assassinations of Cuban revolutionaries, and thousands of others were thrown into concentration camps. As early as 1863, prominent Cubans had petitioned the Spanish Government to grant Cuba the same degree of home rule that was in effect in Puerto Rico, but the petition was denied.

Terrorists activities of the Spanish Volunteers were responsible for a great deal of Cuban immigration to Florida, especially of the leaders of the revolutionary movement. San Carlos Institute was the first and most prominent of the revolutionary organizations in Key West. Its membership grew so rapidly that it soon erected a building which was named San Carlos Institute in honor of the first President of the "Republic in Arms," Carlos Manuel de Cépedes.

San Carlos Institute was dedicated to a twofold purpose: the liberation of Cuba, and the education of Cuban children in Key West. Many of Cuba's most eminent revolutionary leaders visited Key West and spoke from the San Carlos stage. Dramatic productions brought sufficient revenue to operate the school and to outfit several military expeditions which were dispatched to aid the revolutionary fighters in Cuba.

When the fire of 1886 destroyed the Institute, the Cubans immediately began working for its reconstruction-El Templo del Patriotismo they called it at the time. Shortly a new three-story building was erected. Here in 1892 José Martí, the "George Washington of Cuba," founded the Partido Revolutionario Cubano, and from then until the realization of Cuban independence he and many other patriots met frequently in San Carlos and inspired the Key West Cubans with revolutionary zeal.

Martí also made frequent visits to Tampa, where the cigar workers organized the patriotic 24th of February Club and The Avengers of Maceo. In both Key West and Tampa the cigar workers made regular weekly contributions to the cause, and Martí's world-wide junta received its main financial strength from these two cities. Altogether, twenty-seven military expeditions financed and largely manned by the Latins left Tampa to fight in Cuba.

Key West and Tampa were hotbeds of sympathy for the cause of Cuban independence, and in time this sympathy spread throughout the entire country, culminating in the Spanish-American War in 1898 and the establishment of the Republic of Cuba in 1902.

As for the thousands of Italians whom the New Orleans lynchings drove to Florida, most of them settled at Tampa, although some found employment as manual laborers, fishermen, peddlers, and farmers in Jacksonville and other port towns. They rapidly gained a foothold in the Tampa cigar industry and proved skillful operatives; when one Italian had learned to make cigars he taught others at night. Like the Spaniards, and to an even greater degree, many of them were successful in establishing businesses of various kinds. For years they sent their savings to banks in Italy, and this practice was not abandoned until Italians began to operate banks in Tampa.

"The Citizens Lost Their Patience"

During the first ten years of the Tampa industry's existence there was relatively little friction between the manufacturers and workers. One of the first labor organizations was Los Cabaleros del Trabajo (The Gentlemen of Labor), a branch of the national Knights of Labor, which abolished secrecy in 1878 and called for "the organization of all toilers to check the power of wealth." From 1886 until 1901 the dominant Tampa labor group was La Resistencia, a society imported from Cuba. It was in 1898 that the first Tampa local union, with twenty-four members, affiliated with the AFL International Cigarmakers' Union.

Consolidation of the Tampa factories gained momentum in 1899, when ten of the largest combined to form the two-million dollar Havana-American Company. Two years later this company was absorbed by the American Tobacco Company, popularly known as The Trust. The Trust was militantly open-shop and opposed to any recognition of the unions, and consequently incurred their opposition. Many independent manufacturers also regarded the monopolistic Trust with disfavor. Consolidation and removal to Northern manufacturing centers has continued ever since, and is directly responsible for the unemployment of some 4,000 Tampa cigar workers.

The Tampa Cigar manufacturers' Association was formed in 1900 for the usual purposes of such associations including "the group handling of labor relations." The first general strike of the Tampa industry was caused in 1901 by the manufacturers' insistence on weighing out eight or nine ounces of filler tobacco and requiring the cigarmakers to make 50 cigars from this amount-which was difficult and sometimes impossible. The strike was conducted by La Resistencia and opposed by the small Cigarmakers' International Union. The U. S. Immigration Commission, of which Senator Wm. P. Dillingham was chairman, told this story of how the strike was broken:

"Responsibility for every serious strike rested with a limited number of men, who, with pernicious activity in their own behalf, were constantly playing on the prejudice of their irresponsible followers to the common hurt of the workmen, manufacturers, and citizens. When, therefore, the industry had once more come to a standstill and many families lacking the means to withstand a long period of idleness were becoming public charges, the citizens lost their patience. To put an end to the strike and to prevent further trouble a course of action was determined upon which brought about the desired result.

"A committee of citizens, whose names are not on record, visited the homes of the leaders of the strike, gathered about 30 and placed them on board a schooner which had been chartered for the purpose, and instructed the captain to land them on the shore of Honduras. They were advised that a return would invite still more drastic treatment. Of those deported, a majority were Cubans. Work was soon resumed, and since then no leaders have been found willing to assume like responsibilities."

Needless to say, the manufacturers were responsible for this illegal deportation of union leaders. "Italians were escorted into the factories by law enforcement officers, took the strikers' places and proved that they could fill them," the Commission's report continued. "When the bitterness engendered by the strike was allayed and there was danger that the Cubans and others would return and oust them from their places, the Italians bought their jobs by bribing foremen. The close of the strike found the strength of the unions effectively broken."

That report was published in 1909. *The Cigar Industry of Tampa*, published in 1939 by the Bureau of Economic and Business Research declares that the labor leaders were "arrested" rather than "gathered," and gives their number as sixteen instead of "about 30."

In a typical call for a return to work, on September 14, 1901, *the Florida Times-Union and Citizen* of Jacksonville reported:

"TAMPA.-The cigar manufacturers made known the fact yesterday that they would desire to open some factories within the next few days. They stated that representations had been made to them that many cigarmakers wanted to go to work, and that they would do so if proper protection were given them.

"The manufacturers held a meeting and decided that each manufacturer could open as he pleased. The citizens' committee called upon the County Commissioners and had a conference with them, whereupon the commissioners at once called upon Deputy Sheriff L. J. Lester and instructed him to swear in 200 able-bodied men as deputies for duty and to take as many more men as he needed from the body of the county, and to require every good man to serve regardless of his excuses. They stated that if men wanted to work, they should be allowed to do so, and must not be interfered with. They also stated that there must be no disorder in this city over this matter, if there were men enough to keep it down.

"The plans were all carefully gone over and everything is ready. The manufacturers pay the same prices they always have paid. They simply do not recognize a union man or anything else except a workman, and this is the only difference they make. All factories will probably be open by the middle of next week."

The factories did open, and operated with a skeleton force of strikebreakers until November 25, when La Resistencia, weakened by the deportation of its leaders called off the strike. From this time on La Resistencia declined in importance, and was eventually replaced by the International Cigarmakers' Union.

The value of the cigars manufactured in Tampa in 1908 was $17,175,000, and the 10,500 employees received a weekly wage of $200,000-which was seventy-five per cent of the total payroll for the city. Those figures have been frequently quoted, but the following have not appeared often in print. Strippers and stemmers were earning from four dollars to eight dollars per week, and banders from four dollars to twelve dollars. The average yearly earning of the Cubans and Italians was about $820, and for the Spaniards, $850.

In 1910 the Union and the Manufacturers' Association agreed upon a detailed list of labor rates to be paid for approximately 200 different kinds of cigars. This list of rates, known as the *cartabón* (square-the tool), has, with minor adjustments, continued in use. A set of wooden models classifying the various sizes and shapes of cigars, also made in 1910, is also still in use.

The second general strike of the Tampa industry, which lasted seven months from June 25, 1910, to January 26, 1911, was caused by the manufacturers' "noncompliance" with the *cartabón*. The Union conducted a successful organizational campaign in thirty-seven factories, and the manufacturers saw fit to discharge fifty per cent of the selectors and twenty-five per cent of the cigarmakers for union activity. Seeking to avoid a strike, the Union petitioned the Tampa Board of Trade for intervention; but the Board refused to act, and the strike was twofold: to obtain the manufacturers' compliance with the *cartabón*, and to obtain recognition of the Union.

During the strike a bookkeeper at the Bustillo factory was killed, and according to *The Cigar Industry of Tampa* the "local citizens became aroused and an unknown group of lynchers took the lives of two Italians who were allegedly guilty of the crime. In addition, records of the unions were seized by law officials in an effort to prove that prominent strike leaders were accessories to murder." Members of the Unions' Joint Advisory Board were "temporarily place in jail pending the investigation." Once again the Union was deprived of its leaders by illegal methods. The vote to return to work came after the Union had become indebted to the amount of $13,000 disbursed to its members for subsistence during the strike.

Meanwhile in Key West the industry again reached its peak of 100,000,000 cigars in 1911. The greatest growth of the industry throughout Florida took place between 1914-19, when the number of cigar workers increased from 10,791 to 12,280, and their wages increased from $6,638,229 to $11,874,880.

However, in 1920 the Tampa manufacturers precipitated another general strike by refusing to re-employ a number of union delegates discharged the preceding December. The strike began on April 14, and its aims were the re-employment of the union delegates and the establishment of a union shop. More than 11,000 cigar workers participated. The manufacturers, refusing to consider a union shop, organized a company union, Los Torcedores (The Twisters-"anything causing displeasure"). Though it actually consisted of about 200 strikebreakers, Los Torcedores claimed 1,800 members.

As the strike continued the cigar workers established a cooperative union restaurant to feed their families. But according to one of the strikers, "The manufacturers conspired with the police authorities, with the result that policemen came and destroyed our restaurant and threw all the cooked food and groceries into the street. Then the 'Coo-Coo' Klan paraded through Ybor City to try to scare us out of the strike. We just sat on our porches with our guns across our laps and watched the parade. It sure was a quiet parade, and it didn't last very long. Man, it was a good thing the Klan didn't start no trouble-there would have been revolution in Ybor City!"

72.........MEETING OF CIGAR WORKERS ON STRIKE.
Mass meeting of cigar workers on strike, Tampa, Florida 1920. State Library and Archives of Florida.

The strike continued for ten months, and the manufacturers lost nearly half of their trade to competitors, and have never regained it. The Union lost the strike after becoming indebted to the amount of one million dollars paid at the rate of five dollars per week to each striking member.

It was also in 1920 that the readers were first banned from the factories. They were reinstated in 1926 with the provision that all reading matter be sujected to approval, but were again abolished in 1933 "for fomenting strikes and reading material objectionable to the women workers."

The struggle for union recognition for which the cigar workers had suffered so long in the general strikes of 1901, 1910, and 1920, and in numerous smaller strikes, was not won until the New Deal's National Recovery Act of 1933 guaranteed the right of collective bargaining to all American workers.

"We Are Superfluous here"

The effect of the Depression on Florida's Latins was truly terrible. Had they not been staunchly law-abiding there would have been crime waves such as those which swept other sections of the state and nation. Hopefully and patiently they waited for the New Deal's program of direct relief and work relief to develop. Under the Civil Works Authority they were paid about forty dollars per month for construction work, and were greatly encouraged. But with the expiration of the CWA there was a barren period under the Federal Emergency Relief Administration when direct and wholly inadequate relief was given. The Latins objected to the charitable aspects of this dole quite as much as they did to its inadequacy.

"The people of Ybor City are orphans, not only of mother and father, but of everything else in life," it was said. "We call the poor people here 'vacant-house-rats' because they have very little to eat. If they are actually starving, we call them 'hardware-store-rats.'"

"There is much monkey-business going on inside the walls of the relief building," declared one Latin father. "The money intended for the unemployed is being spent on high salaries for administrators and in 'other' ways." An official investigation was conducted when "riots" (protesting demonstrations) took place over contaminated canned beef which the FERA distributed.

"My daughter," complained a widow, "is given one day's work each week in the FERA sewing room, for which she receives two dollars. At first I used this money to pay the rent, and began selling pieces of furniture to feed my seven children. Now the furniture is almost gone, and we all huddle into one bed at night. Since the furniture gave out I have been using the two dollars for food, and I expect to be thrown out of the house any day for not paying the rent. When that happens, where can I go? There are many days when I feed my children, and my oldest daughter and I go hungry." Circumstances such as these made the Latins disillusioned and bitter. "They will not remember the burro until he is dead," they said.

"I cannot believe in anything or anybody; we have endured too much hunger," declared a rebellious mother. "I become frantic when I see my children without shoes, clothes, and proper nutrition-when I think of the great amount of food rotting away in warehouses while my children go to bed without eating. My blood boils within me against those who are responsible for such injustice in the world. Everything should be distributed equitably, and not go only to a few millionaires who exploit the productive class to enrich themselves. The more money they have, the more money they want. I cannot understand such avarice in accumulating money. They cannot take it with them. They are burros overloaded with money; like burros they shall die!"

Yet in spite of their hatred of those responsible for their grim plight, the Latins somehow managed to laugh. At night the men would gather at their clubs and try to outdo one another in telling tall tales.

"When I was working on the sewer project," said one man, "there was a fellow who always had the same thing for lunch. Every day I watched him open his lunch and it was always the same: a bologna sandwich and a banana. Three months I saw him eat that every day. Finally I asked him why. 'Doc Roosevelt's orders,' he said.

"That's the way it is," said another relief worker. "One day on my project a colored man brought a big brown paper bag full of something. Everybody looked at the bag and wondered what was in it. It was shaped like a cake and whatever was in it was soaking through the paper a little. 'It must be a cake,' somebody said. All morning everybody was trying to say something nice to the Negro or do him a favor to get a piece of his cake. We could hardly wait for lunch-time to come. Finally the whistle blew and the Negro went for his lunch bag. Everybody was standing around watching when he opened it. He reached in and pulled out a big pancake of hominy; and that was his lunch: cold hominy and water."

"That's nothing," asserted another man. "The other day my project was cleaning up the beach. When lunch-time came one man reached in his lunch bag and pulled out two big slices of Cuban bread. Everybody looked at him to see if that was all he had to eat. But he reached in again and pulled out a lime; then he cut it and squeezed juice all over his bread. We all looked at him to see if he had gone crazy from the heat. 'What kind of sandwich do you think you're making?' I asked him. 'A fish sandwich,' he said, holding up the bread to catch the *marisco* [fishy sea-breeze]."

In Key West, where more than eighty per cent of the population was dependent upon relief, the state government through the FERA assumed all functions of city and county government, and launched a program to rehabilitate Key West by developing it as a tourist resort. The program was carried out under the slogan: Help to Those Who Help Themselves, and Key Westers helped themselves by contributing 1,749,000 man-hours of voluntary labor in beautifying their city. FERA wages varied from twenty dollars to thirty dollars per month, and the WPA "security wage" for unskilled labor was about forty dollars per month. Material contributions to the relief of the Latins have also been made by the Federal Surplus Commodities Commission. But the combined efforts of relief agencies has been wholly inadequate to meet the basic needs of all those who are certified as being in need of assistance.

Among the Latins, the Cubans were hardest hit by the Depression, and many of them left the Palmetto Country. "With characteristic good nature the Cubans have taught all who wanted to earn the trade of cigarmaking, and this has proved their undoing," it was said. The FERA estimated that some 6,000 of them left Tampa between 1931 and 1935, most of them going to New York City. Various Cubans phrased their reasons for emigrating as follows:

"We are leaving Tampa because we are superfluous here. We cannot find work. We have no funds to meet this situation and though we would like to remain, hunger drives us out. What else is there for us to do? We must leave, though lightning may strike us down in another place."

"Our friends who have gone to New York have written that things are somewhat better there. Some have found work, while others have succeeded in getting on relief, which is more adequate than it is here. We deplore having to leave Tampa, but, to be frank, we are going hungry. We would gladly remain if we could find work digging ditches; but even that is denied us."

"I am leaving because I have eight children, and I must find some way to support them. I cannot understand why the Government has not taken steps to bring new industries to Tampa so that we can support ourselves."

It was only by great sacrifice that the destitute Cubans were able to save the money necessary to leave. A number of automobile owners regularly transported passengers to New York City, charging ten dollars each, although some emigrants simply shared expenses of the trip. Those who were unable to find employment in New York sought to get on relief. To do this it was necessary to produce evidence of having lived the preceding two years in New York City. The Tampans managed to do this by taking a letter addressed to them in New York, and changing the postmark to a date several years earlier. It was also a common practice to arrange with janitors and storekeepers to declare them to be old residents.

When it became known that large numbers of Tampa Cubans had succeeded in getting on New York relief rolls, a campaign to remove them was begun. The New York relief office employed a Cuban FERA official from Tampa, who soon spotted the Tampa families and dropped them from the rolls. The FERA officials were stationed along the highways leading out of Tampa to report on the emigration of relief families.

One Tampa Cuban who returned from New York had this to say: "All that shines in New York is not gold. We who have been accustomed to tranquil life in Tampa found it hard to get used to the agitated life of New York. Life is less friendly in New York than in Tampa; life is more individual there, while here it is more collective. The Tampa Cubans now living in New York have a melancholy longing for the Tampa they knew in the old days. If the depression ever ends these people will return to the city they love; like swallows they will return to build their nests once more in Tampa.

"Some way must be found to put the necessities of life within reach of all. Collective cooperation is necessary instead of individualism. Frankly, I feel communistic; I am desirous of seeing justice prevail, of seeing everyone happy, contented, and enjoying life. God grant that that happy day may arrive, and we may live as we have in other times in Tampa.

Gravy on His Grits

The CIO inclinations of the cigarmakers' unions became manifest during 1938, when R. E. Van Horn, international president of the International Cigarmakers' Union, suspended five of the major leaders of Tampa locals, charging that "they have manifested sympathy for the Committee on Industrial Organization, a rival organization, and have engaged in communistic propaganda contrary to the policy of the Cigarmakers' International Union and the AFL, and have encouraged the violation of the terms of the contract with manufacturers in that they have openly criticized the provisions thereof and have encouraged strikes among the workers."

Van Horn was granted a court injunction restraining the five suspended leaders and eleven other union officials from interfering with "the authority of Van Horn and his representative, Charles M. Norona, and from taking any part in the affairs of the union." The rank-and-file of the union, called together by Van Horn "to fill the vacancies caused by the suspensions," voted not to elect new officers, and instead passed a resolution condemning the action of Van Horn and asking that he immediately reinstate the suspended men.

When this was refused, the cigar workers petitioned the court to dismiss the injunction on the grounds that Van Horn had "no authority under the constitution of the union to suspend local officers; that the laws of the union do not forbid its members to show sympathy for the CIO; and that if the unions changed their affiliation from the AFL to the CIO they would still have the right to benefit by contract with the manufacturers."

The motion was further asserted: "the court cannot take judicial notice of the phrase 'engaged in communistic propaganda.' The Bill of Complaint fails to specify the particular type of Communistic propaganda in which the defendants are engaged; whether the type which certain Tampa police officers charged the late Joseph Shoemaker with promulgating; or the type which the Hearst press charged President Roosevelt with promulgating; or the type a witness before the Dies Committee charged Shirley Temple with aiding and abetting; or the type which Trotsky charges Stalin with spreading; or the type which the repudiated resolutions committee of the last AFL convention charged the U. S. Government with pursuing, or still some other type of 'communistic propaganda.'"

The motion for dismissal of the injunction was refused. Later at a hearing on the injunction, the counsel for the cigar workers said: "The vague and flimsy charge of communism was put into the injunction in order to incite the people of Tampa to riot against the cigarmakers. They know they can get certain people to burn fiery crosses if they talk about engaging in communistic propaganda. We have such people-I can show you the grave of Shoemaker to prove it."

In referring to the injunction's allegation that the suspended men had criticized the contract with the manufacturers, the counsel said, "In Mr. Hitler's Germany, criticism may be called engaging in communistic propaganda, but not in America. But Mr. Van Horn's charges are fascist propaganda of the worst sort. Any criticism of a high official, one of the boys at the top, seems to be a crime under the unwritten laws of the AFL. That's how the royalty exists."

The court refused to dissolve the injunction. Then the wage-hour law became an issue in the dispute. The cigar manufacturers had stated in local papers that if the lower-paid workers, such as stripper, were not exempt, they would be forced to discharge approximately 1,000 of them, and have their tobacco stripped in Cuba. A representative of Van Horn and a representative of the Manufacturers' Association flew to Washington to ask exemption of these workers from the provisions of the act. At the same time, the counsel for the cigar workers wired Washington not to grant the exemption. It was not granted. The following week the manufacturers discharged 350 strippers, reporting in the press that they were "keeping as many as possible for the present in the hope that such workers will be exempt."

In order to maintain the unity of the Tampa cigar workers, particularly in the face of the wage-hour problem, to avoid a strike, and to maintain the influence of the progressive and politically conscious leaders reaffirmed their loyalty to the AFL, and Van Horn in turn reinstated them to union membership, with the provision that they not hold office for one year. It is a significant fact that the new officers elected by the unions were also known (by the membership) to favor the CIO. Commenting on the settlement and labor conditions generally in Tampa, a labor leader said:

"With the suspended men bound, gagged, and hamstrung by a court injunction issued at the behest of enemies of progressive unionism, no better settlement could have been expected. The manufacturers like the AFL much better that the CIO, and that's why they give us a closed shop. Of course the cigarmakers like the CIO, but there is nothing we can do about it right now. It is hard for us to strike, because cigars are not perishable, and all the factories have thousands of cigars stored away to fill orders during a strike.

"In Tampa and other parts of Florida attempts of workers to obtain their rights have always been opposed by certain allied groups who have banded together to keep wages down and to cow the workers. These sinister groups conceal their real purpose by raising the cry of 'communism!' at any demonstration of labor. Every labor organizer is branded an 'agitator' and a 'dangerous radical.'

"These enemies of justice have an organized system of suppressing labor, by means of court injunctions, calling out the national guard, and by sending thugs in nightgowns and Legion caps to beat up strikers, always under the smoke screen of 'suppressing communism.' Any poor devil who wants a little gravy on his grits is called a Communist.

"For years this invisible government by industrial gangsters has controlled the newspapers, law-enforcement agencies and the courts, using them to crack down on workers. As a further help, they hire 100 per cent un-Americans in white robes, blue uniforms, and khaki pants, to intimidate, flog, and murder workers who dare to raise a voice for labor. And all this is done under the hypocritical and bloody cloak of 'Americanism.'

"So you see why a progressive labor movement can get nowhere in Tampa. But don't hang my name onto this. If you do, they'll put me at the top of their next whipping list-if I'm not already there."

"Democracy Is Damned Foolishness!"

That is the expressed opinion of a Florida banker whose attitudes are typical of many bankers, editors, and associated groups throughout the Palmetto Country. He is a genuine homemade fascist (Fifth Columnist) and deserves to be treated as such. His following spiel was delivered privately when the new Deal was at its best.

"The politicians in this town are good examples of how the people govern themselves. Most of them never had a pot to piss in or a window to throw it out of. Not one of them ever had $10,000 of their own to manage, yet they're allowed to handle large sums of other people's money. They've all got their ears to the ground. The way they crawl up to me is disgusting!

"For 32 years I've devoted myself to the best interests of this community, giving freely of my time and energy. And what has it brought me? Absolutely nothing; not even appreciation. The people don't want to be helped. I may not have to live in all the filth in town, but it's no fun living next to it. Roberts has the right idea; he's building a fine house on an island, with only a drawbridge connecting. If I was him I'd keep sharks in the water. With the country in the condition it's in now, I wouldn't put more than $100,000 into a home anywhere.

"The thing holding this town back in the Cubans. They're the most radical and unstable people in the world, always striking. They were brought over here to work in the cigar factories, but they went on strike so often the factories had to close down. For six years they've all been loafing on the WPA, letting the Government feed them.

"A lot of them have been dropped from the relief rolls because they don't have all their citizenship papers. I was certainly glad to see it. The quicker we put an end to such things as the WPA, the safer the country will be. The Government is bleeding the taxpayers to death.

"Crackpot professors have tried to ruin the whole country with their Utopian schemes. Roosevelt is as bad as the rest of them. The man must be crazy-getting on the radio and talking about 'economic royalists,' pitting class against class! He's trying to fix it so no man can make more than $5,000. If he succeeds, this will be one hellova country to live in. The most encouraging thing was when his purge failed. At least the South is still fundamentally American.

"If the U. S. Government was operated with ten pr cent of the efficiency of the U.S. Steel Corporation, the country would be a lot better off. Credit, even Government credit, is like a rubber band. Just a little more stretching by the New Deal and it will snap, and there'll be hell to pay getting it back together again. It looks like the only thing that can save this country is a Hitler or a Mussolini."

"The words of the bank president were reported to a Cuban WPA worker, who had been a cigarmaker. His rebuttal:

"I'm not sure what is autocracy, but I think it means for one man to be in charge of everything and tell everybody else that to do. I guess he would like that, so he could be boss over everybody. This would be a democracy if it wasn't for men like him.

"The politicians here is pretty bad, but I'll tell you why. He picked out the whole damn bunch and bought their way into office so they would run things the way he wanted. I know plenty of people he sent ten dollars and a car to ride to the polls in, so they would vote against Claude Pepper. He sent me ten dollars. Heck yeah, I took it-and voted *for* Pepper.

"No wonder he's kicking about Roosevelt. Roosevelt is on the side of the poor people, and the rich people don't like it. Man, I wish Roosevelt would fix it so everybody can make $5,000 a year! I sure would appreciate it and get satisfied. With that much money every year I could take care of my family fine and we all be plenty happy.

"I wish he would build a house out on an island; that's where he belongs, away from everybody. And he don't need to put no sharks in the water, cause nobody wants to go see him. You see how easy he talks about a house costing $100,000; that proves he's gotten a bank full of money out of this town.

"If only I could get that fat scoundrel to do just one day's work on the WPA I'd show him whether it's loafing or not! We works for what we gets paid. Lots of men have got laid off cause they aint got all their citizenship papers. Some of them has been living here forty years or more, almost all their lives, and didn't even know they had to have more papers. I guess the Government thinks those people and their families don't get hungry like everybody else. It hurt me to see Roosevelt let that happen. You know they are telling the joke now that the Government is going to send José Martí-his statue in the cemetery-back to Cuba because he doesn't have all his papers.

"If you ask me there's no need to worry about the Government's credit breaking if it will just tax some of the money the rich people have got hid away. If those rich mens kill the New Deal they'll need a Hitler or a Mussolini to protect them. Everything will be OK; if the rich mens kill the New Deal they'll have to call up a dictator and if they try that it won't take us long to get rid of them and the dictator too!"

Gato Carried a Gun

The unemployed cigarmakers look back with a great deal of longing to the days when the industry was at its height. "I used to be a hell-raiser," said an ex-cigarmaker named Norberto Díaz, "but I was a good cigarmaker. Whenever I finished making a thousand I'd make me a little one to smoke and then walk around helping those who were slow. In those days there was money everywhere. Sometimes they would pay us in silver dollars-burrr-r-r across the counter, like that. Up to 1930 all of us cigarmakers went to work dressed up like sheiks; a man wouldn't work in dungarees then.

"The factories were as much fun as a carnival; there were always lots of peddlers coming in selling hot *bollos* [pea-meal fritters], *empanadas* [small meat pies], *pirulis* [candy suckers], and all kinds of sweets. Everybody bought all kinds of damned foolishness-they'd buy a chicken head on a stick. There were lots of raffles of shoes, suits, and things. Beggars used to stand in front of the factory, and sometime I give out 100 dimes on payday. Whenever a cigarmaker got sick the reader would stand up on the tribunal and say, "Fellow workers, brother so-and-so needs medicine.' And we'd take up a collection and buy him whatever he needed.

"At first the factories allowed us as many fumas [smokes] as we wanted, but then they put a limit of five smokes for every man per day, then they cut it down to three, and finally they wouldn't give us none at all. So we used to sit on the tobacco to press it, then hide it in our underclothes and take it home to make our smokes

"One time when there was a strike at our factory I didn't know about it till I got there and a girl we called Tiburón [Shark] said, 'You're not going to scab, are you, Bud?' I told her, 'Hell, no-not me.' I was on the picket line when the men that led the scabs came up. One of them was called Manteca [Lard] because he was so fat, and the other one was a tough Puerto Ricaño called Gato [Cat]. Gato always carried a gun.

73.........WPA MURAL.
WPA mural, Orlando Civic Auditorium. Some criticized President Franklin D. Roosevelt's economic stimulus efforts through the WPA as a "Utopian Scheme" that was "bleeding the tax-payers to death." K. Yonge Library, University of Florida.

"He came up with two big cracker cops. They stared serching us and they put my buddy in jail for having a pocket knife. Gato stood there and cussed us out plenty. My buddy turned white but I stood there and looked back at Gato. That night when he was walking across the street to get a sandwich somebody put twenty-one buckshots in him. A man named Joe Pérez went crazy over that thing. He went around acting funny, and one day in a café he said, 'You know who shot Gato? I done it. I shot him.' 'You better not go around talking like that or you'll have the cops in back of you,' said another man. But not long after that Pérez killed himself.

"These days the only way you can get and keep a job in the cigar factories is to pay the foreman something every week. Maybe the factory pays you eighteen dollars a week, but to keep your job sometimes you have to pay the foreman eight dollars a week. And you know a man with a family can't live on ten dollars a week."

Custom Reigns

The cigar industry has been on a continuous decline sinceWorld War I, when cigarettes rose rapidly in popularity. The belief is also general that "the cigar-making machines are at the root of all evil in Ybor City." Between 1927 and 1931 the last of the Key West factories were either closed or moved; the industry was dead in the former cigar capital, and the workers were stranded. There was a consequent decline in Key West's population; 5,048 left between 1920 and 1925, the exodus continued through the Depression; and from 1930 to 1935 an additional 1,200 left the island. In Tampa the number of large factories decreased to seventy in 1929-a reduction of seventy-five per cent as of 1919. The total number of employees has dropped from 11,748 in 1930 to 6,997 in 1939.

A *brujo* witch-doctor who had spent eight years in a Havana prison for practicing black magic did a brisk business in Tampa selling voodoo charms to the cigar workers, with the assurance that, worn around the neck, they would ward off unemployment. For some reason the charms failed to function, and in 1942 there were 5,688 unemployed cigarmakers in Tampa.

As layoffs continued the unions voted to stagger the work-to spread it out so that complete layoffs would be retarded. This means less work and less pay for each member, but it helps protect them from total unemployment.

Probably no group of American workers is more cognizant of what the New Deal means to them than these Florida Latins. "This NLRB, unemployment compensation, WPA, and social security is sure a big help," they say. But if the Tampa cigar industry can never hope to absorb its unemployed workers, it would seem that the only real solution would be to teach them new skills and provide them opportunities to use them. So far nothing practical has been done in this direction. In Key West the conversion into a tourist resort may be accomplished, but there is nothing to indicate that this would solve the problem of employment for the Cubans there.

Golden Jubilee

In 1935 the Tampa cigar industry celebrated its Golden Jubilee. The manufacturers arranged a banquet and invited the pioneer cigarmakers to be guests of honor. The invitation was declined by José Garcia, who said, "This is the crowning-point of the farce. The manufacturers have always treated us like dogs. I, for one, do not intend to sit beside Mr. McKay and the others who are directly responsible for our misery. Almost all of the old pioneer cigarmakers are now wandering the streets in rags, and would welcome the cost of their place at the banquet in order to purchase some groceries."

These pioneer cigarmakers petitioned the Cuban Government to take them back to Cuba and pay them a small pension for the remaining years of their lives. Nothing came of the petition, is spite of the fact that these men had been instrumental in bringing about the independence of Cuba.

ALL FOR ONE
AND
ONE FOR ALL

It is not generally known, even in the Palmetto Country, that co-operative social medicine societies were established by the Tampa Latins as early as 1887 and have flourished ever since. Presumably they were the first such organizations in the United States, and have remained in continuous operation longer than any others in this country. They preceded the establishment of most of the European systems, and the Cuban society which inspired them was founded in 1879, four years before Bismark adopted the idea.

In 1942 there were eleven social medicine societies in Tampa and one in Key West. Their active membership totaled 18,000 persons and their property was worth more than on million dollars. The pioneer Florida group was La Igual (The Equal), formed in Tampa in 1887 by Dr. Guillermo Machado, a Spanish physician. La Igual provided medicines and doctor's care to its members for dues of ten cents weekly. In 1888, El Porvenir (The Future) was organized by a group of cigar manufacturers in an effort to increase production and profits by alleviating the ravages of disease among their workers.

The first large Tampa social-benefit society was El Centro Español, formed by cigar manufacturers in 1891 "to provide education and recreation for its members, whom, it shall protect in the most efficient manner possible against any contingencies to which they may be subjected on account of their nationality." It was originally conceived as a company union to pit against the unions of the Cubans.

In 1898 the Asturian members proposed the establishment of a social medicine plan. But the manufacturers who controlled the club were already operating El Prorvenir, and consequently opposed the inauguration of another plan, particularly since it would be more or less controlled by working men. After violent debate, the Asturians seceded, founded the Centro Asturiano, and immediately established a social medicine plan and began building a hospital. In order not to lose still more members, the directors of El Centro Español decided to do likewise. After a survey of the sanitariums of Cuba, in 1906 the club built a $60,000 hospital on the shore of Tampa Bay.

The state and local units of the American Medical Association launched a violent campaign to kill the social medicine plans. Doctors were threatened with cancellation of their AMA membership if they served the societies, so it was necessary to bring physicians from other countries. Dr. J. R. Avellanal was the first to come and serve the Centro Español. Feeling against him on the part of the American doctors was high. One night he was attacked, and for a long time thereafter he had to ask for police protection and carry a revolver.

In spite of all opposition, the club grew until its membership reached a peak of 2,537 in 1912. In 1911 it built two new clubhouses, costing $90,000 and $80,000, in Ybor City and West Tampa. The young American-born members proposed that the clubhouses include gymnasiums, but the directors replied, "Work hard and you will need no other exercise."

In 1922 the club established clinics and emergency hospitals in Ybor City and West Tampa, and also arranged for its doctors to visit sick members in their homes. La Beneficencia Española was organized to extend the benefits of social medicine to the wives and children of the club's members, and in 1942 this organization boasted 3,600 members in addition to the cub's 2,000 regular members. An affiliate organization provides unemployment insurance for members who become too ill to work; the dues are fifty cents weekly, and the benefit payment of six dollars weekly are paid for a period of 16 weeks. Another department provides for the payment of $280 cash to members who find it necessary to go to Spain or elsewhere to convalesce.

Members who have paid dues for two years or more are entitled to $415 under this plan.

Although the by-laws provide that members whose dues are two months in arrears be dropped, unemployed members more than eighteen months in arrears have been given medical treatment. The service record of the club's social medicine plan is most impressive. During the twenty years following its establishment it provided treatment for 7,781 persons and performed 1,623 surgical operations. In a typical ten-year period, 2,473 members were hospitalized at an average cost to them (in dues paid) of eighteen dollars each. The services they received would have cost an average of one hundred dollars each in private hospitals, so their aggregate saving was nearly two million dollars, or eighty-two dollars each.

The various services which have been described are typical of those offered by the other Latin clubs. Besides the actual money saved by the club members, they also enjoy the benefits of better health and freedom from anxiety. Instead of putting off going to a doctor, they receive skillful attention at the first sign of illness. Not only that, the epidemics which

74.........CENTRO ESPAGNOL.
Centro Espagnol, Ybor City, Tampa. Women were not allowed, except for special events. Florida Collection, University of South Florida.

have periodically swept through the Latin colonies would have caused a great deal more suffering and loss of life had it not been for these societies. And because the Latins have scientific treatment available they have virtually abandoned their vast store of traditional home remedies and herb concoctions.

As has been indicated, the Asturians deserve the credit for launching social medicine on a large scale in Tampa. After seceding from the Centro Espanol, they petitioned the Centro Asturiano of Havana for a charter, which was granted in spite of the fact that a committee of Tampa cigar manufacturers representing the Centro Espanol went to Hvana to oppose the petition. The club had 546 charter members, and is first meeting was devoted to a drawing to determine which one should receive membership card No. 1, as all 546 members wanted it.

This club, too, encountered ferocious opposition from the AMA, and it was only with great difficulty that it finally secured the services of Dr. G. H. Atlee. With the aid of a $3,000 loan from the Centro Asturiano in Havana,

75 .... CENTRO ASTURIANO, YBOR CITY, TAMPA.
Traditional costume ball at the Centro Asturiano, Ybor City, Tampa. Pisso Collection, University of South Florida.

a new hospital was completed in 1905. The first social medicine hospital to be built in the United States, its facilities were the most modern available and its laboratories were the first to cultivate vaccines in the South. Besides making outstanding achievements in the treatment of typhoid, it was instrumental in introducing modern therapeutical methods to the Palmetto Country.

A clubhouse built in 1909 was destroyed by fire, and was rebuilt in 1914 at a cost of $100,000. Younger members proposed a gymnasium and roof garden, but the directors only acceded to the gymnasium.

Whenever strikes have occurred the membership and finances of the clubs have suffered. But the Centro Asturiano has a special department whose function is to conduct benefit dances and picnics whose proceeds are used to pay the dues of unemployed members, who are expected to repay the club when possible.

Two other Tampa clubs-El Círcula Cubano and L'Unione Italiana-do not have hospitals of their own, but the hospital of El Centro Asturiano takes care of their members by blanket contract. The hospital also admits, at popular rates, persons who are not members of any club. The present hospital, built in 1928 at a cost of $175,000, has seventy beds and a staff of twenty-five physicians, surgeons, and nurses. In 1942 the club had 2,500 regular members and 3,200 family members, and they were entitled to the privileges of other units of the Centro Asturiano in Cuba, Spain, and New York. The membership includes not only Asturians, but many other Spaniards, Cubans, Italian, and Anglo-Americans-not to mention politicians of various breeds.

The first Cuban organizations in Florida were largely devoted to furthering the cause of Cuban independence, but many of them also had social, recreational, and educational functions. When the Spanish-American War put an end to the political organizations, the need for the other services remained. To fill this need the Círculo Nacional Cubano was formed in Tampa in 1899. "It admitted both white and Negro Cubans," a member recalls, "and was a sort of black beans and rice." With the founding of the Cuban Republic, the club was reorganized as the Círculo Cubano, leaving out the Negro Cubans, who formed a group of their own, La Union Martí-Maceo.

The Círculo Cubano staged a picnic which brought a profit of $1,000 and this was used to purchase a lot. A mortgage of $18,000 then enabled them to build a clubhouse in 1907. The mortgage was liquidated by dramatic productions staged both by local talent and professional entertainers from Cuba. After considerable opposition from the elderly members, a social medicine plan was launched in 1908. Dues for regular members are fifty cents weekly, while the Sección Familiar dues are thirty-five cents weekly for women and twenty-five cents weekly for children. In addition to the usual services, membership covers burial expenses. And for an added fee of twenty-five cents weekly for a period of at least ten months, women are provided complete services for childbirth.

At one time the club maintained a pharmacy which provided medicines free to members at wholesale cost to the club, and also made sales to the general public. During the influenza epidemics the pharmacy gave large quantities of medicines to indigent members of the community who were not club members. Private druggists conducted an intensive campaign

76 .... CUBANS IN EXILE.
    Seated in front is Major General Mario G. Menocal the former president of Cuba and leader of the Miami exiles. Standing from left to right: Martin G. Menocal, Santiago Cerdeja, German S. Lopez, Julio Rabel, J.M. Lasa, Elicio Arguelles, Luis Hernandez, Pedro M. Fraga, E. Arguelles, Jr., Raoul Menocal, M. Llaneras, E.A. Reuda Martinez and Arturo Mora. State Library and Archives of Florida.

against the pharmacy, and during a general strike the club was forced to sell it.

In 1916 the clubhouse was destroyed by fire, and Mario G. Menocal, then President of the Cuba, contributed $1,000 toward a new building fund. The club members voted to pay ten cents additional weekly dues, and a gigantic picnic brought a profit of $5,200. A loan of $35,000 was negotiated, and the balance needed was raised by a bond issue. The new building was completed in 1918, and was furnished by the proceeds of a bazaar which lasted eight days.

When the United States entered World War I, some 300 members of the club enlisted in the Army. During the wartime influenza epidemic the clubhouse was operated as a hospital, admitting anyone who applied without charge. Many lives were saved, and the club incurred a debt of $35,000, which was liquidated by the members paying double their regular dues. The club also had financial difficulties during the 1920 strike, but members who went to Havana sponsored a dance at the Centro Gallego there, and sent the $1,200 proceeds to the Círculo Cubano.

Like the other Tampa Latin clubs, L'Unione Italiana conducts a social medicine plan. Its beautiful clubhouse of Italian Renaissance architecture was built in 1918 at a cost of $82,000, and it now has 3,800 members. Another Italian club, the Societa de Mutuo Soccorso, has some 500 members and a $10,000 clubhouse.

The success of the social medicine plans has led to the establishment of various other co-operative health insurance organizations. Among these are the Buena Pública (Good Public) Clinic, La Popular Bondad (The Popular Kindness) Hospital, La Más Popular (The Most Popular) Society, Instituto Médico-Quirúrgica de Protectión al Anciano (Medical-Surgical Protection of the Aged), and the Clínico del Niño (Child's Clinic).

In Key West, La Sociedad Cuba provides the advantages of social medicine to some 1,000 members, about one-fourth of whom are non-Latins. The club's property is valued at $30,000, and it has no debts. The club organized its social medicine plan in 1917, but for some time was unable to get a physician to serve it, as local doctors and pharmacists opposed the plan as "socialistic." Finally Armando Mato, president of the club at the time, called a meeting of the doctors and pharmacists and offered them the choice of administering to the poor as charity cases, or being paid for the work by contract with the club. The doctors and pharmacists have been competing for Sociedad Club contracts ever since.

The Bread of Instruction

"The more you say it, the less I believe you."
-Cuban saying.

The Latins of the Palmetto Country have suffered because of the inadequacy of the educational opportunities afforded them in their native and adopted lands. During the four centuries that Spain ruled Cuba, formal education was available only to the small wealthy class. Rural children generally received no education except in their homes, although the few parish schools enrolled children without racial discrimination. However, in the schools conducted by the Church, the catechism was the chief study of the boys, while embroidery and music were taught to the girls.

Reading matter was carefully censored before being admitted to Cuba, and the mass of the population first gained some knowledge of what was taking place in the outside world when a flood of literature was released on the island during the twenty-year period of British rule. The Cubans evinced an especially keen interest in the writers of the French Revolution, and their provincialism was greatly relieved by this stimulus.

The most important educational factor in the life of the cigar workers- and one which affected many aspects of their philosophy and way of life- was the system of having readers in the factories. The custom was begun in Cuba about 1880, and was inaugurated by a manufacturer in an effort to "halt union and political discussion" among his employees. In practice, opposite results were achieved. The readers were paid by the cigar workers, who contributed from ten to twenty-five cents weekly from their wages. The readers were popular because they provided the workers with intellectual stimulation and kept them informed about current events, without requiring them to further strain their eyes by reading. They were not only skilled in the use of Castilian Spanish, but were also able to translate newspapers and other material written in English. They imparted to the cigar workers a broad oral knowledge of Castilian Spanish; even the Italians tended to learn Spanish rather than English at first.

The material to be read was chosen by a vote of the workers. From a platform called the tribunal, the readers read *Don Quixote, Les Misérables,* and works dealing with the French Revolution and Garibaldi's enterprises. Other popular works were those of Gorki, Marx, Malatesta, and Tolstoi. Among the periodicals were *El Internacional,* the Tampa unions' paper; *Despertad* (Awaken), published in Key West and said to have been communistic; *El Machete,* also reportedly communistic; *Aurora* (Dawn), socialist; and *Tierra y Libertad* (Land and Liberty), an anarchist paper published in Barcelona. But frequently heard were the speeches of the Cuban revolutionary leaders, material describing Bolivar's campaigns to free South America, and the stories of other struggles for national independence.

This sort of thing increased the support of the cigar workers for the Cuban revolutionary movement, and consequently the readers were greatly disliked by the Spanish manufacturers. Other factors contributing directly to this dislike were that the readers often acted as union spokesmen, and that the tribunals were utilized by the workers as a place to voice their grievances. When the Tampa manufacturers abolished the readers in 1933, a bitter strike resulted which was lost by the workers. Since then radios have been installed in some factories, but they are no substitute for the readers.

When the Latins arrived in Florida, educational facilities were extremely limited. The Latin clubs, therefore established schools of their own, where reading, writing, arithmetic, commercial subjects, and music were taught in Spanish. These proved so effective that by 1908 only five per cent of the Tampa cigar workers were illiterate. As public education improved, all of these classes were discontinued with the exception of those at the San Carlos Institute in Key West, which enjoys the unique distinction of being the only school in the United States that is owned and operated by a foreign government. In 1900 the Florida Legislature provided that $500 per year should be spent to employ an American teacher at San Carlos to supplement the work of the Cuban teachers, and since that time the students have studied in both Spanish and English.

In its historic role San Carlos was a far more dynamic force that at present. Once the revolutionary purpose to which it was primarily dedicated had been achieved, the Institute settled down to a rather ineffectual

77 .... San Carlos Institute.
    The San Carlos Institute at 516 Duval Stret, Key West Florida. State Library and Archives of Florida.

existence as a grammar school. Classes are conducted from the primary through the seventh grade, and the present enrollment is about 100. The school is open to all children of the white race, without tuition charge. The auditorium is rented as a motion-picture theater, and the proceeds are used to purchase books, uniforms, and hot lunches which are served free to the students each day. Each child is given two uniforms and a pair of shoes every four months.

The most significant thing about San Carlos at present is that its students are taught to be good Cuba-Americans—to become Americanized and yet to maintain their cultural identity as Cubans and Spanish-speaking people. In this policy the school has a lesson for all democracies. Yet with its small enrollment San Carlos cannot compete with the public schools in molding the Cuban children of Key West. The public schools are intent upon a program of "complete Americanization." Their only concern with Cuban and Spanish culture is to obliterate it entirely, and this they threaten to do within a very short time.

Language difficulty has been and is responsible for considerable scholastic retardation among Latin children. In the early days it was not uncommon for boys and girls to remain in grammar school until they were fifteen or sixteen years old. This led to many difficulties. For example, sixteen-year-old girls would come home with the distressing message that "The principal put me over his lap, pulled up my dress, and spanked me with his bare hands!"

A study several years ago in the Key West grammar school revealed that 60.3 per cent of the Cuban children were retarded, while only 29.8 per cent of the non-Cubans were retarded. Of those with mixed Cuban-American parentage, those with American mothers were fifty per cent retarded, and those with Cuban mothers were 45.5 per cent retarded. Horace O'Bryant, principal of the Key West high school, has written, "An average I.Q. of 80 indicates that the Cuban children are definitely a dull group. The majority of them come from homes of semi-skilled and unskilled laborers. Very few brilliant children are to be expected from such homes." He neglected to mention that his I.Q. tests were given in English, and that no attempt was made to determine to what extent language difficulty and other cultural factors handicapped the Cuban children. Tampa schools maintain pre-primer classes where the rudiments of English are taught, but no such service is provided in Key West. Nevertheless Key West Cubans become bilingual, while Tampa Latins are often triligual, speaking Spanish, Italian and English.

Some Florida school officials have always regarded Latins as double trouble. In 1904, J. V. Harris, superintendent of public instruction in Monroe County, (Key West), reported that he considered "compulsory education to be incompatible with personal rights"; and in 1908 he said that "strict legislation is needed for the separation of white and Cuban children." These sentiments were apparently endorsed in 1936 by B. M. Duncan, principal of the Key West grammar school, who wrote, "many other people felt that a public high school would be overcrowded with poorer Cuban children whose parents have as a rule contributed very little to public education in Key West. In the then existing high schools [Catholic and Methodist] only Cubans of the better class could afford to pay tuition fees. Those who desired higher learning might pay for it in one of these schools or send their children to some school elsewhere. There was a skepticism of the masses as to the justice of everybody paying for the advanced education of somebody's child."

Principal Duncan also explained the comparative inefficiency of the Key West schools when he said, "Teachers were usually chosen from the ranks of local applicants regardless of their qualifications for teaching." It is another interesting fact that in 1942 physical punishment was still administered in Key West schools, despite state laws to the contrary.

Relatively few Latin students can afford to finish high school, and only a handful are able to attend college. They are sensibly concentrating on commercial subjects, and quite a number enroll in business schools; but their frequent inability to find employment is most disillusioning. Parents generally appreciate the importance of education for their children, having been handicapped by a lack of it themselves. "It's hard enough to earn a living even if you've got an education, much less without one," they say. As a framed card which appears on the walls of some Cuban homes says in Spanish:

If you don't know that you don't know, you know nothing;
If you know that you don't know, you know something,
Because you know that you don't know.

The Latin youth of Florida have fallen heir to the problems which confront American youth generally, but they are also faced with special problems because of their race and the decline of their traditional industry. In attacking their problems they seem to lack the militant spirit and co-operativeness which has characterized the struggles of their fathers. The older generation still fights for its need through coherent organizations, but the young Latins stand alone.

"God is very Discredited"
"Do you think if there was any God he would let people go hungry?"

The above statement and question, often heard among Florida Latins, are indicative of their disbelief in things theocratic. Yet they are not anti-religious, although there are some ardent anti-religionists among them. They are simply irreligious. Theirs is a profound feeling of disillusion acquired over a period of centuries, but it is not an emotion of hatred such as exists so widely in Spain, Mexico, and other countries where the worldly power of the Catholic Church has oppressed the common people. In the United States the Church has no such power; Church and State, and Church and public education were permanently severed in this country by the American Revolution, whereas this was not accomplished until quite recently in Mexico, and is yet to be achieved in Spain.

In Cuba the Church co-operated with the Spanish authorities in opposing the Cuban revolutionary movement, suppressing Negro slave revolts, denying popular education, and censoring the press. Thus to the Cuban immigrants who came to Florida, Spain represented oppression—and Spain and the Church were well-nigh synonymous. Those who came from small Cuban villages were somewhat more religious than their city-bred brethren, because in the rural areas the priests were an integral part of community life, and lived simple lives among the folk. But in Key West and Tampa there has never been any such affinity between the Catholic clergy and the Latin people.

One of the first acts of the Cuban Republic was to abolish the requirement of the former Spanish Government that all marriages be performed by the Catholic Church. This had the immediate effect of causing the Church in Key West and Tampa to lose almost all of its Cuban communicants. The Cubans came to Florida with a strong desire to find economic security, and this attitude tended to dominate all others. Since the life motive of most Cubans is to enjoy life, they are not overly concerned about the prospect of a hereafter. This preoccupation with the pursuit of worldly happiness is so intense that it often results in an impractical philosophy, which does not include a due regard for even the earthly future. As with most Latins, their time is not commercialized; they believe that by living largely in the present they can savor life to its fullest.

The extent to which the Latins do not attend church is indicated by the following figures. In 1935 less than one per cent of the Tampa Cubans were regular church attendees, while at the same time, thirty-seven per cent were members of clubs. However, some 2,800 claimed to be members of the Catholic Church, 800 were reported to be Methodists, and 350 were Baptists. This means that many of them adhere to the spirit of Catholicism to the extent of claiming to be Church members, yet they fail to attend Church except at Easter and Christmas. Many of them, as they say, are merely "affiliated with the Church by birth." Probably a majority are given a Catholic christening, marriage, and burial, though they seldom attend Church between those events. The Spaniards and Italians are but slightly more religiously inclined. In 1933 there were reported to be but 1,000 Spanish and 400 Italian churchgoers in Tampa.

Less than ten per cent of the churchgoers are men. Within the family group the Latin father often ridicules his wife for her church attendance, and his sons, in order to seem manly, refuse to attend church with their mothers and sisters, and instead go to the clubs with their fathers. "While I was attending church all sorts of ridicule were heaped upon me by my fellowmen," is a common report of the masculine ex-churchgoer. In further derision of the religious propensities of their wives, the men make such supplications as *Dios de los hombres, porque el Dios de las mujeres es el hombre!* (God of men, for the God of women is man!).

"I have not gone to church since I realized that the moneychangers have taken over the temple," a typical Tampa Latin has said. "This does not mean that I do not have religion. My religion is this: to do good to others. If I know of someone who has nothing to eat, I cannot sit at my table. The anguish of anyone is my anguish; I feel it as much as the one who is actually suffering. This is my religion and the one which I have taught my children. I do not believe in the preachers who with their little book in hand

78 .... SIGNS OF THE TIMES.
  Signs of the times like this one were prevalent on trees and barns all over the Palmetto Country. P.S. He never made it. From the Stetson Kennedy collection.

will cross themselves reverently and do harm to anyone. They are the parasites of religion.

"I remember an old Negro who died so poor he did not have a place to fall dead. Some of us took up a collection to bury him, but the preacher would give nothing. We took the Negro to the burial-place, and the day was hot enough to crack stones. The preacher stayed at a distance under a shade tree. After we had buried the Negro the preacher came and said, 'Ashes you are, ashes you will be through the centuries of centuries; Amen.' Then he clapped on his hat and left hurriedly. If it had been the funeral of a rich man he would have delivered a sermon for two hours that would have put everyone to sleep."

The Latins have evidently found that their worldly institutions-unions, political organizations, social-benefit societies—are best designed to meet their worldly needs. This is conclusively demonstrated by the comparison of 18,000 club members and 9,000 union members to the several hundred church attenders. Of course the economic factor has had a hand in this; the Latins prefer to pay a small sum each week for job and health protection, rather than make donations to the Church which renders them no tangible service in return.

There are still other reasons why the Catholic Church has lost favor with the Latins. For one thing, Masonic orders are quite popular with the men, and members of such societies are excommunicated by the Church. Then there is the Church's opposition to birth control. Another serious blow to the Church's influence was its collaboration with the fascist conquest of the Spanish Republic. Various Protestant churches have sought to recruit Latins through "mission" work, but their awkward efforts have met with little success.

Though a tendency to gamble usually goes hand in hand with religious piety, this is not the case with the Florida Latin, who is thoroughly addicted to games of chance but not to religious creeds. "When I see a prostitute I play number twelve in bolita," he says—and on such a plane his propitiation of the supernatural ends. In such matters he is an unswerving conformist, and will go to great pains to do whatever he considers necessary to enlist the gods of fortune on his side.

Such acts of adjusting conduct according to some traditionally approved method of approach or conciliation are a primitive form of worship, and place the uneducated Latins who follow the prescribed modes in the same category with the hosts of other Christians who take more stock in juggling the material fixtures of their ritual than they do in "living the life." The concept of the Christian deity, being quite complex at best, causes many Christians to resort to the symbolism and ritualism which have always been an essential part of organized worship.

Among the Latins this finds expression in various ways. Most remarkable is the way in which both men and women wear a crucifix or image of some saint. There does not seem to be any belief in the efficacy of the objects to ward off evil, nor in many cases is there any genuine piety. When asked for a reason, one woman wearer replied, "I wear it for pretty. My husband wears one too, I don't know for why. Bit it's not for any kind of protection-he's no sissy!"

Other simplifications are the superstitions which cling to the body of religion. One of the most popular of these is the belief that bread should be kissed before being thrown away "because that bread is the face of God." Another version of this kissing game has it that the bread should be kissed "because the dead want it." A particularly puzzling superstition bans sweeping at night "for fear of sweeping out the Virgin Mary." Still another, of the wish-fulfillment type, declares that when you see a white horse, if you will tie a knot in your handkerchief and leave it tied until you see a preacher, and then untie it while looking at the preacher, your wish will come true.

The proverbial fatalism of the Latins further militates against religious teaching. The possibility of any dire occurrence is likely to be dismissed with a shrug and the remark, "If it is in the book to happen, it will happen, and there is nothing to be done about it." It is important to note that eventualities are attributed to "the book" (identity unknown), and not to any sort of guiding hand or divine providence. This spirit-inoperative in political and union matters-even finds expression in small framed cards such as the following:

> *Whichever way the wind doth blow,*
> *Some heart is glad to have it so;*
> *So blow it East, or blow it West,*
> *The way it blows, that way is best.*

"Cuba Call Your Children"

In the early days social affairs were mostly family gatherings with music-making, singing, and dancing. Groups of young men strolled about the streets in the late afternoon and evening, strumming guitars and singing ancient folksongs. Known *as cantantes callejeros*, they are the modern equivalents of the wandering troubadours of Europe, and, like their predecessors, are important folk characters. The Latins have recently provided a good demonstration of the relation between bread and song; with the slight betterment of their condition incident to the war production program, a host of them broke forth into song who had not hummed a note in years.

With the organization of their clubs the social life of the Latin colonies boomed, and the satisfaction which they derived from seeing substantial club buildings arise through their cooperative efforts did much to dispel their early longing to return to their native lands. Most of the clubhouses have elaborate recreational facilities, such as card rooms, billiard rooms, gymnasiums, bowling alleys, and libraries. The libraries contain many valuable books in Spanish and Italian, and also files of magazines and newspapers in those languages. The Tampa public library maintains branches in the Latin colonies, with foreign-language material, but Key West does not even have a free public library.

An extraordinary spectacle was the "exhibition bull fight" announced by El Círculo Cubano for January 1, 1926. Following the announcement there was such an enormous storm of protest that the Governor of Florida ordered that the fight be canceled. The El Círculo Cubano maintained that it was to be merely a "mock fight," with all the color and pageantry of the real thing, but "without danger to man or bull." After an investigation by State officials, the plans proceeded. Professional *matadors* were brought from Mexico and Spain, some choice Florida bulls were rounded up, and three "mock fights" were staged. No blood was shed, and tremendous crowds of spectators, who came from all over the Palmetto Country, were highly pleased.

The recreation divisions of the clubs have sought to keep alive the national customs of their members. The picnics were identical with the

European *romerias* of folk festivals given on saints' days, and consisted of bounteous outdoor feasts, followed by programs of folk music, singing, and dancing. The *verbenas* were somewhat similar, but were held at night and included dramatic tragedies. Some of the world's leading grand-opera singers have appeared on the stages of the Tampa clubs.

Picnic and verbenas have been sadly lacking since the decline of the cigar industry, and there has been no adequate substitute for the entertainment of the elderly people.

Perhaps the most conspicuous of the Latins' folkways is their custom of promenading. This is the sole form of recreation for many people, who dress in their best clothes and walk up one side of the main street and down the other, speaking with friends, window-shopping, and ocassionally making purchases. Girls who are looking for sweethearts make *buscanovio* (looking-for-sweetheart) curl by plastering a lock of hair into a curl over their temple. The young men gather in groups and call out such things *as* "*Cuba, llama sus hijas!*" [Cuba, call your children!] as the girls go by with twinkling legs and a flutter of skirts and eyelids.

By nature the Latins are inclined to celebrate any and all occasions with marked enthusiasm, but their festive spirits have been sadly dampened by their economic plight.

The national holidays of Cuba, Spain, and Italy are still observed by the respective clubs. This is especially true of the Cubans, many of whom participated in and have not forgotten their country's comparatively recent struggle for freedom.

The traditional Latin methods of celebrating Christmas are quite different from the American. "In celebrating Christmas we hold many *rumbitas*," says a Tampa Cuban. "One time we were rhumba-ing for a whole week. We would come out of the factory and go to the house of Pablo to continue the rhumba, day after day. On New Year's Eve we make a practice of burning the old year. We gather together, and a puppet symbolizing the old year is burned while we say, '*Vete año malo; a ver si el que viene es mejor*' [Go bad year; let us see if the coming one is better]."

Numerous Cuban superstitions are connected with Good Friday. It is believed by some that a mirror held over a pan of water will reflect the image of Christ if He is called upon. Another belief has it that all eggs laid on Good Friday will last one year without spoiling. Still another belief is that if a girl before retiring cuts several potatoes in halves, thirds, and quarters, and places them with a whole potato beneath her bed, and upon reaching for them in the morning she should first grasp the whole potato, then she will soon be married.

The Latins have adopted Valentine's Day *con mucho gusto*, and Halloween is celebrated with masquerade balls and pranks. Thanksgiving too, is observed, but usually with road pork and black beans rather than America's traditional turkey and cranberry sauce. The Fourth of July is celebrated in true American style, with firecrackers, picnics and parades. They have always observed Mother's Day, but only recently adopted Father's Day. And traditionally they have celebrated the internationally observed revolutionary May Day, but now have given precedence to the American Labor Day.

Tampa Latins annually observe La Verbena del Tabaco (Tobacco Festival) and a Latin-American Carnival. These affairs, though originated by commercial interests for tourist consumption, are celebrated in true folk style, with typical Cuban, Spanish, and Italian folk music and dancing in native costumes. The Gasparilla Festival is widely known as a rival of New Orleans' Mardi Gras. In "honor" of the pirate José Gaspar, this tourist attraction features an invasion by a "motley crewe" of the socially elite, who play their piratical parts with great aptitude. The crew enters Tampa Bay in an ancient sailing vessel, with their true colors (skull and crossbones) flying. They take over the city, and parades, pageants, and costume balls are held climaxed by a king-and-queen crowning.

A legend has grown up about a beautiful Cuban girl whose scantily clad body was covered with gold paint so that she could decorate a cigar factory float in the 1930 Gasparilla parade. Shortly after the parade she was poisoned by the paint and died two days later. The cigar company did not pay her funeral expenses, though her family was destitute.

When the FERA took over Key West it found that, among other things, the town lacked a festival. So La Semana Alegre (The Week of Joy) was concocted. But so many of the Cubans have been subsisting on the WPA "security" wage, it is not surprising that The Week of Joy has not been all that its name implies.

Lolita Likes Bolita

"There are two things I like in this world, and bolita is one of them."
-Lolita.

The world *bolita* is Spanish, and means "little ball." It is a Cuban adaptation of the age-old Chinese game of *charada,* and has inherited much of that game's symbolism, especially as regards the interpretation-in terms of winning numbers—of dreams and objects actually seen. The 100 objects and their corresponding numbers are definitely fixed in *charada,* and have been carried over unchanged in bolita. Charts, calendars, and booklets listing these objects and numbers are published widely in Cuba and find their way to the Palmetto Country, but most Latins memorize the combinations at an early age.

Probably bolita was fist played in this country by a Cuban named Francisco Gonzáles, also know as Pancho Macaro, in Key West about 1885. In 1942, Key West bolita houses listed the following establishments on their blackboards: Curro, Orange Inn, Trumbo, Two Friends, Nancy, Broadway, Sunlight, Red House, Rocky Road, Duval, The Club, Cuba, and 8 O'clock House. A notice on the wall read:

WE PAY WHAT THE TICKET CALLS FOR.
EXAMINE YOUR TICKET BEFORE YOU LEAVE.

Bolita tickets, numbered from one to a hundred, are sold at the bolita houses or by agents who go from door to door. The tickets cost five cents each, and each winning ticket pays the holder four dollars. At the bolita throwings a crowd of players gathers in the bolita house, and a tray holding one hundred small balls consecutively numbered is displayed for examination. The balls are then placed in a bag, which is passed around and thoroughly examined and thoroughly shaken; finally it is tossed by the operator and caught by a player by one of the balls inside. Closely watched to prevent sleight-of-hand tricks, the operator cuts the bag, releasing the ball held by the player—and the number on that ball is the winner.

The winning numbers of each bolita house are telephoned to all other houses and to barrooms, where they are posted on blackboards. This and the grapevine method soon make the winning numbers widely known. Winners collect directly from the bolita house or from their agent.

The popularity of bolita has spread until it has become one of America's most favored gambling games. The *Baltimore Afro-American*, quoting the magazine *Business*, reported that in 1935 Negroes alone gambled one and a half billion dollars on bolita and similar games. These players won slightly over a million dollars—one dollar for each $1,500 spent. In the Palmetto Country as elsewhere, this illegal racket is made possible by the payment of "hush" money to public officials. Some bolita operators pay the policemen on their beat a regular weekly protection fee, while other operators hold a 'police night," on which the officers are tipped off about what number will be "fixed" as the winner. Periodic anti-bolita campaigns almost always result in the ballyhooed sentencing of one or two smalltime agents, while the actual operators are seldom arrested.

79 .... HARLAN BLACKBURN, GAMBLING KINGPIN.
Harlan Blackburn, seated in the far left of photograph, was the gambling kingpin of Orange and Polk Counties in the 1950s. State Library and Archives of Florida.

Since the Depression another form of bolita, called *pajarito* (little bird), has been popular. In this game, tickets cost one cent instead of five cents, and winning numbers—which are determined by the final numbers listed in the daily stock market quotations—receive six dollars. Still another type of bolita is *guiguí*; the player gets three numbers on his five-cent ticket, and twelve winning numbers are drawn; if the player's three numbers are all among the winners, he receives fifteen dollars.

The *Lotería Nacional Cubano* is also very popular. The results of the lottery are announced by radio from Havana each Wednesday, a day on which the majority of Latin-owned radios in Key West and Tampa are tuned to that station, whether inhabitants of the house have bought lottery tickets or not. The winning numbers are announced by orphans, wards of the Cuban Government, who are benefited by the net proceeds. Their sing-song chant reverberates throughout the Latin quarters for several hours.

"Heck Yeah, I'm an American!"

The Cuban mother in Tampa who made that declaration and then asked "Aint I on the WPA?" was offering very sound evidence of her citizenship, since aliens have been purged from relief rolls. Her daughter, however, retorted, "You may be an American citizen, but real Americans consider you a Cuban just the same." But there was no answer to her mother's final words: "What do I care what they consider me, so long as I am an American?"

A typical example of how racial antagonism is stirred up for anti-social purposes occurred in Key West during the 1935 WPA wage strike. During a strikers' meeting an Anglo-American supervisor (whose job was at stake) cried: "Don't be led around by a bunch of Cuban niggers!" He was promptly seized, the strikers separated into two groups, and violence seemed imminent. Then Luis Avila, the strike leader spoke alternately in Spanish and English. "Wait boys," he pleased. "Can't you see he's trying to split us up to end our strike? Don't pay any attention to him." The meeting and the strike continued.

Of course the press had played its customary part in molding race relations. The editor of the *Key West Citizen* has said, "The trouble with Key

West is that too many people have gotten the idea it's a Cuban town; we want to correct that impression if we can." This he seeks to do by publishing a minimum of matter relating to Cubans. The major bus system of the State has tourist-sense enough to advertise Key West as "The Cuba of the United States." Politicians, too, have found it profitable to play upon the pride of the Latin-Americans and the prejudice of the Anglo-Americans.

The public schools have also done their bit in perpetuating interracial friction. Horace O'Bryant, principal of the Key West high school, has written, "Among the first Cubans to come to Key West were the political refugees. They were few in number and intellectually superior. As such they were welcomed. Later, many of the lower classes came to Key West. When this large influx of the lowest grade Cuban—the tobacco roller—took place, the situation changed."

As is usually true in such matters, the attitude toward Latins is not one of invariable antipathy, but is adjusted to correspond with the economic status of the particular individuals being appraised. Thus, those Latins who have achieved a "respectable" economic status, and who display the appurtenances appropriate thereto, are respectfully regarded. On the other hand, Latins who earn meager wages, live in poor surroundings, and wear working clothes suffer the full measure of racial prejudice.

For reasons not purely esthetic the Latins desire light complexions. This leads to some of the women to resort to heavy applications of a light shade of face powder. Even with the men the effect of sun-tan is often more than skin-deep. For example, a young Cuban-American working as a clerk in Key West was warned by his Spanish employer not to go swimming in the sun any more if he wanted to keep his job. The employer was afraid that customers might suspect the clerk of having Negro blood.

Despite some opposition from the foreign-born immigrants, intermarriage of the Latin groups has proceeded at an increasing rate. There has also been a great deal of intermarriage between Latin-Americans and Anglo-Americans; in Key West alone there are now 2,093 persons of mixed Cuban-American parentage. More than twice as many American men are married to Latin women as there are Latin men married to American women. Comparatively speaking, Latin women are glad to marry American men for the freedom obtained, while on the other hand American women are reluctant to marry Latin men who still retain the idea that the woman's place is almost exclusively in the home.

It is said that Cuba achieved the closest approximation to equality between laboring folk of the white and black races. Be that as it may, it is always a distinct shock to the Anglo-Americans in Key West to see Cuban naval vessels arrive with white and Negro Cubans on deck, and still more of a shock to see them march side by side in parades. This equality is reflected among Florida Cubans, whose attitude toward Negroes is far less prejudiced than that of the average Southerner. In Ybor City many Latin children play with their Negro neighbors.

In recent years many poor whites from rural sections of the Palmetto Country have settled in Ybor City to work in the cigar factories. They have come in intimate contact with the Latins, often living under the same roof. The two cultures collided headlong, then settled down to good-natured adjustment; they have poverty and its attendant problems in common. At first the Latins were afraid the crackers would seek to break up their unions. "Them cracker people will work for anything," they complained. "They work for enough to by a little fat bacon and a sack of flour and they get satisfied." But the crackers have joined the unions and there has been but little friction. "The only thing wrong with them cracker people is that they been used to living so far out the running water aint got there yet." The Latins say with a grin.

The Americanization of the Latins continues apace, despite the absence of any organized or practical assistance from the country of their adoption. As a matter of fact, the Latins are qualified to teach many of their Anglo-American neighbors how to be better citizens in a democracy. Those traditional customs which the Latins still retain have been compared and found preferable. There is, however, an over-all tendency toward cultural homogeneity. That the American environment has made profound changes in the Latins who have lived here is clearly brought out when they visit their native lands, where they are easily identified by their differences of speech, customs and mannerisms.

An Unhealthy Place for Fascists

"The Left is the side of the heart; the Right is the side of the liver."
Spanish proverb.

The Latins are by far the most politically minded folk in the Palmetto Country. During the hey-day of the cigar industry they elected members of their group to the Florida Legislature, the mayorship of Tampa and Key West, and to numerous smaller positions. Although their influence has declined considerably with their payroll, they continue to vote solidly for the candidates endorsed by their unions, clubs and newspapers, and therefore are a force commanding respect.

However, it is in the field of national and international politics that they excel. Their political movement is conducted in conjunction with their unions, which keep a watchful eye on current events. Lively discussions take place at their Labor Temple, and the telegrams of condemnation or praise which are the usual result are not without effect upon their recipients. The unions are also noted for their telegramed expressions of sympathy for all justified strikes which occur in the Palmetto Country. They have been exceptionally active in taking a stand on legislation affecting the New Deal, the rights of labor, civil liberties, and related matter.

There is a story told that Leon Trotsky, after haranguing an audience of workers in Spain for hours without arousing much enthusiasm, finally asked in desperation, "What kind of government do you want?" The answer came back from many throats, "We want no government!" Such an attitude is not difficult to understand in view of the Spaniards' centuries of suffering under despotic governments. The old Spanish proverb that "no evil can last a hundred years" may be true, but it seems that in Spain new evils have always succeeded the old.

Nothing approaching such a spirit of anarchy prevails among the Latins of the Palmetto Country, although radical terminology and habits of thought are traditional with them, a heritage from the anarchists and syndicalists among their forebears (not to mention their exploitation). It is said that many Tampa Latins have embraced the comprehensive creed and strict discipline of the Communist Party. Diego Riviera, the, the Mexican artist, has said that the official and living Mexican Revolution is "a Bour-geois revolution employing the language of Marx instead of Robespierre." His remark ignores, however, that the motive power of the Mexican Revolution is derived from the exploited Mexican workers and peons. A somewhat analogous situation obtains among Florida Latins, who use Marxian terms while calling for nothing more drastic than extension of the New Deal.

They still take an interest in the politics of their native countries, and their colonies have always been a haven for exiled leaders of the revolutionary organizations, which have periodically sought to better social and economic conditions in Cuba. When the family of the deposed Cuban dictator Gerardo Machado fled to Key West a large crowd of angry local Cubans gathered at the docks, and the National Guard was called out to maintain order. The Tampa Italians are similarly opposed to Mussolini, and always boo him loudly when he appears on the screen. With the entry of America into World War II, the FBI in its search for enemy aliens found no Axis sympathizers in the large Tampa Italian colony. As for the Spaniards, most of the working men are antagonistic to the Franco regime, although some of the manufacturers are on the other side of the fence.

The Latins have always been confident of the ultimate victory of democratic forces throughout the world, and have been united on the firm basis of anti-fascism ever since the advent of that dread disease as a world force. During the pre-Munich era, posters throughout the Latin colonies called for *Solidarity With the Victims of World Fascism!* In particular, the conspiracy against the democratic Spanish Republic by the coalition of Spanish Falangists, Italian Fascists, German Nazis, Moorish mercenaries, and French-British-American non-interventionists, with blessing of the Roman Catholic Church, served to unite the Latins in support of the Spanish Government.

Not since the struggle for Cuban freedom had the Florida Latins been so aroused. Organized in a local unit of the North American Committee to Aid Spanish Democracy, they contributed regularly and generously from their meager wages. "It was almost like playing bolita the way they took up those collections for Spain," a cigarmaker reported. "You could buy a five-cent receipt or as much more as you want. Every week they printed in the union paper how much each man gave." Altogether the per-capita aid rendered

341

by the cigar workers was greater than that of any other group in the United States. They sent nearly $200,000, two ambulances, tons of food and clothing, and six million cigarettes to the war-torn Spanish Republicans. They made the cigarettes themselves, purchasing the tobacco and working after hours in the factories. In Key West the Cubans were too poor to contribute much, but meetings were held for the benefit of Spanish children, and Ernest Hemingway, then a resident of Key West, served as sponsor.

During a meeting held by the Committee in Ybor City, George O. Pershing, field representative of the national organization, read an anonymous note he had received which said, "Tampa is an unhealthy place for liberals." Someone in the audience shouted back, "Whoever wrote that note should be sent a reply saying, 'Ybor City is an unhealthy place for fascists!'" The crowd roared its approval.

The support of Tampa Latins for the cause of Spanish Republicanism did not end with the physical conquest of Spain. They reorganized to aid Spanish refugees, sending materials to those in French concentration camps and doing everything possible to aid in bringing them to Mexico and the United States. David Lord, a director of the Spanish institute of Florida, visited Mexico City in 1939 and met the intellectual leaders of the Spanish refugees. These cultural leaders are united in an international organization, the Junta de Cultura Española. José Bergaman, the famous Catholic writer who is president of the Junta, has said, "Of all the activities now being driven out of Spain, those which affect science, literature, and art are representative of the national and popular Spanish spirit, and their preservation in America is of great significance to Spain and America as well." Upon his return, Lord established a chapter of the Junta in Tampa.

The Spanish conflict taught the Florida Latins, among many other things, how to identify Fifth Columnists, and this is a lesson that should not be lost upon all freedom-loving people; they have not forgotten that Franco's fascist General Mola created the phrase, and that his reference was to the *reactionaries* in Madrid whom he knew he could depend upon to betray the Republic and help him wipe out democracy in Spain.

One of the Florida Latins' outstanding leaders has been Pedro Rimirez Moya, long-time editor of *El Internacional*. Moya went to Washington in 1938 as a delegate to the Congress for Peace and Democracy. "I went around with a delegation to ask the Congressmen to vote for lifting the embargo on Spain," he reported. "One Congressman told us, 'You are from Florida and are not my constituents, but in your request you represent the majority of the American people, and so do I.' You should have seen us when we went into Senator George's office from Georgia. We almost got thrown out. I don't guess there has been a Spaniard in Georgia since De Soto marched through. I learned a lot in Washington, all right. I watched those guys work and I know there are very few real liberals among them. Most of them are uneducated and crooked politicians controlled by the big interests."

Shotgun Shacks

"The chief industries of Ybor City are cigar-making and bolita, and the chief recreations are love-making and arguing."

That saying has been popularized by the Chamber of Commerce, but the inhabitants tell a different story: "We live in Ybor City because we can't afford to live nowhere else. That's the only reason anybody lives here." And so it is that economic necessity, quite apart from cultural affinity, requires that the Latins concentrate in compact settlements where the cost (and standard) of living is lowest. A typically Latin atmosphere is created by a combination of factors. Besides some beautiful examples of Spanish and Italian architecture, cows and goats grazing in vacant lots add an exotic touch. Spanish continues to be the predominant language, and many shop signs are also in Spanish. "Tampa was once a small Havana," it is said. "At first our customs were typically Cuban and Spanish. Then the Italians and Americans came, and everything was a mixture. Everyone helped each other, until Tampa became cosmopolitan."

Street venders, whose low operating cost enables them to undersell the markets, are an important part of the food supply system. Many families depend on them for fruit, vegetables and fish, while the children listen anxiously for vendors of *piruli* suckers, *empanada* meat pies, and tropical fruit ice creams. The venders announce their wares in poetic chants, sometimes combining Spanish and English, according to the neighborhood. One of the most colorful of the Ybor City venders was an old Frenchman.

Wherever he went he would be met by children who would approach him cautiously and then infuriate him by singing this doggerel mocking the peculiar rhythm of his walk: *Tranquitro, tranquitro, tranqui trique, trique, tro.* The children were convinced that the old vender ate sand. The taunting song died with him, but it is said that the mockingbirds of Ybor City still whistle the refrain.

In 1942 a popular Cuban vender of pirili suckers announced his wares in a Spanish verse which translated:

> *Wake up folks: this may sound funny,*
> *But I sell for, or without money,*
> *Four coupons—one piruli;*
> *One cigar—three pirulis.*

"I've Done My Duty by Uncle Sam"

"Marriage is like a lottery: you don't know whether you win or lose until it's all over."

—Cuban saying.

Because the proximity of Cuba enabled them to bring their wives with them, the Cubans of Florida have multiplied rapidly. Other factors making for their rapid increase were favorable economic conditions during the first decades, the tendency to marry at an early age, and an ignorance of contraceptive methods. There is still a tendency for girls to marry while in their middle teens, but this has been somewhat mitigated by economic stress and the increasing desire to obtain a high school education. Nevertheless, some marriages still take place at the ages of fourteen to sixteen, especially among the most poverty-stricken. Many such nuptials are explained by the popular saying, *Se casaron porque no tenían otra cosa que hacer* (They got married because they had nothing else to do).

When a marriage takes place between two people of vastly different ages, or if one or both of them have been married before, they are give *la lata* (the can). This is the tin-pan serenade, or *charivari*, which the French introduced to New Orleans and which has spread throughout the Palmetto Country as the "shivaree." A large group, consisting mostly of young boys, parades through the streets beating loudly and in unison with sticks on all sorts of pans, buckets, and tubs. As the unearthly sound spreads, new recruits hasten to join the parade and add to the din. Eventually the parade arrives at the house of the newlyweds, where the mock serenade continues indefinitely until the groom treats the assembly to cake and beer. The custom has been revived since the repeal of Prohibition, with the enthusiastic approval of the barkeepers.

The customs of Latin courtship are most elaborate. Before a young man is able to begin courting a girl openly he must first have the approval of the girl's family. Once accepted as a suitor, he is expected to call on the girl several times each week for a period of time specified by her parents, before asking for her hand in marriage. One of the most tenacious of the Italian customs (besides the red bandana) is that of having the nearest relative of the suitor ask the parents for their permission and arrange a wedding date; as a face-saving device, literally and figuratively, this custom must have considerable merit.

Until recently, the girl was kept under close surveillance from the time she learned to walk until she was turned over to her husband. When a girl went to a dance, picnic, or other social functions she was invariably chaperoned. Besides rendering lovemaking extremely difficult if not impossible, the chaperon was an added expense to the escort.

The American custom of taking dates to dances is rapidly supplanting the chaperon system. This change has been brought about by continuous pressure on the part of the young people, who seek to convince their parents that the chaperon custom is backward and "un-American." Probably the principal reason for the custom's longevity is that it has afforded older women almost their sole opportunity to attend social affairs. Yet the Latin girls are far from enjoying the liberties of their Anglo-American counterparts; the mere suggestion of such things as "late dates" and "dawn dances" would shatter the best of Latin reputations. Moreover, Latin temperament almost always prevents the Latin girl from enjoying the luxury of more than one boy-friend at a time.

Just how radically customs of courtship have changed is shown by the following conversation between a typical Latin mother and her grown daughter. "I wasn't allowed to go anywhere without a chaperon," said the mother, "and even when my boy-friend came to see me at the house we had to just sit in the parlor and hold conversation. I would ask my chaperon if me and my boy-friend could go back to the kitchen to get a drink of water, but she always made me go get it by myself. I couldn't even go to the door with him to tell him goodbye."

"Cuban customs are crazy anyway." Her daughter replied. "I'm glad I was born in America. I'm going to marry Nicky and go to New York. Of course I would like to marry an American, but I can't do nothing about it. The only way to get an American husband is to live over in Hyde Park and be hightoned, and I can't do that. I don't want any of them damn crackers from out of the woods, either. They're wild people. You can grow potatoes in their ears and scrape their heels."

"Well, all I can say for myself is that I've done my duty by Uncle Sam," her mother said, "I had four kids before I was twenty years old. That was fast work. But them days is gone forever. There aint any sense in having kids unless you can give them some of the things they need. The more kids you have, the less there is to give them. When I got married my mother hadn't never told me nothing about life. I was as innocent as the day I was born. When she used to want to talk about those things she would look at me and I would have to leave the room. I didn't know nothing about how not to have babies—no wonder I had so many."

Another interesting statement about home training was made by a Cuban girl upon returning from the NYA camp at Ocala, Florida. "The American girls were always walking around the dormitory stark naked!" she reported in shocked amazement. "That's one thing I wouldn't do even in front of my own mother, I was raised different."

However, Latin home life has suffered because of the custom, which prescribes that the men spend their evenings and Sundays at their clubs. The man who stays at home is thought to be but half a man. This practice does an injustice to the women, who are left at home with the children to amuse themselves as best they can. Latin wives are generally faithful to their husbands, but it is fairly common for the men to indulge in extramarital relations. When this occurs it is said that the man is "jumping the fence" and "putting horns on" his wife. This characteristic of the male is usually tolerated by wives because the prospect of divorce and separate maintenance is too grim.

When death occurs in a Cuban family, custom requires that curtains and doors on the front of the house be kept closed for several days. Funeral services are usually conducted in the home, with the women of the immediate family retiring to a back room to weep. It is the duty of the men to escort the body to the cemetery, while the women remain in the house. Shops close their doors as the funeral procession passes. During the mourning no one in the family is expected to participate in social activities, but even this custom is being modified. As an aged Cuban woman said, "When I die all I ask is that my family bury me. Remaining in a downcast spirit would do them no good, and certainly would not help me any. I want them to enjoy life, for life is very short."

"I Destroyed the Cigarmakers' Union"

This is the life story of Enrique Pendas, owner of the Lozano Pendas & Company cigar factory. The research worker who obtained the story first applied to Fermin Souto, secretary of the Centro Español, for a letter of introduction to Mr. Pendas.

"No, I cannot do that!" exclaimed Mr. Souto. "Mr. Pendas has the highest regard for me, but he is a man of strange moods. He is a porcupine—you cannot touch him. He is not a man to sit down and open his heart like me; he is too proud. He is a man who carries his head far back, and only considers those who have a high position in life. However, if you go to his home after he has had his supper—he might be in a good mood then. But for all that you hold sacred—not the slightest reference to me!"

In spite of this advice, the interviewer called upon Mr. Pendas at his factory. There he was received civilly, but Mr. Pendas said he was too busy to see him. The interviewer suggested that he see Mr. Pendas at his home that night; but Mr. Pendas said, "No, I go to bed early." Then the interviewer said he would call every day until Mr. Pendas could spare a few minutes. Mr. Pendas smiled at this, and said, "Come to the office Sunday morning and I will see you."

At the beginning of the interview, Mr. Pendas tore up the interviewer's paper, so he wrote the story from memory.

"My name is Enrique Pendas. I was born in the province of Asturias, Spain, in 1865, which makes me about as old as Christopher Columbus. I went to Cuba when I was still very young, and was amazed by the beauty of the land, which yields three crops a year, a thing equaled by no other coun-

347

try. Above all is the hospitality of the people, who are always trying to please; it is second nature to them.

I founded the Centro Español, and although I hold membership card number 1, I have retired from the club altogether. They have sent committee after committee to get me to go back, but I have principle in my life. The reason for this action of mine is that the Centro Español once gave a reception for the former Cuban President, Ramon Grau San Martín. They acted like dogs that lick the hand that whips them! [San Martin enforced a law in Cuba requiring that at least fifty per cent of the employees of all persons and establishments be Cubans.]

I attend many meetings of the Cuban Club. At one meeting I brought up the matter of sending a committee to the officials of the City of Tampa. No one wanted to go; they were all afraid. So I appointed myself the committee and went myself. It is absurd to be afraid to voice your rights before those who came here after we founded the city. I might say that I do not consider myself a Spaniard, but a Spanish-American, as all other persons of Spanish blood in the Americas should be called.

"Every year I make substantial donations to all worthy charitable causes. When the terrible storm destroyed the entire town of Santa Cruz del Sur, Cuba, I immediately organized a movement to succor the inhabitants. I was afterwards awarded a certificate in recognition of my act, which I still hold. I also pay the dues of many members of the clubs when they are out of work.

When the beautiful santorium of the Centro Asturiano was built, the president fell ill so I took charge and organized the hospital. Since the first of these social medicine societies were formed the private doctors have been carrying on a most brutal war against them. They are a bunch of shameless rascals. At least sixty per cent of the people in cemeteries have been killed by such doctors.

"During one of the long strikes here I went back to my home town in Spain. I thought I would find my old friends and relatives, but I knew no one. Upon my return to Tampa an old mulatto man, who had worked in my factory for years, died. I attired myself in a tight coat and tall top hat— it still makes me laugh to think how I was dressed for his funeral. In those days I was alone here, without my family, so you can be sure I wasn't too good. I did as I pleased.

"Mr. D. B. McKay was raised in Ybor City. As a boy he was always among us. He has not forgotten his friends, and attends all the social functions of the different Latin clubs. When he first ran for mayor of Tampa I was his chief supporter. I, myself, placed him as mayor of Tampa. Peter O. Knight is another one of the 'strong men' of Tampa. He visits all the clubs on Christmas day, and he visits me at my home.

"The cigarmaking machines are ruining not only the cigarmakers, but the manufacturers as well. The Tampa factories must compete with other factories in the country, which are producing a very large cigar to retail at two for five cents. This competition is ruinous.

"The Cigar Manufacturers' Association here is composed of pirates of the industry. They are not human; they can only think of new ways of squeezing the cigarmakers more and more. At one time there were false rumors that I had said something about one of the manufacturers. So at one of our meetings I got up and said that whoever said such a thing about me was an *apestoso hijo de perra* [stinking son of a bitch!]. No one got up to contest this.

"Of Mr. Davis of Scwab Davis & Company, I can't say much. It is best to ignore him altogether. He wanted to have the cigarmakers produce panatelas at thirteen dollars per thousand, and thought he could do it by threatening them. How little he knows the nature of the cigarmakers! I told him he could sooner starve them to death than make them submit to any threats. I have always treated the cigarmakers as human beings, not as animals. I thoroughly understand their nature.

"Most of the strikes in Tampa have been originated by the Cigarmakers International Union. One of the things causing the strike was the readers in the factories. I advised the manufacturers to take out the readers and there would be no more strikes. The readers were abolished forever through my efforts. In the big strike of 1910, the cigarmakers demanded recognition of the union. I headed the manufacturers' Association, and although the cigarmakers lost, they still had hopes of forcing recognition. In 1920 they struck again. This strike lasted ten months, and I completely destroyed the International for all time.

"Of the pioneer settlers of Ybor City, only a few remain. Most of them are in their graves, and that is the only place I can go to see them. Many of the younger generation are leaving. I do not intend to leave, however, for I have lived here practically all my life, and I intend to die with the cigar industry in Tampa."

"Man Sould Not Be Enslaved"

"I wish to ask that my readers be tolerant, since they will not have the pleasure of reading the words of an upright literary man, but those of a humble worker who by many sacrifices has been able to take a little instruction.

"My name is Gerardo Corina y Piñera, and I was born in Havana in 1912. I am the son of honorable and laborious Spaniards. My father was a poor but honest grocer. He died when I was six, and four years later my mother died, leaving five children without any means of support. My older brothers and sisters were cared for by relatives, and I was placed in a Catholic school where I studied for five years. Forced to leave school for financial reasons, I became an apprentice line-maker in La Habañera printing house. I worked in this shop until 1928, when I boarded the steamship *Cuba* and came to the City of Tampa in this hospitable land of America.

"Upon my arrival I found employment as a reader in the cigar factory of Gradiaz Annis & Company. In 1931 I contracted nuptials with Esther Gemis, daughter of a respected Tampa family, but toward the end of the year I was struck with unemployment sickness—the cigar manufacturers voted to abolish the readers in all factories.

"The manufacturers gave the excuse that the readers were reading pernicious radical works and communistic papers. My opinion—and it is very humble but gifted with the sincerity that characterizes a Christian—is that since the Government guarantees freedom of the press and permits communistic material to be distributed through the mails, these manufacturers—who are of foreign origin—have no justification for restricting the democratic rights granted by this country in allowing the people to read whatever they wish.

"Through the readers the cigarmakers increased their cultural knowledge, and were given an opportunity to clearly comprehend the plan of President Roosevelt, who upon his inauguration addressed himself to the workers of the country and strongly urged them to unite in organizations which would assist him in carrying out his plans for bettering their condition.

"The manufacturers actually abolished the readers for a reason, which they lack the moral courage to publicly admit: the readers were a powerful force in maintaining the unity of the workers in labor unions.

"Leaving aside this anti-democratic action of the manufacturers, I return to the account of my life. My wife presented me with a beautiful daughter, whom we named Sofia in memory of my departed mother. But the following year was a sad one for me, because my daughter, the angel of my home, departed from this world. It was impossible for me to follow the Christian faith, which asks resignation of man in the face of Divine Will, and to this day I have not found consolation for the death of my beloved daughter.

"It is my hope that mankind will soon gather sufficient force to defend with the required energy their right to benefit from what they and the earth produce. It is to be lamented that some men have persisted in enslaving their fellow men, because Christ said that. That all mankind should benefit from what the earth produces, and that man should not be enslaved. In the present system, so inappropriate, man finds himself worse-off than the beasts; but a day will arrive in which justice shall be done, and I trust this will not long be delayed."

"Este dolor no se cura con resignación."

-La Pasionaria.

Afterword

Retropect and Prospect

Almost three-quarters of a century after writing *Palmetto Country*, I am still here, looking back, around, and ahead—and hardly knowing what to say. Perhaps this much at least can be said with certainty: the palmetto has fared rather better than the country.

It is good that the book was written when both Florida and I were seventy years younger. Even though I had graduated into the abyss of the Great Depression, my generation was nevertheless imbued with a vision of progress—the fond notion that man's path lay onward and upward, with every difficulty overcome and every gain leading toward a better world. If I had to write it over today, when we don't know which destructive trend, or combination thereof, will put an end to it all, this book would be far less lyrical.

Of course time means different things to different people and places. John Muir, the eminent naturalist who sauntered from Jacksonville to Cedar Key in 1867, once spoke in awe of the Yosemite as a place where a day seemed like a thousand years, and a thousand years but a day. Nature has created many such places on earth, and Florida has been one of them.

But timelessness means little since our species appeared upon the scene. Carlos Castaneda's Don Juan admonishes us to "Leave Earth as you found it — undisturbed." But it is far too late for that, in Florida as elsewhere. It was already late when Muir was here and swore to devote the remainder of his life to saving humans *for* the wilderness and the wilderness *from* them.

The Florida Man Made

Disturbance of the peninsula dates back just a few centuries to the coming of Europeans and the Africans they brought later. People have always been attracted to Florida, for one reason or another. Prehistoric man came in pursuit of the mastodon and other game. Later, Native Americans saw

353

the peninsula as a fabulous raw bar. European explorers came in search of a Fountain of Youth and Cities of Gold; they found neither but were nonetheless rhapsodic about the wealth of natural beauty. American settlers came seeking runaway slaves, the Indians' herds and pastures, and as much farm and timberland as they could lay hands on.

My father in the early 1920s safaried into the wilderness that was to become Miami, and came back to Jacksonville to report, "Nothing down there but skeeters and 'gators." Toward the end of the decade he loaded five Kennedy kids into the family phaeton and drove back down to see what the real estate boom had wrought. This time, all he could say was, "My God, what money has done to this country!"

Eighty years later, I feel much the same way about what has been happening to the entirety of my native state. When we think of the Florida nature built, as opposed to the one man has built upon it, we envision an expansive scene of air, sun, seacoast, islands, lakes, streams, pinelands, hardwood hammocks, cypress swamps, scrub, groves of cedar and palm, mangrove swamps, marshland, and palmetto thickets. But our species has a peculiar notion of what constitutes a natural resource: something that can be converted into cash.

Marjorie Kinnan Rawlings, in her autobiographical *Cross Creek*, remarked how ridiculous it was to be celebrating the burning of the mortgage to her place "when in reality it belongs to the redbirds." I was there for the Rawlings Commemoration of 1988 and can attest that, seventy redbird generations later, they were still in active possession of the premises, especially the chicken coop.

The flora and fauna of Florida did indeed get here long before we did, and all the fences, walls, moats, and private property signs we have installed are no more than ephemeral clouds upon the inalienable title to the land that all living things hold in common.

The gratuitous assertion by our species of a right of stewardship over the world of nature, if it is to have any validity whatever, must be predicated upon faithful fulfillment of the responsibilities of stewardship. To date, we are grievously in default. In some instances despoliation has already passed the point of no return; in others it looms just around the corner.

The paroquet and Key pigeon were already long gone when *Palmetto Country* was written, and since then such species as the pileated woodpecker and seaside sparrow have joined them in limbo or wherever it is that species go. The endangered list for Florida, headed by the panther, makes lengthy reading. So, too, would any further listing of what damage Florida has incurred, from its minerals to its sparrows. Some may say that species come and go but Florida will go on forever—but I say not necessarily.

Many of the politely-called "extractive industries" have literally extracted themselves to death. The live-oak lumber barons and yellow pine kings cut out and got out, and the road from Jacksonville to St. Augustine would never again "lie stirrup-deep through a carpet of pine needles."

Where once forests of yellow pine, life oak, cypress and cedar stood, scraggly slash pine has taken over, only to be ground up by pulp mills serving America's insatiable demand for paper for all manner of purposes, from newsprint to toilet tissue, boxes to store our "stuff," the junk mail that fills the mailboxes, and the advertising inserts that crowd the news out of the newspapers.

80 .... SHUCKING OYSTERS, APALACHICOLA.
Once the keyword for excellence in oysters, the Apalachicola oyster is not what it once was, thanks to pollution. State Library and Archives of Florida.

There is still a lot of phosphate to be mined, but its production has created vast holding ponds of toxic water, just waiting for flimsy dams to break and kill some of the peninsula's major river systems.

The diversity and abundance of Florida's seafood was once the envy of the world. Now we deem ourselves lucky if a menu lists even one "catch of the day" along with Alaskan king crab and Hawaiian mahi mahi.

Some industries disappeared because technology found substitutes. The pogey fishing fleet turned to something else when someone discovered other ways to make fertilizer. Few folks use natural sponges any more. The turpentine industry went out when artificial paint-thinning solvents came in. Cigar sales fell when health concerns changed the nation's smoking behavior.

The blights that laid low Florida's coconut palms, Key limes, and sponges were bad, but not nearly so devastating as the man-made structural blight that threatens to engulf the entire state. While spoiling the natural habitat with one hand, we have been building an oft-times monstrous human habitat upon the ruins with the other. Architecture anywhere ought to include the elements of aesthetics, be compatible with the human spirit, utilize to the extent possible natural and native building materials, be compatible with the environment, and incorporate traditional features when they seem to merit it.

Florida still has a lot of open space, but vast areas have become congested to the bumper-to-bumper point. On a recent low-level flight from Orlando to Key West I was dismayed to look down upon the unbroken paisley-like pattern of more or less uniform housing that had replaced the mangrove swamps that long provided homes to wildlife and protection to communities when hurricanes roared in from the Florida Straits.

Another problem lies in the fact that most developers think of "site preparation" as stripping the area of every vestige of verdure, from every noble tree down to the last sandspur. "Makes construction easier and cheaper," they say. "Don't worry about the loss of habitat. We will replace it with even nicer trees and shrubs." But of course they don't do anything of the sort. A few cheap saplings are the most you can hope for, and fondly trust that by the time your children are grown the saplings will have grown some too.

Stretches or even snatches of unspoiled nature are becoming more and more scarce. Anyone who has seen Florida from the air in recent times must have been struck by the extent to which mile after mile has been blanketed with row after row of almost identical "cracker boxes" looking for all the world like rabbit hutches and huddled so close together that the occupants can hear their neighbors' plumbing.

Already a Great White Way consisting of condo canyons, gated communities, and plastic logos of motels, fast food, convenience stores and strip malls has girdled Florida's seacoast from Fernandina to Key West to Pensacola—and much the same can be said of the entire inland network of highways and byways. This is of course not confined to the region, but afflicts the entire nation. The cherished characteristics which long identified communities have been swallowed up to such an extent that if you were to drop from the air all you would be able to say is "I'm in Anywhere, USA."

So much for what has been happening to man-made Florida. The damage being done to the Florida nature made is no less devastating, and is also no secret. Numerous public and private agencies have occupied themselves with producing blueprints for salvation, a recent example being the Century Commission for Sustainable Florida's study called the "Critical Lands/Waters Identification Project."

So the problem lies not so much in not knowing what needs protection, as it does in the fact that almost anything a developer wants he can get. To the old adage that "money talks," I would add "and megabucks dictate!"

If nothing else, the Meltdown of 2009 should teach us that the so-called "private sector" governs our lives and fates even more than government itself. From which it follows that if we know what's good for us we need to get and keep oversight and handles on it too.

Otherwise, the otherwise-laudable profit motive is apt to give way to unbridled greed and economic anarchy, with devastating consequences for us all. Along with self-determination and political democracy, all the peoples on the planet are entitled to see to it that their economic establishment is not given a license-to-loot investors and public.

Getting back to nature, if we could just figure out ways to make preservation more profitable than despoliation, we would have it made.

It has long been my conviction and contention that the human habitat and natural habitat need not be mutually exclusive. If we would but accommodate them, they would adapt us. Already we are requiring developers to provide holding ponds for surface water; why not holding ravines and greenways to enable wildlife to coexist with us? Arctic falcons are nesting atop the skyscrapers of New York and feasting handsomely on pigeon; seagulls are forsaking the sea in favor of shopping malls; osprey are looking upon powerline towers as nesting places of preference; raccoons have gone suburban; and so it goes. Given a place in a food chain, wild things are adept at adapting to changes in habitat. In other words, if you want more eagles, breed more rabbits.

On the other hand, for many species, conservation is no longer enough; the need is for propagation as well. Mother Nature is very prolific, but we need to give her a helping hand by providing nurseries as well as hatcheries to enhance survival ratios.

We-the-people must insist upon sustainable development. To that end, it appears that we must also insist upon our right to be heard. For example, in July of 2009 the St. Johns Water Management District scheduled a public hearing on a request by Seminole County to draw down 5.5 million gallons of water per day from the St. Johns River. My wife Sandra Parks and I joined hundreds of others to voice our opposition.

Since the facility would only accommodate a fraction of the individuals and organizations seeking to address the board, the rest of us were locked out under a hot sun. Despite overwhelming public opposition, the Commission voted five to four to grant the permit. Sandra and I filed suit, asking that the courts void the meeting and its decision on the grounds that the board's failure to provide adequately for public comment violated the definition of a public hearing under the Florida Sunshine Law.

Since my lifetime spans two Florida land booms and two economic busts, I have seen the results of both. Back in the boom of the '20s, real estate agents wore knee-length golf knickers and flattop Panama straw hats. Today the salesperson is most apt to be a sweet-young-thing driving a company van.

But artifacts of overdevelopment remain for a long time after the sales-pitch. For example, after the first Big Bust there was a ten-story structure on the outskirts of Miami, abandoned in mid-air with a roof but no windows. Tourists drove by for years, gazing with awe and wondering what had happened. And then along came an entrepreneur, who put wire screening over the windows and turned it into a ten-story chicken coop!

Now, I am driving past half-finished shopping malls far out in the boondocks, with little hope that the developments they were intended to serve will materialize any time soon. ---Which reminds me of a billboard left standing far out in the water near Jacksonville after the first bust, reading:

ON THIS SITE WILL BE CREATED ISLANDA, JEWEL OF THE ST. JOHNS!

It stood there for years and years, before finally falling down and becoming a favorite sunning platform for alligators.

Florida's People Today

As industries went, the people who had done the work went with them. A great many of the folks you met in this book--the tree cutters, turpentine dippers, cigar makers, sponge divers, fur trappers, moss gatherers--are long gone. Clam diggers are learning how to "grow their own," and many fisherfolk have taken up carpentering.

The Florida of today owes its population even more to the urge to migrate than to the urge to procreate. Native whites and blacks of southern origin have long since been outnumbered by newcomers from other states and lands.

As I approach my 93rd birthday. I am gratified that real progress was made in the field of human relations, glad above all that black Americans have at long last overthrown the tyranny of white rule, white supremacy, and Jim Crow apartheid. Die-hard redoubts of discrimination continue to exist, but by-and-large the folks in Palmetto Country—along with the rest of the region and nation—have discovered that they enjoy their newfound fairness and fraternity. (I was startled when friends and strangers called to congratulate *me* on the election of Barack Obama as President of the United States. Upon reflection, I realized I *had* been working on his campaign ever since 1932.)

When the "Meltdown" of 2009 precipitated America and the world into Big Bust II, I remembered too well when Big Bust I made its debut. I saw with my own eyes a mother give her newborn babe to the family dog to suckle. My recorder was turned on when the Black Sea Islands preacher prayed, "Hear us, O Lord—we're down here gnawin' on dry bones!"

Here's hoping that this Bust doesn't come to such as that. But the potential is there, for human privation and suffering on a scale comparable with what might be wrought by an atomic attack and foreign occupation. Hurricane Katrina and 9/11 wouldn't hold a candle to it.

Foreclosure isn't the only way that people in the Palmetto Country and elsewhere are losing their homes. Even if you got born into a beautiful home in a beautiful community with a beautiful view, you stand to lose it all if rich folks decide they want it. All they have to do is bid up property values and taxes with it, and you can kiss it goodbye! In the first Bust folks worried about being tractored off their land; nowadays they're being taxed off.

The evolution throughout America of a mutual rip-off economy, facilitated by plastic card purchasing power, gave rise to a degree of pseudo prosperity. During the Great Depression Floridians knew one another, lived simpler lives, bought less, and knew how to make, fix, or make do with what they had or needed. For today's Floridian, poverty in Paradise will be much harder to take.

Who Is a Floridian?

All the changes in Florida's demographic map have posed, and will increasingly pose, questions concerning Florida's traditional cultural pattern and its sense of community and identity. Does it matter whether the people who live here consider themselves to be Floridians? Or does shifting one's residence from one state to another entail nothing more than a new auto tag and tax collector?

If we agree that a sense of belonging to the place we call home adds to the quality of life, then it follows that we all—whether we arrive by stork, land, sea, or air—stand in need of some "fotchin-up."

The Florida depicted in *Palmetto Country*--and even more in the contemporaneous works of Marjorie Kinnan Rawlings and Zora Neale Hurston--had an Arcadian quality, and there are still a lot of places that are about as Arcadian as you can get in the 21st century. I couldn't help but take notice that somehow Marjorie's whites never lynched, and Zora's Blacks never got lynched, despite the fact hat Florida was always running neck-and-neck with Mississippi when it came to lynching. In any case, the good ole boys and gals are alive and kicking, and just as pleased with themselves and their culture as they ever were.

Not as much can be said of some of the ethnic cultures that were flourishing in Florida when this book was written. Their names are still in the telephone books, and their DNA is still getting around, but much of their cultures have fallen into the American melting pot.

At the same time, new waves of immigration from Central and South America, the Caribbean, India, Southeast Asia, and elsewhere have been enriching Florida's ethnic and cultural mosaic.

It is my hope that we will be more hospitable to these than we were to those who came earlier, and will make it public policy to hold in mutual esteem every people and culture under the Florida sun.

The Florida reflected in *Palmetto Country* was a folksy one, and we were doubly blessed in having a Rawlings and Hurston (not to mention the WPA Writers Project) around to immortalize it. Zora once described folklore as the "boiled-down juice, or pot-likker, of human living." There was a lot of it around back then, and there still is, albeit in modern settings.

We will be eternally indebted too to some others who took it upon themselves to record Florida's folksongs and tales: John and Alan Lomax, who went among the cane-cutters, gandydancers, stevedores, and chaingangers; Francis Densmore among the Seminoles; Ralph Boggs with the Latins of Ybor City; and Alton Morris in pursuit of British ballads. The folklore unit of the WPA Florida Writers Project was in the field too, and as its head I was privileged to work with Alan, Zora, and Alton. All of this Florida material can now be accessed on the Library of Congress website.

It is true, though, that the family hearth is no longer the purveyor of folk culture it once was, and only the classroom is in a position to fill this vacuum. "London Bridge" and "Banbury Cross" will always be important to us, but Florida schools should also be offering "Miami Hairycane," "Hug Em in Sebring," "Lost Boys of East Bay." "Collier in the Scrub," and "Look Out for the Big Gator." Paul Bunyan, John Henry, Casey Jones, and Woody Guthrie will always inspire, but how about some of our Florida folk heroes, such as Captain Coker, Cockeye Billy, Roy Tyle, Quevedo, Daddy Mention, Mama Duck, Uncle Monday, Aunt Memory, Old Pete, and Father Abraham?

Today new generations of Florida troubadours recount Florida's history, celebrate her unique characters, and exhort us to preserve her natural heritage. Will McLean composed ballads about Seminole Wars, hurricanes, and folk heroes. Gamble Rogers sang and told humorous tales about a mythical Florida site called Oklawaha County. Frank and Ann Thomas made up and sang hundreds of songs about Florida characters and critters.

Steve Blackwell wrote music to honor those who have protected Florida's environment and human rights. Dale Crider educates, while he entertains his listeners with rousing songs about Florida's rivers and wildlife. And there are a host of others, singing their hearts out in praise of and defense of the Florida they love.

It's not just up to them. but to all of us, to save Florida and not trash it. The media have a major role to play in this effort and are doing their part. So long as we keep the Florida shelf in our homes, schools, and libraries well stocked, Florida will be secure, and the people who live here will be true Floridians no matter where they come from.

I asked my good friend Bobby Billie, spiritual leader of the traditional off-reservation Seminoles, why they refuse to touch the millions that were set-aside for them at the time of forced tribal incorporation.

"No way!" he said.

"What *do* you want," I persisted.

"Florida," he replied.

As a native Floridian myself, I know just how Bobby feels. There's really no other place on earth quite like it.

I can speak with authority, because I spent eight years overseas, traveling through some 31 countries, with one eye on the lookout for some place more Floridian than Florida. I found palm trees enough, and some bathing beauties, but I finally had to come on home because the weeds weren't right.

When I get to Heaven, I guess I will just have to make-do.

Stetson Kennedy
Beluthahatchee Park
Fruit Cove, August 2009

INDEX

A

African Methodist Episcopal Church, 104, 176
alligators, 64, 253, 291, 359
American Medical Association, 316
American Revolution, 11, 61, 262, 327
American Tobacco Company, 297
Anderson, Judgy I. Muncy, 205, 206
Archive of American Folksong, 156, 278
Arrotomakaw, 57
Ashton, Corp. Adam, 95
Atlanta Constitution, 215
Atlee, Dr. G. H., 318
Audubon, John James, 11
Aury, Luis, 63
Avellanal, Dr. J. R., 316
Avengers of Maceo, The, 296
Avila, Luis, 337

B

Baker, Ma, 121
baptismal ceremonies, 84
Barbee, Rev. James E., 205, 206
Bartram, John, 1, 2
Bartram, William, 21
bathing beauty, 4, 258
bear hunts, 25, 71
Belgians, 125
Bell, Vereen, 20
Beluthahatchee, xi, 160, 162
Benét, Stephen Vincent, 61
Bergamin, José, 342
Big Cypress Swamp, 10
Big John the Conqueror, 131—132, 137—141, 160
Big Scrub, 7
Billygoat Hill, 196
Black Bottom, 194, 199
Black, Justice Hugo L., 217
Blondie, 204
Boarman, Judge Alex, 295
bolita, 175, 330, 335, 336, 337,
341, 343
Boom, 9, 41, 60, 118, 267, 272, 354, 358
Botsford, Gardner, 209
Bowlegs, Billy, 17, 24, 239
Brennen, Jean, 205
Bronson, Irlo, 231, 232
Bronson, Judy, 142
Browne, Jefferson B., 294, 295
Browne, Thomas, 61
brujeria, 169, 181, 182, 183
buckeye cigar factories, 289
bull fight, 332
Bull, Uncle George, 79
Burgoigne, Nicholas, 56

C

Camp Blanding, 189
Cape Sable, 158, 159, 160
cartabón, 300
Castellano, Gerardo, 294—295
catch dogs, 229, 254
catfish, 120, 255, 256
Catholic Church, 21, 50, 55, 62, 82, 322, 326—331, 350
cattle industry, 17, 62, 223—251
Cattlemen's Association, Florida, 232, 245, 247, 248
Centro Asturiano, 316, 318, 319, 348
Centro Español, 315—318, 347, 348
Cépedes, Carlos Manuel de, 296
chain gang, 215—217
chambers of commerce, 26, 32, 248, 343
Chambers, Izell, 217
chaperon, 345
charada, 335
charivari, 344
Church of God, Pentecostal, 272
Cibola, 53
cigar industry, 287—351
Cigar Industry of Tampa, The, 298, 300
Cigar Manufacturers' Association, Tampa, The, 297—302, 306—308,
314, 323, 349—350
Círculo Cabano, 319—321, 332
Círculo Nacional Cabano, 319
Cities of Gold, 50, 51, 53, 354
Civil Liberties League, 246
Civil War, 11, 24, 71, 75, 77, 92—96, 264
Civil Works Authority, 302
Clinch, Gen. Duncan, 64
Comité Nivelador, 293
commissary, 277—278, 281—283
    commissary wedding, 286
communism, 105, 246, 305—308, 323, 340, 350
conch (shellfish), 118, 256, 260, 262, 270, 271
Conchs, 15, 125, 260—264
Condition of Affairs in the Late Insurrectionary States, The, 100, 111
Confederacy, 11, 20, 92, 93, 94, 97, 101, 264
Congress for Peace and Democracy, 342
Congress of Industrial Organizations (CIO), 306—308
conquistadores, 288
Constitutional League, 106
co-operative, 125, 129, 244, 267
Copperheads, 115
copra, 4
Coronado expedition, 51
Couch, W. T., 35
cow attorney, 249
Cow Ford, 11, 67
cowboy songs, 250—251
Crider, Dale, 362
Cross-State Canal, 145
cuácaros, 65
curfew, 41, 78
cypress, 6, 7, 8, 9, 10, 20, 25, 355
Czechs, 125, 129

D

Dacy, George, 224, 245, 246
Danes, 125

Dann, Carl, 26
Davis, Charlie, 217
Davis, Jefferson, 91, 92, 116
Davis, Kay, 239
Debatable Land, 96
Democratic Party, 92, 109, 111—116
Depression, 46, 302—305, 313
Díaz, Norberto, 311
Dickens, Jonathan, 4
Diddy-Wah-Diddy, 160, 161
Dies Committee, 306
Dillingham, William P., 298
Disston, Hamilton, 18
Douglass, Frederick, 87
Drake, Sir Francis, 56
Duncan, B. M., 326
Dutch, 125

E

Egan, Squire, 265, 266
Eleutheran Adventurers, 260—262
Emerson, Ralph Waldo, 69
Estebanico, 51
Eureka Store, 172, 173
Everglades, 10, 15—20, 36, 267

F

fairy stones, 172
Falangists, 341
farming, 18, 25, 32, 43, 44, 55, 77, 101, 129, 143, 251
Fascists, 307, 308, 330, 340, 341, 342
Feast of Epiphany, 125, 183
Federal Emergency Releif Agency (FERA), 302, 303, 304, 305, 334
Federal Security Administration, 206
Federal Surplus Commodities Commission, 304
fence laws, 249
fence wars, 245
Fernandina, 21, 55, 63, 81, 83, 95, 357
Fifth Column, 308, 342
Filor, James, 78
Finns, 125
fires, brush, 12, 241—243
fires, muck, 18
fish-fry, 258
Flagler, Henry M., 35
floating islands, 31
Florida Cattleman, 246
Florida Facts, 103

Florida Keys, 4, 6, 34, 40, 46, 86, 125, 225, 260—266
Florida Times-Union, 88, 299
Florida, A Winter in, 103
Floridian Plateau, 27
folklore, xi, 7, 14, 56, 120, 155—157, 277, 361
folksongs
  Barney McCoy, 66
  Bellamena, 269
  Big Jim in the Barroom, 250
  Bonefish is Bitin, 186
  Bottle on the Horse, 251
  Chain Gang Theme Song, 219
  Chillun of God, 83
  Collier in the Scrub, 361
  Come All You Rounders, 213
  Conchy Joes, 260
  Crab is a Better Man than Man, 270
  Feet Too Big, 197
  Filor will get you, 78
  Fishy, Fishy Bite, 255
  floryda, 56
  From Cracow I Am Driving, 130
  Gainesville Storm, 46
  Go down to Bimini, 186
  Good God, with a Bounty, 7
  Great Big Bars, 221
  Ho, Ho, Come Along, 81
  Hoist Up The John B Sail, 268
  Hug Em in Sebring, 361
  Hush, Little Baby, 14
  I Can Whip The Scoundrel, 94
  I Want To Go Back To Georgy, 68
  I Want to Go to Abaco, 272
  I'se Gwine To Georgy, 276
  In All My Mother's Children, 118
  Jeff Davis Rides, 91
  Johnnie, Fill Up The Bowl, 96
  Just a Jitterbug, 281
  Look Out for the Big Gator, 361
  Lost Boys of East Bay, 361
  Louise, 197
  Miami Hairycane, 361
  Miami Hurricane, 42
  Mosquito Had a Spree, 270
  My Cindy, 250
  My Dear Mother, 280
  Nigger in the Kitchen, 80

  Old Demos, 128
  Ole Sow in the Corner, 251
  Over There, 71
  Pass My Old Gold Ring, 272
  Poverty, 126
  Run, Nigger, Run, 75
  Sittin on a cow-horse, 243
  Snow James, 119
  Song Ballad of the Lost Boy, 7
  Sponger Money, 267
  That was Irish too, 67
  The 1928, or West Palm Beach, Storm, 44
  The Crow, 187
  The Homespun Dress, 92
  The Lost Boys of East Bay, 259
  The Mosquito's Wedding Day, 128
  Them Johnson Gals, 257
  Three Grains Of Corn, 70
  Turkey Hammock, 250
  Uncle Bud, 131
  When A Slovak Left His Country, 129
  When I Was Young, 166
  Where the Climate Suits, 32
  Whoa Larry, Whoa, 66
Fort Caroline, 53, 54, 55
Fort Lauderdale, 259
Fort Moosa, 57, 59
Fort San Carlos, 58
Fort San Marco, 55, 57, 58, 59
Fort San Mateo, 55
Fortune, Emmanuel, 101, 102, 104, 108, 111
fossils, 28
Fountain of Youth, 35, 49, 354
Four Centuries of Florida Ranching, 224, 245
Franco, Gen. Francisco, 341, 342
Freedmen's Bureau, 103, 104, 116
freezes, 34
fruit fly, Mediterranean, 15

G

Garcia, José, 314
Gaspar, José, 334
Gasparilla Festival, 334
Geechees, 118, 257
Gibbs, Jonathan, 107, 108, 113
Ginny-Gall, 160, 161, 162
God's Protective Providence, 4
Gorrie, Dr. John, 34
Gourgues, Dominique de,, 55

Graveyard Dirt, 174, 185
Greeks, 60, 125, 126, 127, 266
green benches, 34
Gulf Stream, 32

H
hairydicks, 236
handicraft, 9, 272
Harris, J. V., 121, 326
Hawkins, Sir John, 53, 54
Heaven, 160, 161
Hebard Lumber Company, 24
Hemingway, Ernest, 342
Hendry, cattle king, 253
Herty, Charles H., 12
Higgenson, Col. T. W., 94—96
Hitler, Adolf, 249, 307, 310
hogs, 85, 137, 139, 226, 245, 251—254
Homestead, 159
Hooker, William B., 235
hookworm, 71, 253
Hope, Jessie, 234
Houston Street, 201, 204
Huguenots, 53—54
Hungarians, 125
hurricanes, 36—47, 356, 361
Hurston, Zora Neale, iv, xi, 40, 360, 361
hyacinths, 13, 14, 226

I
Ibor, Vincente Martínez, 289
ice, artificial, 34
Indians, 2, 17—24, 30, 31, 34, 35, 50
Inquisition, 288
Insects, 14, 15, 270, 291
Internacional, El, 323
Intracoastal Waterway, 30
iron spider, 80
iron-clad oath, 97, 98
Irwin, Jared, 63
Italians, 60, 126, 287, 288, 297, 298, 300, 319, 322, 328, 341, 343

J
Jackson, Gen. Andrew, 64
Jacksonville, xiii, 11, 13, 29, 32, 35, 94, 95, 96, 152, 172, 193, 195, 196, 197, 201—209, 212, 215, 216, 255, 287, 297, 299, 353, 354, 355, 359
Jacksonville Journal, 209
Jai, Anna Madgigiane, 87, 89

Jefferson, Thomas, 62
jerking poles, 83
Jews, 121
Johnston, John H., 64
jooks, 189—199, 204, 209
Junta de Cultura Española, 342
Junta Revolucionario Cubano, 295

K
Key West, 4, 78, 79, 86, 116, 121, 134, 158, 160, 170, 183, 184, 260—267, 268, 271, 287, 288, 289, 290, 291, 293, 294, 295, 300, 304, 313, 314, 315, 321, 323, 324, 325, 326, 334, 335, 337, 338, 341, 342, 356, 357
Key West Citizen, 158, 337
Key West Rifles, 290
Key West–The Old and the New, 294—295
King, Zibe and Bet, 232, 234
King's Road, 60
Kingsley, Zephaniah, 88—91
Knight, Peter O., 349
Knights of Labor, 297
Korona, 130
Ku Klux Klan, xii, 106, 113, 114, 189, 204

L
L'Unione Italiana, 319, 321
La Fitte, Pierre and Jean, 63
labor unions, 287—293, 297—302, 306—308, 340, 347—350
lakes
    Blue Sink, 131, 141, 142, 143
    disappearing, 31
    Maitland, 141
    Okeechobee, 6, 7, 15, 18, 27, 28, 30, 38, 43, 58, 121, 223, 258
Latin-American Carnival, 334
Laudonnière, René de, 53
Lee, Dan, 24
Lehman, P. E., 227
León, Ponce de, 32, 49, 50
Lincoln Brotherhood, 104
Lincoln, Abraham, 91, 96, 97
Little Alcatraz, 215
Live-Oakers, 11
Lockler, Irving, 235
Lomax, John A. and Alan, 156, 361
Lopez, David, 158
Lord, David, 342
Lotería Nacional Cubano, 337

Loyal League, 104—105, 106
Loyalist, 62, 262
lumber industry, 6, 9, 10, 11, 12, 24
lynching, 40, 86, 236, 297, 360

M
Macaro, Pancho, 335
MacGregor, Gregor, 63
Machado, Dr. Guillermo, 315
Machado, Pres. Gerardo, 341
malaria, 14, 15, 291
Maloney, Mayor W. C., 79
mangrove, 6, 36, 46, 354, 356
Mann, Tappan, 235
Maroons, 57, 59, 63, 64, 141, 224
Martí, José, 296, 310
Marx, Karl, 323, 341
Mathews, George, 63
Mato, Armando, 321
McGillivray, Alexander, 61
McGirth, Daniel, 61
McGuire, Will, 192
McIntosh, John, 63
McKay, Capt. Donald, 225
McKay, D. B., 314, 349
McLean, Will, 361
McQueen, A. S., 24
Meacham, Robert, 80, 100, 104, 111, 116
Menéndez, Pedro, 10, 54, 55, 56
Miami, 4, 18, 19, 34, 35, 38, 39, 40, 42, 46, 47, 80, 121, 123, 159, 170, 178, 189, 204, 239, 259, 287, 320, 354, 358
Miami Beach, 38, 123
Miami Herald, 124, 206, 216
Miami Hurricanes, 37
miasma, 6
mining industry, 29
Minorcans, 4, 60, 62, 287
Mizell, Bone, 233
Mizell, Hamp, 25
Mobile (Ala.), 51, 57, 58, 265, 287
moccasins, 14, 18, 19, 253
mockingbird, 14, 26, 344
moonshine, 26, 190, 212, 285
Moore, Gov. James, 57
mosquitoes, 17, 35, 87, 142, 157, 160, 230, 245, 291
Motivos de Cayo Hueseo, 294
Moya, Pedro Rimirez, 342
Mussolini, Benito, 310, 341

N

ñáñigo, 169, 183, 184
Narváez, Pánfilo de, 50, 51
Nassau dinghy, 269
Nassau niggers, 118
National Labor Relations Board (NLRB), 314
Native Son, xiii, 212
Naval Stores Industry, 283
Negro Fort, 64, 224, 225
Negros Brujos, 181
New Deal, 302, 309, 310, 311, 340
New Orleans, 13, 65, 175, 179, 265, 283, 288, 297, 334, 344
North Georgia Review, 190
Norwegians, 125
NYA (National Youth Administration), 346

O

O'Berry, Cleo Wynn, 7
O'Bryant, Horace, 325, 338
Oats, Joe, 106
obeah, 169, 178, 184, 185
Ocala, 29, 30, 145, 146, 235, 346
Oglethorpe, Gov. James, 59, 62
Okefenokee Swamp, 20—26, 147
Old Senator, 9
Original Sacred Harp, 71
Ortiz, Dr. Fernando, 181
Osborne, Col. Thomas W., 104, 108, 114
Oversea Railroad, 40, 265
Overseas Highway, 46
oxen, 9, 28, 66, 230, 237

P

Palm Beach, 239
Palmer, Col. George, 58, 59
palms, 2, 4, 6, 356
Panton, Leslie (and Company), 61, 62
Partido Revolucionario Cubano, 296
Pasionaria, La, 351
Patriarchal System of Society, The, 91
Patriots' Rebellion, 63, 91
patrollers, 75
Pendas, Enrique, 347—349
Pensacola, xiii, 11, 40, 55, 58, 59, 61, 62, 64, 79, 86, 105, 124, 255, 357
Pensacola Gazette, 86

Pepper, Senator Claude, 310
Perez, Bienvenido, 170
Pershing, George O., 342
Piñera, Gerardo Corina y, 350—351
piruli, 311, 343
Poles, 125, 130
Porvenir, El, 315
Pratt, Theodore, 40
prison life, 211—222
Proctor, George, 77
Prohibition, 190, 237, 345
promenading, 333
prostitution, 194, 201, 205, 206, 208, 210
pulp industry, 12, 355

Q

Quevedo (folk character), 131, 135—137, 361
Quevedo, Los Pícaros de, 136

R

railroads, 11, 24, 39, 42, 46, 47, 67, 104, 150, 151, 213, 249
Rawlings, Marjorie Kinnan, 7, 354, 360, 361
readers (in cigar factories), 302, 322, 323, 349, 350
Reconstruction period, 79, 97—116, 226, 253
Reed, Gov. Harrison, 107, 108
Reed, Henry, 109
Remington, Frederic, 226, 227
rivers
   Apalachicola, 30, 64
   Choctawhatchee, 30
   Escambia, 30
   Miami, 41
   St. Johns, 13, 53, 88, 90, 152, 235, 358
   St. Mary's, 65, 94
   Suwannee, 24, 51, 64, 234
   underground, 30
Riviera, Diego, 340
Roberts, Bull, 158
Roberts, Uncle Steve, 157
Rogers, Gamble, 361
Rolle, Denys, 60
romerias, 333
Roosevelt, Franklin D., 26, 306, 309, 310, 350
Roosevelt, Theodore, 172
rustling, 236, 237

S

salt works, 93

Sam-Jones-Be-Damned, 17
San Carlos Institute, 296, 323
San Martín, Ramon Grau, 348
sandspur, 15, 356
Savannah, 12, 58, 61, 63, 106, 190, 232
Sawgrass, 36
sawgrass, 17
Sayle, Capt. William, 260
schools, 281—285
Scott, John R., 115
Scottish Chief, 225, 226
sea-chanteys, 257, 258
segregation, 108, 208, 272
Seminole, 2, 10, 17—23, 36, 62, 64, 67, 68, 141, 157, 225, 239, 361, 362
sharecropping, 103
Shoemaker, Joseph, 306, 307
Silver Springs, 30
Silver, Harry, 205
singing festivals, 71
Slovaks, 128
Social Security, 278, 282, 283, 314
Sociedad Cuba, 321
Soto, Hernando de, 51, 343
Souto, Fermin, 347
Spaniards, 50, 51, 53, 54, 55, 56, 57, 59, 65, 263, 287, 288, 290, 294, 295, 297, 300, 319, 328, 341, 350
Spanish Democracy, North American Committee to Aid, 341
Spanish moss, 10, 12, 227
Spanish Volunteers, 296
Spanish-American War, 297, 319
sponge industry, 125, 126, 131, 134, 266, 267, 268, 270
spongers, 267
springs, 30, 35
St, 88
St. Augustine, 4, 10, 21, 47, 54—59, 61, 62, 77, 82, 161, 262, 287, 355
St. Johns Ri, 88
St. Marks, 55
St. Petersburg, 34, 239
Stacy, Cull, 148
Stearns, M. L., 109, 114, 115
Stolbrandt, Col. V. E., 35
Summerlin, Jake, 225, 226
Sutton, Corporal Robert, 95
Suwannee Canal Company, 23

swamp buggy, 19, 20
Swamp Water, 20, 20
sweat-box, 78, 143, 214, 215
syphilis, 206, 207, 214

T

Tallahassee, 58, 67, 69, 75, 77, 92, 105, 106, 113, 116, 178, 193, 194
Talmadge, Gov. Eugene, 214
Tamiami Trail, 18, 20
Tampa, 18, 50, 51, 73, 129, 144, 145, 150, 151, 183, 184, 197, 225, 234, 235, 236, 239, 255, 287, 288, 291, 292, 293, 295, 296, 297, 298, 299, 300, 304, 305, 306, 307, 308, 313, 314, 315, 316, 318, 319, 321, 323, 325, 327, 332, 333, 334, 337, 340, 342, 343, 348, 350
Taylor, Judge Robert R., 39
Ten Thousand Islands, 4, 6, 158
Thirteenth Amendment, 98
Thomas, Frank and Ann, 361
tobacco, 67, 71, 190, 225, 288, 290, 291, 294, 298, 307, 311, 334, 338, 342
    smoking, 53
Tomlinson, Ellis, 158
Torcedores, Los, 301

Tories, 59, 61, 64, 262
tourists, 26, 28, 34, 37, 50, 119—124, 125, 130, 194, 202, 209, 239, 258, 272, 275, 304, 314, 334, 338, 358
Tournament of Love and Beauty, 69
trees, 6—17
Trotsky, Leon, 306, 340
troubadours, 332, 361
Turks, 125
Turnbull, Dr. Andrew J., 60
Turpentine Corporation, South Florida, 282
turtleburger, 271

U

underground railroad, 86
Union Martí-Maceo, La, 319
Unionists, 97—101
University of Florida, 32, 136, 204
    Bureau of Business and Economic Research, 283
University of Miami, 37

V

Vaca, Alvar Núñez Cabeza de, 51
Van Horn, R. E., 306, 307
Veaux, Maj. Andrew de, 262, 263
venders, street, 343
Verbena del Tabaco, 334

verbenas, 333
voodoo, 143, 169—187

W

wage-hour law, 307
Walker, David S., 98
Walker, J., 108
Walker, Jonathan, 85, 86, 87
Walkin Jawbone, 192
Warren, Fuller, 247, 249
Washington, George, 62, 63, 85
Week of Joy, 334
Wheeler, Hughlette, 235, 236
Whidden, Bob, 235
Williamson, Jack, 217
Woodward, Walter, 217
World War I, 46, 118, 206, 313, 321
World War II, 30, 118, 123, 267, 341
WPA (Works Projects Administration), 304, 309, 310, 314, 334, 337, 361
Wright, Richard, xiii, 212

Z

Zar, 160, 162
Zebu, 238
zombies, 182